Our Whole Life Is Our Whole
Responsibility

By
Michael G. Kamau

Life Energy Publishing
Cincinnati, Ohio

Copyright ©2023 by Michael G. Kamau

All rights reserved. This book or any portion thereof may not be reproduced or used in any manner whatsoever without the express written permission of the publisher except for the use of brief quotations in a book review or formal literary citation. Life Energy Publishing is a subsidiary of Worldvoice Business Resources, Inc.

Printed in the United States of America

Second Printing 2023

First Printing, 2011

ISBN 978-0-578-09448-9

Life Energy Publishing
5111Hawaiian Terrace #8
Cincinnati, Ohio 45223

Library of Congress Cataloging-in-Publication information is available upon request.

Cover design concept by Life Energy Publishing.

Table of Contents

ACKNOWLEDGEMENTS vii
PREFACE viii
INTRODUCTION... ix
It May Not Be Our Fault…But It Is Surely Our Responsibility 1
    Accept Full Responsibility 7
    Understand the Role Mass Media News...................................... 9
    She Let Other People Make Excuses 11
Why We Don't Accept Responsibility 14
    Abandon Excuses Not Responsibility 22
    We Are Wasting Technology.. 24
    How Enablers Damage Us 25
Our Education Does Not Stop Because We Graduate 29
    Gain a Financial Education 33
    The Good Ole Days 34
    Keep a Distance Regarding Foolish People 38
The Essence of Our Character 41
    What We Believe... 41
    Character Influences 42
    Beware of "Experts".. 44
    Decide Who We Are.. 50
We Are Never Too Young To Accept Responsibility 53
    Our Reputation and Public Image 61
Become Obsessed With Wellness 64
    Basic Care of Our Physical Self.. 68
    Our Amazing Emotional Faculty.. 74
    Our Mental Faculty 79
    Solidifying Our Spiritual Health 81
    Our Social Development 83
    Reasons to Share.. 85
    Reduce Stress to Improve Our Health 86

- Creating Our Personal Health Management System ... 88
- Our Personal Health Plan ... 91

Embrace and Respect Work ... 94
- Make Your Resume Useful ... 96
- A Few Interview Tips ... 99
- There Is Always Something To Do ... 103

What We Do Want Out of Life ... 105
- Courage and Acceptance ... 107
- Selling Our Souls ... 108

Being A Better Example Today ... 111
- We Are All Role Models ... 113
- Develop Discipline ... 115
- Treasure Accountability ... 116
- What We Bring To Others ... 117
- Help Create Our Healthiest Environment ... 125

Our Life and Our World ... 128
- Our Transition Among Worlds ... 129
- What To Expect Tomorrow ... 133
- Take Proactive Control ... 135
- When Minor Things Just Go Wrong ... 136
- Know When To End A Matter But Never Quit ... 138
- Crushed and Rejected ... 140

Value Relationships As Great Wealth ... 143
- Women's Relationship Choices ... 146
- Marginal Mate Selection Standards ... 146
- What Men Fear ... 148
- How to Identify An Abuser ... 150
- Wisdom from a Professional Dater ... 153
- Study Your Intended Mate's Character ... 157
- Unaddressed Trauma Can Damage Our Relationship ... 158

Use The Power of Your Spiritual Energy ... 162

Religious Education versus Spiritual Education 163

Our Spiritual Energy 165

Access The Power of Your Spiritual Ability 167

Discovering Our Dharma 173

Our Sense of Entitlement 176

The Power of Our Natural Freedom 187

Always Side With Responsible Public Opinion 188

The Satan Experiment 198

My Search for Religious and Spiritual Truth 200

My Search For Satan: The Experiment 202

…Because That's What GOD Wants… 207

Bibliography ....**Error! Bookmark not defined.**

Index 214

ACKNOWLEDGEMENTS

I must extend my full gratitude and appreciation to the many thousands of students and participants, who have allowed me to teach, tutor, mentor and/or instruct through classrooms, seminars, workshops, support groups and presentations over the years. I have appreciated your support and friendship in ways that I may never be able to express appropriately.

I must thank the Riley family of Cincinnati, Ohio – Renita, Desmond, Lanay and Jasmine-Reneé for providing me with the family that I have always needed at a crucial time in my life. The four of you mean everything to me. I will always love you and be grateful.

I also thank my life-long friends from childhood and those I have made in my adulthood to whom I rarely remembered to say thank you for all that you brought to my life. I count my blessings, regarding your presence in my life, often.

Thank you to you, Julie E. Brent, founder of Earth Heart Reiki for your eleventh-hour support in encouraging me to complete this work at this time.

Finally, I dedicate this, my first book, to my parents, the late Ralph A. Smith (1937-2004), Vera G. Smith and my brother Addiction Specialist Dr. Greg A. Smith, M.D. for being living examples of the spirit of this book and who demonstrated the patience to tolerate someone in the family who was so very different from each them. Thank you.

PREFACE

Every condition of our life is not necessarily our fault; however, it is definitely our responsibility.

This book is about choosing to accept responsibility for the condition of our life, no matter how it became that way. If we didn't get a fair start in life or someone intentionally set out to ruin our life and succeeded, it is still our issue. If, by a series of poor decisions, we found ourselves in a place in our life where we are completely unhappy, still, it is our issue, no one else's.

We can choose to blame others, seek revenge, gossip and wish ill to others and make our life even worse by driving away the few people who still care for us and want to see our life situation improve or we can choose to accept responsibility for where we find ourselves, take charge of our life and make ourselves a better, stronger and more successful person. The legacy we leave is completely our choice, no matter where and how we started.

This book is designed to provide important information about how we make our choices in life, encouragement for each of us to make positive changes where we identify the need and practical ideas, techniques and methodologies for correcting the direction of our life path to where we desire it to be. So far as this book is concerned, making excuses, blaming others and self-pity are not acceptable actions for any area of life improvement.

While reading this book, it is important to remember that many areas of discussion will be very personal to us for a variety of reasons. It is not intended to open old wounds, taunt or ridicule anyone. It is intended to encourage each of us to make the decision to move forward to a significantly better place in our life.

How each of us chooses to effect those important, positive life changes is why this book was written. There is no "one-size-fits-all" approach to making our life better. Throughout this book, we are encouraged to draw upon the many resources around us, within us and available to us to make our life what we once wished and expected it to be.

We can get our lives back on track if we truly desire to do so. Our personal welfare and wellbeing are at stake as well as that of our loved ones, extended family, friends, community, and nation and world community. The better we make ourselves, personally, the better we make our human race.

I wish you love and light as you continue your life's journey.

Michael

INTRODUCTION

Why Our Whole Life Matters

If we are completely happy with every facet of our life, this book is probably is not for us. Give it as a gift to someone who is dissatisfied with his or her place in life, relationships, social circle, employment situation, state of health or family situation.

We are taught dependence on others from time we try to speak our first words. Most of us worked hard at being independent and responsible for ourselves as we developed from infancy. We tried to feed ourselves, hold our own bottles, travel without help (even if we had to crawl) and investigate our world in every way to establish our independence.

As we grew, we paid close attention to our parents and our other caregivers to learn how we should behave, deal with conflict, work through adversity, take care of ourselves, socialize with others, communicate with others and so on.

By age seven, virtually, everything we know and understand about the world, right or wrong, was taught to us by our parents, caregivers, family members and teachers. Collectively, they were responsible for all that we knew at that point in our lives – how to dress and feed ourselves, how to bathe and groom ourselves, how to share and socialize with others, how to assess problems, evaluate alternatives and make important decisions.

From age seven to fourteen, our foundation for survival skills in life had been established. We had developed a battery of survival skills that we believed would work for us. We were able to recognize situations where physical defense (or attack) might serve us better than silence or verbal negotiation.

We had mastered lying, deception, manipulation, passive, assertive and aggressive behaviors. We understood the value of excuses, blaming others and victim behavior as well as we understood the value of exaggerated confidence, grandstanding and abject arrogance. For so many of us, it is amazing how our social, educational and mental maturity seems to plateau at this stage of our lives.

We seem to trust and use the same sources of information that brought us to this stage of life. We tend to suspend our life explorations regarding our health issues, family matters, career options, social behavior, financial, religious and political convictions, lifestyle choices and ability to determine our own destiny in life. Over the next seven years of our lives, instead of testing what we have been taught about life, maturity and adulthood, so many of us tend to solidify our beliefs around what we have been taught with minimal challenges.

Perhaps, we have become equally acquainted with being saddled with ridicule for being too inquisitive. Maybe we experienced just enough sarcasm and criticism for dreaming out loud about what else we might be other than what we have been told we should be. In so many cases, we have been indoctrinated not to step outside of the established family identity. For example, "We're mechanics in this family not artists;" "We're musicians not athletes;" "We have always been caterers, not construction workers." (Armstrong, 1993)

Some families have made career paths for their offspring as welfare recipients, drug traffickers, street hustlers, prostitutes and petty thieves. Despite the consequence of constant legal entanglements and jail sentences, so many people, who have taken this road, appear not to be interested in evaluating any other career paths regardless of the improved quality of life that is attainable.

Socially, the same appears to be true. Teens experiment with smoking, alcohol and drug activity because they see it as adult behavior. However, in great numbers, those who began these behaviors as teens often continue such habits for several decades; even while they are experiencing, first hand, the negative consequences to their physical, emotional and mental health. Despite public health warnings, warnings from medical personnel, coworkers and dying relatives, they still do not seriously consider changing the habits that are clearly most damaging to their overall wellbeing.

Nutritionally, many people never seem to mature past their teen years mentality. We love our fast food, processed canned and boxed foods, junk foods, nutritionally unbalanced meals, and pre-made deserts. Within about twenty years later in life, when we look at our teen photographs, we often do not see any resemblance to our present self because we are several pounds over the weight that our skeletal structure was designed to carry.

We have an array of health issues that we are trying to remedy with handfuls of prescription medications. We ache all over; we have health issues that we have never had before and yet we refuse to change our nutritional habits; we refuse to get regular exercise; many of us refuse to drink a clear glass of water. Again, many of us never stop to consider the improved health benefits of changing what we're doing to create a healthier lifestyle.

Career wise, this social, educational and mental maturity (or lack thereof) seems unchanged. We will plod along in a career path that isn't fulfilling nor rewarding in any way that is important to us for decades. We will complain; we will call off; we will use our sick time; we will use all of our personal and vacation time each year. Still, we are miserable and unhappy. Although, we aren't happy where we are, until we are out of options, we refuse to consider learning anything new that could create a new, more fulfilling, career path.

If you have found that any part of your life has been perpetually unfulfilling for any number of years and that you have found it difficult to create the changes that you desire for yourself, then, this book was written for you. It was written for you to see that you are the master of every area of your life. It is empowering in every way. In every chapter, you are encouraged to open your eyes a bit wider; scrutinize your surroundings more closely and study your available options more seriously.

This work does not conflict with your chosen religion. Your power of choice is discussed fully, however. Exercising this power will allow you to rise above all negative programming from your youth; your self-imposed learning limitations, the fear and anxiety you experience from watching news programs; your dysfunctional relationships, any low self-esteem issues; involvement in self-damaging habits and so on.

Conspiracy theories, government plots, other worldly beings and secret societies have absolutely no bearing on the personal choices we have available to us that will markedly improve the quality of our lives. For those who choose to engage in this form of journalistic investigations, I only ask that your efforts demonstrate responsibility, integrity and ethical exposure for the sole benefit of the masses of people, worldwide. Delivering the truth is always honorable. Anything less is corrupt, divisive and irresponsible.

Regardless of where you find yourself on your life journey, you are now called to accept responsibility for every subsequent decision you make and each step you take from today forward. You will find that your confidence and power to direct your own life in a positive and productive direction will strengthen daily.

You will find people, systems and resources available to you that you never realized as you become a proactive force for positive change in your own life. By improving your situation, you improve the quality of life for those around you in immeasurable ways. Once, you are well into your journey, you will see for yourself.

Thank you for choosing to embark upon this journey of personal transformation. Simply internalizing the mentality of taking ultimate responsibility for every area of your life creates confidence and inner strength. You will be a better person while improving your home, family, community, nation and the world. It is among the best decisions that you will ever make.

Chapter 1

"You must take personal responsibility. You cannot change the circumstances, the seasons, or the wind, but you can change yourself."
— *Jim Rohn*

It May Not Be Our Fault…But It Is Surely Our Responsibility

It was November, about three weeks into the late fall term and I was passing back assignments, the second of the term, when I noticed that Christina wasn't in class. She was a tall, 19 year old blonde who seemed to have given up on life in virtually every way imaginable.

I was teaching a Composition class with rather challenging and unconventional assignments. You see, some students were buying their prepared assignments off of the internet; it was a new trend among high school and college students and I would have none of that. I created all of my own assignments. My assignments forced my students to actually think.

Christina was the only person in the class who earned an "A" on this assignment. The quality of her writing was easily on the level of a college senior. Although she was quite reserved, I did not suspect that she was cheating or receiving any special help; that simply wasn't in her character.

I just wanted to find out, from her, why she was enrolled at a community college as a Technical Writing major. Her writing abilities far exceeded what she was required to eventually learn for this area of study. I just did not see the fit.

Christina attended a later section of the next class that day. After I finished teaching class, I asked Christina for a few minutes of her time. She did not have another class for at least an hour and neither did I.

I congratulated her for such a superior writing effort, her second in a row. She was very humble. Then I started the conversation that I thought might satisfy my curiosity. We were both unaware of how deeply our lives would be altered on that day.

I explained that, in my years of teaching, it is rare that someone comes out of a public high school with such a proficient writing aptitude to enroll in Technical Writing as a concentration. She replied that she couldn't find anything else for a major where she might make enough money to support herself.

I explained that technical writing is specific to every industry; it is simply a bi-product of the specialized work that any of us would have to do and that it is difficult to secure gainful employment with just a Technical Writing degree. Her faced had a sad, dismal look. She was immediately filled with disappointment and regret. She began to verbally punish herself.

I stopped her to interject that I just thought she would be better off at a university that would have the resources to develop her talents to a much further extent than we were prepared to do at a community college. I thought this would make her feel better. Instead, her eyes began to well with tears. I demanded to know what happened that no university had accepted her. Her answer brought tears to my eyes.

Christina told me that she would never be able to go to a university because she had no money. I explained to her the steps her parents needed to take to arrange her financial aid. She told me that her mother was a recovering alcoholic who was still in rehabilitation and her father was in prison. She had been living with her boyfriend and his father for a quite a while.

As you can imagine, her extended family relationships were somewhat strained as a result of her predicament. It was obvious to me that Christina loved her parents very much but circumstances had developed that left her, literally, without a supportive family and a home of her own.

After Christina explained her situation to me, I simply stared at her in silence. Her eyes grew wide and hopeful. I think that she thought I was working on some master plan that would make her troubles disappear. The truth is that my heart was breaking for her. I could not imagine facing life with such daunting expectations of the future at her age. I decided to take a proactive approach in deciding what to do in her case.

I asked, "Christina, when you were younger, what did you want to be when you grew up?" She had virtually no practical answer. Again, I tried, "when you were in the 9th grade, what did you want to be?" The response was the same. Eventually, I did learn that her home was relatively stable while she was in the 6th and 7th grades.

"Christina, when you were in the 7th grade, what did you want to be when you grew up!" I demanded. Her sad faced perked up. Her persona became that of a thirteen year old. "That's easy!" she replied, "I wanted to be a newspaper journalist more than anything else in the world." I breathed a sigh of relief.

I probed into Christina's background further and found that she was active on her school's newspapers at each grade, from that time, until her graduation from high school, often serving as editor. She was active on the yearbook staff each year as well. She took part in fundraisers and literally every opportunity to improve her writing skills.

She even volunteered to write articles for community newspapers. I now understood the reasons for her superior writing skills; mentally, she had been a practicing professional for years. She was still explaining her many accomplishments when I interrupted her, "My dear, we have work to do!" Now, she did see answers on my face and in my eyes.

Over the next nine months, I witnessed a transformation that left me speechless but studying every book I could find about successful people, mystical secrets for manifesting our desires, success techniques, mental transformations and sacred writings containing ancient secrets from a variety of religions and so on. This is what happened.

I asked Christina, where she wanted to attend college to become a journalist. She gave me that blank look again. I rephrased my question. "When you were in the 7th grade, where did you want to go to college?" I coaxed. Again, with no hesitation, she said, "the Scripps Howard School of Journalism."

She added that she wasn't sure where it was but it was probably too far away. I grinned and told her that one of my favorite professors from college accepted a position there after I graduated. I told her, "I think we have a way in!" Now, she looked like she had seen a ghost.

I corresponded with the Dean of the Scripps Howard School of Journalism, at Ohio University in Athens, Ohio, to explain that I had a treasure of a student for them. Christina kept close contact with me for the next three months. She would point out details to me like the fact that the school was passed the acceptance deadline for the next year. "I know," I told her.

"All of the financial aid is depleted at the school for the upcoming year," she added. Again, I said, "I know." She grew more and more puzzled that I was pushing forward with this effort. I could sense that she was bracing for a letdown as disappointment had become her most familiar companion, in recent years.

Periodically, I would tell her that she needed to "complete this application" or "fill out that form." You will need to have your high school transcripts forwarded to this office and you need to get letters of recommendations from these people. Now you have to write an essay about this or that. She stayed so busy that her expectations, about her future, soon fell in line with mine.

We stayed in contact though the Winter break. Classes resumed in January and in early February, my car engine failed so I was relegated to public transportation for a while. It would cost a substantial sum of money to have my car repaired and I just happened to not have the money. It was going to be quite a while before I could get my car repaired – perhaps late March.

Christina came to me a few days later to tell me that they [Ohio University] were having an "Information Day" on Friday, February 27th. I said that I had no transportation because my car died. "I think we should be there," she added as she turned to walk away. I began to explain," I won't have the money to get my car repaired until..." "**THIS IS IMPORTANT**!" she said as she walked away, without looking back.

Christina had transformed from someone who saw herself as a powerless victim of circumstances into someone who realized that she was entitled to the adult life she saw herself leading as a thirteen year old. She was focused, driven and intolerant of excuses from herself or anyone else that would derail her dreams for herself any longer. Christina's attitude and lack of interest in my personal issues forced me to examine the wisdom of making transportation excuses, and thus risking disappointing a driven woman.

I received my car in good repair the night before our journey. To this day, my mind is a blank as to how everything worked out. We departed for our three-hour drive, to Athens, Ohio, through the hills of eastern Ohio at 6am. When we arrived, the parking areas were completely full so we created a parking spot. We made our way, quickly, to the auditorium also to find that, it too, was full as the presenters were about to begin.

We burst into the auditorium somewhat excitedly. Someone from the stage area realized that we were not going to shrink into the background quietly so they announced on the microphone that there were two seats available in the front row. We made our way to the front and we took those seats.

As the information session concluded and tours were about to begin, we learned that we were sitting next to the Dean for the Scripps Howard School of Journalism. Across from where we were sitting, were all of the members of the admitting committee for the school.

Christina and I were both focused and driven at this point. We were somehow working as a single unit. We took full advantage of every opportunity that we could create. We arranged for an impromptu interview with the Dean who subsequently arranged an interview for Christina with all of the members of the admitting committee. Everything went well.

We went on a couple of guided tours on campus. During the tours, Christina was suspiciously quiet throughout. Before we departed for home, I suggested that we stop by the campus bookstore so that she could purchase some souvenirs for herself and some of her friends. She agreed. We entered the bookstore.

Obviously, I had no money [the car] so I browsed. Christina disappeared for a while. When she reappeared, she was wearing a white "OU" baseball cap with Green Letters. She paid for some key chains, mugs and other items and only took off the ball cap just long enough to pay for it. I never saw it off of her head again.

Christina changed on that day. She went from hoping for a dream to come true to accepting full responsibility for her life condition. At least, that is when I noticed it. It may have happened when she would not accept my car-repair excuses.

Whatever the case, my experience with her and the transformation I witnessed in her, caused me to push others who I encounterd since to their desired fate as well. I have amassed enough stories since then, literally, to fill a book. After this wonderful day, I only saw Christina sporadically around the college when she would volunteer her updates to me.

The updates went this way: "they found $12,000 for my tuition but no living expenses... I received a $2,000 scholarship from _____ organization that I applied for last December... I received a _____ grant from the State of Ohio for $3,500... I found a part-time job on campus doing such and such...

I found a place to live that will only cost me $__ each month; my part-time income will cover that... I still have to save money for furnishing my place... My cousin at Miami University is getting married and she is giving me all of her dorm furnishings: linens, blankets, pillows, television, stereo, storage containers – everything."

Christina was attracting literally everything she needed to herself. (Hicks, 2006) She was a bit apprehensive about being away in an unfamiliar environment and not knowing anyone. The university housing department paired her with one of my teaching colleague's daughters, who had also been accepted there. Christina worked hard and made the best of her opportunity. She went on to graduate with honors.

Aside from Christina's extraordinary writing skills, there wasn't much different about her from anyone else. At an early age, Christina did something that many adults never learned to do; she accepted full responsibility for her life condition. She never complained to me about the circumstances in which she found herself.

None of it was her doing directly. She was simply trying to make the best of her situation. She was working a job to cover her expenses and her college classes when I met her. Once she realized that she could make a long-held life goal materialize, she pursued it with all the vigor and enthusiasm that anyone who valued such an opportunity would. I was so proud to have met her.

Wanting our lives to get better is an important start but that is not enough. It is very easy to complain about how unfair life is and who is to blame. The condition of our lives is not always our own doing directly. Often those, upon whom we are dependent, make choices over which we have no control and at some point, we suffer from it.

When the consequences of those choices adversely affect our personal situations, it puts us at a tremendous disadvantage in terms of our prospects for success. Christina had no control over her parent's choices and subsequent consequences that clearly affected her life. She dealt with it just the same.

When we find that our quality of life has deteriorated beyond what we personally find to be acceptable, it is easy to develop an escapist mentality. This involves permitting ourselves to engage in activities, behavior and habits which are often self damaging.

Engaging this mentality often forces us to make necessary lifestyle changes in order to continue to support this mentality. Had Christina chosen to begin smoking, consuming alcohol and using drugs as an outlet for her stress and frustrations, she may have found herself in a far worse circumstance. To my knowledge, she never allowed herself to explore these negative options.

Christina had a range of popular negative choices she could have made. She did not prostitute herself nor compromise her self-respect in anyway. She managed to stay in school and challenged herself to do well. From what I learned from her teachers in high school, she did not make excuses. She demonstrated good character in the most challenging of circumstances.

She found a way to deliver on her commitments. Apparently, she was aware of the wrongness of engaging in spreading gossip and rumors. She managed to stay out of trouble with the law enforcement officials. She did not knowingly engage in any self-damaging behavior.

When we embrace an escapist mentality and accept a lower-quality lifestyle, we can begin believing that certain avenues to success are permanently closed to us. We, then, make choices that are further damaging to ourselves, our loved ones and our own reputation.

Such behaviors might include street hustling, criminal involvement and public assistance schemes among other things. Soon, we find that we are having frequent contact with law enforcement officials. Whatever the condition of your life now, whether is it was your own doing or someone else's negligence, you are still responsible for everything in your life now, no matter how unfair it may seem.

No matter where we find ourselves in life, we must make the decision to accept full responsibility for the way and direction the rest of our life will develop. If we do not, someone else or some institution, that may not have our best interest as a priority, will decide our fate for us and we will have no right to complain.

Accepting such a passive mentality about the fate of our lives will never lead us to a happy and fulfilling existence. We must be assertive and proactive in directing our lives to where we would like it to go.

Having our life develop the way we want requires that we want: 1) a specific quality of life; 2) to fulfill a specific life purpose; 3) the discipline to create a mentality that is positive and productive; 4) to value ourselves by learning and practicing good character. Then, we live it daily until we are where we want to be.

Also, we must accept the responsibility to be a resource to others who want what we have to share. The progress, understanding and wisdom that we gain through our journey must be shared with others who are also seeking answers just as others share freely with us, when we ask.

Accept Full Responsibility

Think about how we can ruin our reputation, for example, by simply disregarding its importance as a priority. It is easy to forget about important promises and debts that we made, especially those made out of desperation. We see it all the time. A friend calls us up with an emergency, usually a financial emergency. They make the promise that they will have it back to us by late next week or their next payday. If we really want to help our friend and we can spare some money we will usually make a contribution. The emergency is usually legitimate; often the promise to repay, although sincere, is not.

When the time arrives to make good on the promise to repay, we often learn that our friend does not have the resources to keep the promise or repay the debt. This creates an extremely uncomfortable position for both us and our friend. If we normally spend time around each other on a daily basis, it will strain the normally free flow of conversation as we will want some assurances of repayment and our friend will want to avoid the subject for as long as possible.

Eventually, such as life is, there will be another emergency. If our friend has not repaid his (or her) debt to us, we will remove ourselves from consideration as an emergency resource in the future. Our friend is clearly in need and cannot discuss the matter with us for fear that we will bring up the fact that we never received repayment from the "last emergency."

If our friend continues this trend with others, we can figure out that, soon, all of our friend's resources will be depleted. At some point, there will have to be a resolution of this situation if our friend is to continue to subsist in his or her current surroundings.

Now take the above situation with our friend and extend our friend's mentality to credit situations, unfulfilled commitments with family and friends, unreliable behavior in parental roles, irresponsible actions in the spousal or mate relationship and the partaking in personally, self-damaging personal habits and behavior. It is a relatively short journey to a life of chaos and instability. At any time up to this point, our friend could have owned up to any issues faced that would have prevented him or her from being able to honor the agreed-upon commitments.

The point here is that our friend could dig as deep a hole in life as he is willing until his reputation and history prevent him from going any further. Our friend will become paralyzed from being unable to progress through life based on his word – that means bad credit, bad reputation and a deeply negative history.

Eventually, our friend will only be welcome in the company of others who are the same way and who suffer from the same disgraces. Of course, things can get worse, much worse. The truth is that no one really desires for his life to become worse from this point.

When we surpass this point willingly, it is usually out of our own ignorance about what to do to rectify our situation. When we look back at what we have created, it seems overwhelming. Our debts seem impossible to repay, the damage we have done to our relationships seem unforgivable, the setbacks our reputation has suffered seems irreparable and the personally self-damaging habits and lifestyle we have assumed, has left us with very unattractive prospects for a bright future. It is easy to contemplate giving up all together.

Most of us don't think about it but there is always someone watching us – children, adults who are afraid of us, adults who are struggling to not become what we have become, law enforcement officials, people who are in worse situations, business owners, people who only know us by reputation and so on. Taking such a negative journey will draw the proportionate negative attention.

This is exactly why we must accept responsibility for the condition of our lives, now. Whether we created our circumstances or we found ourselves at a tremendous disadvantage in life by someone else's hand, we must accept responsibility for cleaning up the mess that is our life. No one is going to do it for us – no one else should.

This is our chance to be a superstar in our community and among those who know us personally and by reputation. The choice is ours: we can allow our previous choices to define us for the rest of our existence as weak, inadequate, cheap, irresponsible, untrustworthy and unimportant; or we can own up to our reputation and admit that we made specific mistakes for which we accept full responsibility. Whether we realize it, we will gain a tremendous measure of public respect for doing this. Now, we are in a position to take control of the direction of our life and guide it to a positive and productive state.

In this way, we become a beacon of inspiration to those struggling with the same issues that brought us to this point. We become a role model for others who want to turn their lives around. We teach the at-risk youth by example, what a person who commits to practicing good character and responsible behavior can accomplish by creating a life that anyone would envy.

It will not be easy and it will take all of our energy everyday for several months as we will encounter many who doubt our sincerity. They will not hesitate to remind us of our past. Only our sincere acts and deeds, not our words, will silence those doubters. So we must be prepared to earn every measure of respect that we garner.

Our personal reputation is not the only area of our life for which we must be responsible. The same disregard for the condition of our health, finances, education, employment and any other area will yield similar results in those respective areas of our life. Everyone wants to be happy, accepted and respected. The only way to assure that we can create these positive aspects in our lives is to take active responsibility for every area of life that we cherish.

Let's take a look at the best way to move forward in turning our life around. We can change our mentality, the way we think, to a positive and productive one. Then, we can become fully responsible for our own life condition with no apologies or excuses. We can set some goals that we want to reach and work on reaching them, religiously, every day until we have achieved them. We can learn to be a positive and uplifting influence, to those around us, throughout this process by practicing on ourselves each day.

Understand the Role Mass Media News

We have become a world community of consumers who accept what we see and hear from our mainstream news sources, virtually without question. That does not mean that we always agree with what we are presented but we rarely question that which is covered. The television and radio news organizations are run by the wealthiest people on every continent. Fullness and accuracy of newsworthy items vary somewhat from country to country. (Merton, 2000)

We should always remember that most news organizations have a limited window of time to get information to its audience. Also, we are not tuned in to these sources at the same time, as an audience, so the news sources do a great deal of repeating of their stories. Even when there are in-depth news specials, we must understand that all of the information covered, is still filtered through one final authority at the organization before it goes to air. So let us explore why this is important.

Many news organizations are dependent upon advertisers (companies that create commercials to teach you about their products and services) to sponsor (pay for the airing) their news programs. Advertisers are sensitive to the news content as some items might reflect negatively on their products or services that are scheduled to air in commercials, perhaps in that particular season.

If an advertiser is at all offended by the news content for a particular broadcast, they will not sponsor the news program for that time slot. If the news organization's salespeople cannot find new advertisers for that time slot, then, technically, the journalists, editors, producers, technical staff and so on would not be paid. This is not acceptable to any of these professionals.

Because of this advertiser/sponsorship arrangement, news organizations do not like to show images or give offensive information to its viewers. For example, you may never see bloodied corpses shown in a news story with a sponsor that is advertising spaghetti sauce in its commercial. The commercial, which was scheduled to air weeks and sometimes months in advance, will air; the offensive news images, of bloody corpses, will simply not be shown – they would be edited out of the news content. Everyone is happy. Children do not have to be exposed to the reality of what kind of damage a deadly weapon can do to a body. Parents don't have to explain it or censor the news for the family.

The primary purpose of television and radio news is to entertain and its secondary purpose is to inform its audience. For this reason, do not expect a great deal of substantive support from the mainstream news organizations in always doing the right things in life. (Siegel-Maier, 2009)

Other entertainment style programs will often attempt to include some socially responsible programming that may address many of our concerns. It should be taken in the spirit that it was intended – another point of view and nothing more.

Since mainstream television and radio news organizations have so many constraints, they cannot be relied upon to give us unbiased advice on such matters as the dangers of harmful pollutants found in processed foods how microwaves alter our foods' nutritional integrity harmful effects of pharmaceutical drugs, dangerous effects of cleaning products and insecticides, encourage responsible behavior concerning gaming, alcohol and objectifying women. When we choose to accept a more responsible role in managing our lives, we must take it upon ourselves to do our own research and gather our own body of information to assess. (Fox, 2009)

For more controversial issues, there are always smaller investigative news services that will create in-depth reports, usually in recorded form, for home viewing, that mainstream organizations just do not have the time and budgetary freedom to explore. (Smallstorm, 2007)

These may not have a direct impact on our life personally; their primary purpose is to correct the historical record so that all information is available for educational purposes. Always explore these sources for supplemental and detailed information. Be willing to verify the accuracy of the information they present, for you, from the sources they give. After all, it is our responsibility.

So where do we go to get the most complete sources of information when we need to find solutions to our unique issues? The answer is to evaluate a variety of sources, even those presented by people with whom we may not agree. For example, suppose we are a parent for the first time and you want to do it right.

In searching for a definitive resource on how to rear children properly, it is wise to study as many authoritative sources as we can find. Like anyone who is driven to do their best, we would consult a cross-section of resources: books, magazines, articles, expert interviews and presentations, knowledgeable talk show guests, trusted family and friends and so on.

In fact, this is one of the key points of this book: take responsibility for the condition of our life by finding sufficient, reliable information. With this information, we can decide on the solutions that we can use in formulating a customized strategy to get our life condition where we want it to be.

To consult only a few resources, to validate what we already believe, is not being responsible to and for ourselves. We are essentially giving our responsibility and our control away to others and accepting their solutions. Then, we attempt to force ourselves to fit their solutions.

This is exactly what we do when we look for weight-loss solutions and solutions to a variety of other health issues. Instead, we must always be willing to learn enough about ourselves and gather sufficient information about our area of concern so that we can create customized solutions for our own personal benefit. In this way, we take responsible control of our life direction and its condition. Since we are all characteristically different physically, nutritionally, emotionally, motivationally and mentally, it stands to reason that we might require customized weight management.

She Let Other People Make Excuses

Every so often, someone wanders into and out of our life, who without realizing it, both inspires and motivates us; they change us for the better. Such was the case with a cleaning lady who I met on the bus.

I had just finished my schedule of classes for the day and I was on my way home. I boarded my bus for home. It was crowded on that day. Eventually, there was standing room only. The driver made a stop to pick up one last passenger.

There was a seat available beside me for perhaps a child or a small adult. That last passenger was an elderly woman who may not have weighed one hundred pounds. I called out to her that there was a seat beside me. I pick up my belongings from the seat so that she could sit.

"Oh God, Thank you," she panted, "I am so tired, I can't take it anymore today." I adjusted myself to give her a little more room. "Are you ok? " I asked. She went on about how long and difficult her day was and how much she needed rest. She raised her hand to adjust her hair out her eye when I noticed that she had no fingers – not one. I spied her other hand, slyly and saw that she had no fingers on that hand either. I am not sure if this was a genetic condition or the result of some tragic event in her life.

I asked her why she was so tired. She told me that she cleaned houses for a living. She had been doing it for several years. The company she started with went out of business but her two clients liked her work so much that they kept calling her. Over the years, her clientele had grown to over 23 households. She said that they liked her because she didn't charge a lot and she was very thorough. In this particular year, she had more work than she could handle, she insisted.

"Why don't you just charge more?" I offered. She said, "I am up to 50 dollars an hour now." Every time she went up on her rate, her business would double. At this point, the fact that she had no fingers meant virtually nothing to me. I toyed with having her teach me how she cleaned so that I could get in on this business but we were at her stop. She was pleasant and better rested. She departed the bus like someone who was going to take a hot bath and go right to bed.

Just like you, my heart went out to this "poor" elderly lady who had no fingers. That is who I saw; but that is not who she was. She saw herself as someone who needed to be productive while making a good living and have the kind of life she wanted.

It was clear to me that she had dealt with her lack of fingers rather early in her life. Clearly, she did not let it deter her from reaching any goals that she had set for herself. Actually, after meeting and interacting with her, I would not have been shocked if she told me that she had found a way to learn to play a piano.

Dynamite comes in small packages and this lady was no exception. This lovely woman has been my inspiration for so many endeavors since. I would often share this brief encounter with those who felt down, trapped and unmotivated to work toward the goals they have established for themselves. Nearly everyone is fascinated by this woman because, like me, they did not, initially, understand the truth about this woman.

The truth is that this woman, perhaps as a child, made a decision that she wasn't going to spend the precious years of her life whining about the condition of her hands and life. She would like to have completed her life with fully functioning hands; but she did not have that luxury. It may have been a birth defect or a tragic accident; once it was done, it did not matter to her. She took responsibility for her life condition and then control of her destiny.

Few people on that bus that day would have guessed that this frail, elderly lady out earned the most of them and enjoyed a lifestyle most of them would envy. It was her decision to do so. Imagine how many opportunities she must have had in her life to use the condition of her hands as an excuse for not working or drawing public assistance or suing whoever allowed this to happen to her. Obviously, that was not her character, her reputation or her history. We can all live a positive and productive "no-excuses" life the way she did if we adopt her mindset.

It does not matter who we are or what we have, it can all be removed instantly. We see this resulting from natural disasters, various accidents, economic trends, industrial shifts, political changes, health emergencies, criminal activity and poor decision making. We must remember this when we allow our ego to guide our thinking in seeing one another as separate and unequal.

We all need each other at one time or another. We need each other's assistance, understanding and compassion. Whether we realize it, we inspire, influence and are examples to others wherever we go. It is up to us if we are inspiring, influential examples in a positive or negative way. When we choose a positive and up-building mindset, we make the world a better place to live, for everyone we encounter. It is an important way that we accept responsibility for who we are and the quality of life we exemplify to others.

Chapter 2

"Ninety-nine percent of all failures come from people who have a habit of making excuses."
— George Washington Carver

Why We Don't Accept Responsibility

It seems like common sense that if we simply take responsibility for the most important challenges facing us, that we will dramatically transform the quality of our lives. We can solve our most pressing matters by just committing to accept responsibility for common issues; for example, our financial situation or for getting our health issues under control.

No one wants to be miserable and plagued by back problems or social phobias. No matter whom we are discussing, paramount in everyone's life is the desire for happiness (however each of us chooses to define it). Many of us just figure out that it is better to take control, now, and be responsible for creating the outcome that we want.

There are thousands of us who have received unpleasant news from our most trusted physician that "there is no cure for our condition," or "that there is nothing more they can do for us." Now, we are faced with a decision: do we want to live the rest of our lives with this issue and possibly die from it or do we, actively, take matters into our own hands? It really is comes down to this question: Is our desire for more life and full health stronger than any discomfort we may have with ending our issue(s) through death?

Out of sheer desperation, many of us have continued our quest, for better health, with nothing more than a commitment to do anything and everything, in our power, to make a full recovery. Once we align with this mentality, there is no such thing as a bad idea to us. We will investigate every option we find and exhaust every remedy within our reach. Surprisingly, many of us actually find the solutions we were seeking. Those solutions are usually unconventional and creative. Here are some examples:

> Every time I have attended a marathon or walk-a-thon, for a cure of some common public health concern, I have found literally hundreds of people who have a life-changing story about eminent doom, in their lives, for a health condition that they chose not to accept.
>
> They found alternative, often all natural treatments, with the most unlikely people, in professions that are usually ridiculed by the mainstream medical establishment. These survivors are everywhere. They are literally all

around us: in our school system, in our workplace, at our place of worship, where we run our errands and throughout in our community.

Nearly all of us know someone who is, or has, struggled with the challenge of obesity. It may have affected our marriage, our health, our social life or our self image. Every so many weeks, we tell our friends that we are on the latest diet. Sometimes we try fasting or walking more. We usually lose a few noticeable pounds and yet the obesity challenge seems to remain.

Ultimately, we do find a method of losing the weight that works for us, in the wake of a life-altering crisis like a divorce, the pronouncement of impending death from our physician, deep and long episodes of depression stemming from obesity issues and so on. In short, when we feel that we have no other alternative, we find our solutions.

Often, it is only out of desperation that we finally decide to accept full responsibility for the condition of our health. The methodology that we find for achieving our objective, of transformed health, is usually a customized solution of our own creation. It may be a collection of ideas, from the variety diets we have tried, in an unimaginable combination, that we find works for us.

Maybe we have settled on a combination of exercise and diet ideas. What we have come up with, as a solution, for ourselves may not work for everyone, or anyone else, but it works for us. As long as we establish and maintain good health and a healthy state of mind, no one can argue with our results.

Our inquiry, at this point, concerns the triggers within us that signal to us that we must take responsible action for our situation at all costs. For many of us, we must be placed in a circumstance where we have no other choice and no options before we decide to act on our own behalf.

Then, there are others of us, who have learned through the experience of others, that we must take full responsibility in creating our own solutions. We watch them struggle. We watch them fall and then get up to try again and again. We note their persistence and their resolve to win their battle. We come to admire and support them in their efforts. These people serve as a perfect example of what happens when we make the commitment to accept full responsibility for a particular area of life.

There are those of us, around the world, who want to take a more responsible role in guiding our own lives to the destination that we desire. This is not always possible because of cultural, economic and political constraints in their country of birth. The desire to take full responsible control of their life is strong but limited to the extent that they would be willing to suffer the indignities of lower class citizenship in a foreign country that allows them the opportunity to take complete charge of their own life.

For so many people, that is exactly the case. That is why whole families leave the country of their birth to create a better life somewhere else (by the way, not everyone chooses to go to the United States of America). If we are in a society that affords its citizens (and or residents) opportunities to live the highest quality of life we desire, we need only understand that we can have the life we want by accepting complete responsibility for our life.

Many of us have been the victims of horrendous circumstances as children, spouses, employees and community members. We did not consciously desire or create the horrors that we faced. We survived them and we are usually damaged by them. Whether we choose to live with such damage is our choice. We can make the decision to seek assistance through a variety of options. We must actively seek them and uncover the information that we can use to ultimately settle on a solution that fits were we want to take our lives.

Because our situation is unfavorable, at this time, does not mean that we have to suffer, often in silence, with it if we don't want to do so. We always have the option of taking responsibility and focusing our energies on bringing about the needed changes to improve the quality of our lives. We do not ever have to, permanently, live a less than favorable existence. It is always our choice balanced with our desire for the quality, of life, that we want.

We are one hundred percent capable of changing our life circumstances to become far more fulfilling no matter what our situations. There are several issues that stop us from making these changes.

Here are at least six common areas of concern which we, all, can examine in our lives that impede our ability to accept full responsibility of our lives; they are these:

> **The 'Good Enough' mentality** – This way of thinking is characterized by embracing low standards and marginal expectations for our life. We don't feel a sense of entitlement to the better things that are available in life. We feel that we are relegated to a predestined standard of living. This mentality is often consistent with a person's self-esteem and self-image. Such a mentality may be the result of our experiences or teaching from our childhood. Regardless of how it came to be, it is there and it is preventing us from accepting responsibility for our own life condition and enjoying a better life experience. We can choose to change this.
>
> **Impatience** – Technological improvements in society have so many of us accustomed to getting measurable, definable results immediately. Even our plants and pets are engineered to grow more quickly and in greater variety. We are able to access information and answers quickly via the internet. Our entertainment is filled with rapidity, creativity and convenience. Our communications and purchases are delivered faster than ever and just as conveniently.

We must learn to suspend our developed sense of impatience in favor of investing in our own personal development and progress. In fact, this is a necessity. Changing our life conditions, circumstances and direction will take some time. Patience is crucial to success in this area of our lives.

Lack of Discipline – This is common to even the most successful people. However, our discipline really comes down to our priorities. We have to decide that it is worth it for us to limit our shopping totals in favor of adhering to our monthly budget. We can get by on a few less cigarettes or cans of beer in favor of building a savings and investment program for ourselves and our family.

We must be willing to substitute fresh fruit for the bakery items that are causing us our health problems. We can spend a day of recreation with our mate each week and one less evening, out socializing with our friends each week, to improve our relationship with that someone who wants our sincere appreciation.

If we can change our priorities to support our commitment to accept responsibility for the particular area of our life on which we are focused, we can get around some of those discipline issues that have been stopping our progress.

Commitment – This is an area where most of us have less trouble than we think. When we think about it, we find that we have no trouble committing to automobile payments, cell phone contracts, school loans, fitness facility membership contracts, school activities, sports organizations, social organizations and so on. All of the above have at least one thing in common: we see an immediate benefit to making such a commitment.

For most of us, anything we perceive as actually helping us to enjoy a better standard of living, count us in! That is why we are slow to pay off our financial commitments, committing to long-term personal relationships, doing homework, laundry or dishes. Generally, we see these as 'just no fun.' We don't see the glory and excitement.

When we are able to convince ourselves of the benefits of accepting full responsibility for every area of our lives, we will have no trouble making such commitments to rescue our future selves from the excessive neglect we now find in our lives.

Quality of Knowledge – "Ignorance is Bliss" is a theme that has become a popular mentality for those of us who want to excuse ourselves for not taking responsibility for challenges that retard progress in various areas of our lives. It sounds like a witty response upon first hearing; it even seems kind of clever.

The truth is that there is no honor in willful ignorance at all. When we are willfully resistant to information, this is a form of fear. There are those who will actually try to convince us that we are better off not knowing the truth about certain matters. We see it in movies, on television, in novels and even in interviews on our news programs.

Many of us buy into this mentality under the guise of patriotism and good citizenship. However, eventually the truth usually does come out. After the fact, we often find that suppressing information only benefited those who were withholding the information but not the rest of us, who were kept ignorant. We commonly find this to be the case in food processing, medical treatments, historical events, environmental issues, consumer goods manufacturing, automobile safety and building products. (Smallstorm, 2007)

How many issues from the past can we recall where we were better off not knowing the truth once it was revealed? I have pondered this question for several decades and I am unable to come up with a single example. Perhaps, some of you can. Willfully not learning about something that could help us or our loved one, is never a good idea.

We often hear people, who are in poor health, make statements like, "I don't want to know what's in that; I would have to stop eating it." Or, "I don't want to know what this is doing to my body; I just want to enjoy it." If some area of our life is not going the way we want, let the alarms go off.

We must let ourselves feel the urgency of gaining the information we need. We will always be better off for knowing the facts and we will eventually find solutions for healthier replacement soon enough, after we begin our diligent research.

Quality of Execution – This concerns how much effort we put into the approach that we take in putting our plans into action, when we choose to take control of our life condition, and guide it to a positive and productive state. Some will approach this phase with great enthusiasm and persistence, while others of us may seem to be sloppy in our approach with an uncommitted heart. This may not actually be the case. There are reasons for this approach that, if dealt with early, can be overcome so that the quality of our planned execution will be much higher.

> *Distractions* – If we allow it, we will find a convenient reason to get out of doing virtually anything: It is too noisy in here; it is too early or too late. I am tired from working so much. I am hungry and I haven't eaten yet. I just ate too much and I am sleepy. It is too hot or cold. I am going to miss my television shows. The game is on tonight.

We can allow anything to be a distraction. The question we must answer is, "what is this opportunity worth to us?" Exactly how important is this for me to do? If we do not see the value in doing what it takes to change our life condition, we will suffer according to our own mental shortcomings.

At some point, we will grow tired of watching those around us, slowly and methodically, pass us by, while working toward their goals until they are completely out of our life.

Eventually, we will find that we are the only one who is left, who is being controlled by controllable distractions. Very soon, we will find that we are attracting other people, into our lives, who are allowing themselves to be distracted as easily as we are.

We will find that the reasons we use, for not choosing to take control of our life condition, are being echoed from the new acquaintances that we have attracted - like attracts like.

Our new, excuse-making acquaintances will be in our life until we take ourselves out of this trap by finally overcoming the distractions that we, so conveniently, embraced earlier.

Time Constraints –We must realize that nothing is going to change until we change it. If we are already very busy, we must be the one to create time-saving ideas, strategies and shortcuts so that we can begin reaching our goals.

We can make and pack the school lunches the night before; have everyone go to bed 30 minutes earlier each night and get up 10 minutes earlier each morning. Let's find whatever works for us in our situation. We can enlist the assistance of all of our family and friends to help us.

Whenever our employer cuts staff and our wages, then adds more work for us to do in the same time period each day, we find a way to get that done. We become creative in our approach to do our job and usually, we find better ways to do our job.

The same thinking applies in our personal life when we commit to accepting full responsibility for our life condition and take active control in driving it to where we want it to be. We can do that for ourselves and our loved ones.

Lack of exposure – If we grew up (or are growing up) in an environment where we are not provided opportunities to formally learn about music, athletics, travel, home care, religious, spiritual and political education, mainstream social etiquette and so on, then we must be especially vigilant in getting the exposure in life that we need.

Our parents may not have been in a position to give us the exposure that we required so that we might have an informed view of the world. How much did we learn about farming and how we replenish our food supply? How does banking and investing work? How is our transportation system structured to move people and freight to where they need to be? What is the purpose of our political system? Why is the study of economics important? What do we know of manufacturing processes that create the foods and consumer products that we purchase?

If a lack of exposure is an issue in our background, we can always do something about it. We can self-educate ourselves about these matters at our local library. There are books, videos and online courses on all of these subjects and many more. We can check them out, or study them for a limited time, at no charge.

Also, we can seek out mentors (people who have the knowledge and experience we want to know) to meet with periodically. We can have breakfast or lunch with them periodically just to talk things over. Whatever the case, we must take responsibility to remedy this deficiency in our background. We must, each, want do it though.

Mentality – Our mentality is how we think and see the world. If we see the world as a hostile and dangerous place, it will be for us because we will attract others into our lives who think the same way. If we see the world as a good place with basically good people but that sometimes unpleasant things happen, our mentality will adjust accordingly and we will attract like-minded people into our lives.

We can improve our mentality by thinking of ourselves to be in an ever-improving position in life. We can focus on opportunities and positive challenges to come our way each day. We will be surprised how often we will begin to identify them. We will discover chances to make new friends with people who can teach us new things that can help us along in reaching our goals. We will discover opportunities for personal growth as well as opportunities to help others in reaching their goals coming to us more often.

We must still practice intelligence when maneuvering through our environment, however. We cannot put ourselves in positions to be victimized or align ourselves with those who do not share our aspirations for a better life condition. We must give priority to and accept those new acquaintances who are also taking active control of their lives, in a positive and productive way. Gravitate toward those who are going the same direction that we are going and who understand the wisdom in doing it the way we are doing it.

Poor Social Skills – This concerns our ability to get along with others. If we revel in engaging in gossip, rumors and drama, we must leave this lifestyle behind if we are serious about getting our life condition where we desire it to be. Just as we may enjoy such socialization, it does nothing to further our personal development. It hurts the reputation and self esteem of others even when the basis is true.

Instead of enjoying someone else's misery through gossip, we can seize the opportunity reach out to that person, and make a new friend to invite along on our journey to create a better life condition by accepting full responsibility and taking positive control. Be friendly. Show a good a sense of humor. Be polite, considerate and accepting.

Please note that if we insist on keeping close company with people who do stupid and foolish things that create opportunties to interact with law enforcement officials and other legal system personnel, the more we will find ourselves in circumstances that damage our public image and personal reputation.

Reputation – If our life history is such that it contains legal entrapments (felonies), social labels (convict, deviant, offender, alcoholic, addict, abuser) and an unflattering reputation (drunk driver, trouble maker, jail bird, thief, cheat, whore, thug), then we will have a great deal more to overcome than many others but it is still not impossible.

Once people who know us and some who we have openly wronged, learn that we want to change the condition and direction of our life to one that is positive and productive, they may not take our declaration very seriously. Therefore, we will have to make extra special efforts in a variety of areas.

The first place to start is with us. Let's look at ourselves in the mirror. As we stare into our own eyes, we can note honestly what we see. If we do not trust someone with that look and those eyes, then we can work on changing our expressions which are a reflection of our mental state.

Let's stare and observe until we figure out what is wrong and start adjusting our thinking, daily, until we see the kind of person that we would trust. If, before, we gave everyone so many reasons to think poorly of us, then each day we must give those same people reasons to think well of us. It can be done.

We must make sincere positive and productive changes for the better in our heart and mind. Then we must act on that sincerity as often as we have the opportunity to do so. Behavior is always the strongest indicator of inner change. We want to internalize this mentality each day.

If our changes are sincere and real, people will let us know. If we have to tell people that we have changed, we haven't changed at all and the fact that we feel the need to say that we have, proves it. Attractive people never have to tell us that they are attractive. Great athletes never have to tell us that they are great athletes.

To effect real change, we must actually live it. That means thinking it, feeling it, becoming it daily. For example, if we are known, by reputation, to be negative, uncaring and unfriendly, then, we must become positive, caring and friendly in our thoughts (mentality), in how we express our emotions and in our actions.

If we are perceived as being irresponsible and dishonest then we must seize every opportunity to learn to change. As we might expect, our first few efforts will be met with deep suspicion. That is part of the price that we must pay to repair the damage resulting from our earlier decisions and thinking. Accept full responsibility!

If our reputation is extremely poor because of our own doing, never forget that it is completely worth the effort that we put into repairing our reputation. We may have to relocate to a different community to gain a fair start though. Regardless of what our history contains, we can own up to it. We can apologize, when and if we feel the need, but move forward in getting our life where we want it to be.

None of us are extraordinary in any particular way aside from our desire repair some important concerns in our lives. As we work to move our lives in a positive direction, we will be met with countless opportunities, in a variety of areas of our lives, to secure lasting changes for the better. We can choose to embrace these opportunities with gratitude and a loving heart. This will do more to provide self support in moving forward than any praise we can win from those around us.

Abandon Excuses Not Responsibility

In this age of ever-improving technology, we are learning to give responsibility for our life condition to businesses, institutions, consultants, advisors, counselors, media sources and other people we really don't know. We are literally, being taught by business people to give away responsibility in virtually every part of our lives, yet we are becoming increasingly frustrated with the condition of our lives. With each responsibility that we delegate, we also relinquish our freedom that is associated with it.

Think about the people we know:

> We know people who place the complete responsibility for their child's education (academics, life skills, discipline and social skills) with the teachers at their school. The teachers will tell us (nearly always) that they cannot be effective without the support of the parents in the home.

> A common complaint among public school teachers is that they don't see the parents of their most challenging students until there is a crisis. Yet, the student's parents are the first to blame the school system for the issues that their child is facing.

> A married couple enlist the services a therapist because they are not happy in their relationship. They actually do love each other and they do want their relationship to be better. After several months of this therapy, both complain that it is not working and that it is pointless to continue. They complain that the therapist isn't competent or is no good because they don't feel 'all gooey' inside about each other.

> Someone from our workplace joins a weight loss/fitness center to "get in shape." After six months of membership, there is virtually no change in our coworker's appearance. When we inquire about how things are progressing, our coworker responds that it wasn't worth it because all that the trainer wanted to do was "torture me and complain about my eating habits."

In each of the above scenarios, those who appeared to desire positive results the most, gave away their responsibility for success to someone else. In every case, the results were marginal and each party became frustrated with new condition of his or her life. Once we give away responsibility for any area of our life, we also give away our power and ability to control the outcomes in that area of our life that we say that we ultimately want. How could this possibly be the case?

Actually, it is quite easy. Let's take a look at our own life right now. It doesn't matter what our lifestyle, income level, background, social circle or education level may be. We can observe where we have taken full responsibility for our lives and where we have given some areas away. Note those areas. For example, are we satisfied with the state of our health? Are we happy? How is the quality of our social life? What about our primary relationship? Are things the way we want at work? Are we satisfied with our spiritual development?

When we allow others to decide the ultimate fate of any area of our lives, we are not being true to ourselves and we pay for it with our frustration and disappointment when those areas produce marginal satisfaction for us. This does not mean that we should micro-manage every area of our lives. It simply means this: if any part of our life isn't going the way we want, no other person should care about this more than we do. No one else can figure out what is right for us better than us, as long as we have all of the facts that we need. This does not mean that we have to do it all ourselves; absolutely not!

We may have a family physician, dentist, financial advisor, tax consultant, place of worship and so on, where we go to solicit advice regarding so many areas of our well being. There is nothing wrong with that at all. When we ask them for their help in their respective fields of expertise, we can accept and act on that counsel alone or we can accept the information as a part of what we need to know to make an informed decision. In other words, continue to seek other points of view until we have all angles covered.

We can ask where else we would find additional information. We can inquire about others with whom we might discuss our matter of concern. We need not be afraid that this approach would offend any our trusted professionals. Remember, they respect inquiring minds, as they have themselves. Any professional is flattered to be a part of your quest for knowledge. In observing how serious we are to make an informed decision, any of these trusted professionals would take us or our situation even more seriously in the future.

Let's take some time, later today, to examine any areas of our life that have been nagging at our thoughts. It might be anxiety over health issues, periodic stressful situations, quality of our nutritional intake, an unresolved matter with a friend, the fact that we haven't created a realistic household budget; or whatever the case. Let's give some heart-felt thought to the areas of our life that we have been neglecting or for which we have been giving responsibility away to someone else. We can make the decision to take active control of any of these areas immediately.

We Are Wasting Technology

Have you ever known anyone who lived with an uncomfortable condition for a long period of time only to learn that a treatment or remedy for that specific condition was discovered years earlier? Of course, they wanted to get their turn for treatment as soon as they are able to do so. Imagine how much of that person's suffering could have been prevented if that treatment were made public at the time of discovery. (Christy, 1994)

Because so many of us haven't committed to taking full responsibility for the condition of our lives, countless solutions for our health and wellbeing are going undiscovered and thereby retarding technological improvement and progress of these many solutions. There are millions of small business people, technicians, inventers and specialists who have found or created solutions to unique complications that we all share in every area of our existence. (Trudeau, 2004)

Unfortunately, these people do not possess substantial advertising budgets and therefore, they cannot afford to create commercial spots and infomercials that can be run often enough to let the rest of us know about what they have to offer. Even a small newspaper ad in a city newspaper can cost several thousands of dollars each week to run and the results are often very unpredictable. Virtually, the best and lowest cost solution is a well-designed website (which also can run several thousand dollars plus advertising costs).

A properly designed website should contain thorough information about the business, its history, business philosophy, products or services, policies and procedures, purchase and shipping information, contact options information and customer service guarantee options.

Use the internet to find out about these businesses and professionals that can help us. They hold fairs, expositions and conventions in virtually any area for our specific concern. Go to them! We will meet extraordinary professionals and business people. We will meet others who, like us, who are at various stages of finding solutions to their life issues.

Be prepared to be deluged with information about products, services, support groups, educational opportunities, special invitations and amazing product samples. Not only will we enjoy this new experience, we will find a whole new world of resources for when we have questions. Our options for finding solutions, as our life perspective, will be broadened, considerably. (Anderson G., 1995)

In our active search for answers, we will help ourselves, the professionals that we meet, the industry that we are investigating and those who are employed in that industry. We also place ourselves in a position to help others with whom we come in contact in our community, at our place of worship, in our workplace, at our school and among our social circle.

In taking an active interest in finding solutions for the issues affecting our life condition, we change our outlook on life, our expectations for ourselves and our future as well as how we see ourselves. Our contact can effect new and very valuable relationships, future business growth, health breakthroughs and tremendous resource networks. We must always be willing to investigate, listen, explore and experiment. The opportunities for personal enrichment, in a variety of areas and on a variety of levels in our lives, are boundless. (Williams, 1988)

How Enablers Damage Us

Enablers are well-meaning people, who under the guise of love and caring for a particular person, consistently intervenes into that person's life to prevent or stave off harm to that person. They typically make excuses for goals not reached by that person. They cover for their wrong acts and coddle that person as being good and not really meaning to do what it appears that they did. These people do things like these:

- Give money to a person who is ill from excessive smoking, alcohol consumption or illegal substance abuse when they should encourage treatment.
- Consistently bail a person out of jail who has been arrested multiple times for the same offense.
- Make excuses for their child's disruptive behavior in the classroom or on the playground.
- Make excuses for the offensive actions of an abusive spouse.
- Lie to a person about the true condition of their appearance or health so that they don't "hurt" that person's feelings.
- Constantly find employment for a person who keeps getting terminated from one employment opportunity after another.
- "Loan" money to people who have virtually no means to repay their debts.
- Consistently trust someone who has demonstrated no ability to keep a promise or commitment.
- Pretend to believe a person who obviously makes up lies to get what (or out of) he or she wants for the time.
- Do chores or homework for a child who has been reminded multiple times that _they_ (the child) need to complete.
- Tell a person multiple times to do or stop doing a particular thing (note that law enforcement officials are in the habit of telling a person one time before they choose to administer a more forceful means of compliance to their commands).
- Trust the word of an addict or abuser by covering for, supporting and financing them.

If we find ourselves to be engaging in "enabler" behavior for anyone, STOP IT! Our actions are not helpful to the person we think we are helping. It does not matter if the person is our mate, sibling, child or a close friend. Anyone who learns to be responsible for his or her own life condition must come into that realization through personal recognition.

We cannot do this for him or her. We must allow circumstances to develop without our interference that will teach that person, convincingly, that he or she must change the direction of his or her life by accepting full responsibility for it.

When we cover for, coddle or do any task for another person that he should do for himself, we are robbing that person of the dignity and self respect he would claim as a result of the tremendous effort he would put forth in turning his life situation to a positive and productive direction.

When we intervene with unsolicited counsel, instruction or wisdom, we only prolong our loved one's period of suffering. We delay their day of clearly understanding that they, themselves, must make the decision to commit to accepting full responsibility for bringing their life condition to where they desire it to be (not where **_we_** desire it to be).

Everyone wants to tell stories of triumph, war stories from our lives that made us who and what we are today. Our education, both formal and informal, combined with our experiences, produces some measure of wisdom in each of us, depending on how much we grasp from our life lessons.

Ideally, we will mature to the extent that we develop the desire to pass on what we know to those who might benefit from or at least appreciate our guidance. If we have been an enabler to someone who we thought we were helping, we must free ourselves from this impediment and allow the person we were trying to help to begin the journey through this important and life-changing experience.

Some of us reading this section today have figured out that we, ourselves, are the enabled party. We have made a complete mess of our lives. We have become addicted, abusive and predatorial. We have created a terrible reputation for ourselves. We are not trusted nor respected by those who we know still love us.

We know that we are generally tolerated instead of accepted by those people in our family and social circle. We know exactly who we can go to when we need money, a ride, a good meal, sex and place to sleep. For everyone who enables us, we have learned exactly what to say and how to behave to get what we want from them.

Until now, we haven't even considered that it might require courage to admit that we engage in shameful manipulations of other people's guilt to get our way with them. When that doesn't work, we attempt to use flattery, false praise, fear and other intimidating tactics to get what we want. To this point, in our dealings with people, we have openly demonstrated an absence of good character and ethics at every turn.

Anyone can surmise that this is an unsustainable path in life that will only bring greater misery and isolation with each passing day. We are only continuing down this road because we don't trust ourselves to keep any of our commitments, if we chose to accept full responsibility for our lives. We don't believe anyone would truly respect and support our decision if we found the strength within to make it.

The only way we can end the slide, of a toxic lifestyle, is to make a commitment to ourselves today. We must allow our attitude of resolve to be foremost in our minds, today. There is neither tomorrow nor yesterday, only today. We can decide to be fully responsible for our lives today, all day, from this moment. Every day, is today. We must internalize this commitment and live it moment to moment.

When we require help from others, we must do so with full respect for that other person. If we accept money, we must do so with the understanding that we earn it by performing a chore or task of the paying person's choosing. If we enlist another person's time or resources because we need his or her help, we must repay that person in kind, again according to that other person's choosing. (Dyer, 2009)

Learning to repay, immediately, the people who have been enabling us is the first step in accepting responsibility for ourselves. Volunteering to help others by giving our time and physical energy, with no expectations, is a great second step for us to take in demonstrating responsibility for our lives. The third step is critical in establishing ourselves as responsible people. It requires us to develop our independence by earning our own space within our current place of residence.

This means paying our fair share of expenses for the use of the facilities. This act alone, speaks volumes about our commitment to become responsible influences where we are as we respect those who have already been on this path long before us.

Obviously, we will transition onto greater feats of demonstrated responsibility. The above-mentioned steps are important to take to begin. They are 'character-building' steps. As we observe the change in respect from others who are watching our behavior, we will build greater character qualities that will allow us to take subsequent steps with ever-growing confidence. We will become one of those who have a story to tell that encourages others to do the same. We can put ourselves into the category of people who choose to take responsibility for their lives, with no excuses and without manipulation.

Chapter 3

Education is a progressive discovery of our own ignorance.

- Will Durant

Our Education Does Not Stop Because We Graduate

Traditional public school education does not necessarily prepare us for success in life; it only prepares us to continue our education, whether in a college, on a job, in the military or on a path of our own choosing. We have only learned enough to understand that we need to learn so much more, to make our life a productive one.

When we sit through our graduation ceremony, our speakers, many of them were the same teachers who we consistently disappointed in our classroom, encouraged us as though we were going to go out and save the world from evil and corruption.

So often, we find that we struggle through life because of an obvious lack of knowledge concerning our options in life. We don't appear to know exactly where we want to go; or, how to get there if we did. We seem to do everything, in the most difficult fashion possible.

If someone were to observe us long enough, their heart would go out to us and yet we are too proud to ask for help. No doubt, if not us, we know someone who is like this. After some examination, we might decide that, in some cases, this is us more often than we care to admit.

Many of us are proficient in certain areas of life and we might think of ourselves as just "plain dumb" in others. For example, some of us are intellectual giants and yet we have only marginal athletic skills. For others of us, we are great at making money and terrible at personal relationships. Writing and verbal skills comes easier for many of us, yet we have virtually no ability to outfit our home intelligently (or ourselves for that matter). We might be artistically inclined but have extremely poor money management skills.

It is important to understand that education comes to each of us in many forms. If we are one of those who has used the excuse that we never had the opportunity to go to college to explain why we haven't become the success, in life, that we know that we could have become, pay close attention. Formal education has less to do with being successful and more to do with developing thinking skills.

We often confuse formal education with respect for learning. Formal education is concerned with a broad exposure to various concepts over a variety of disciplines. Formal education teaches us to ask specific types of questions, assess issues, weigh options and alternatives, make decisions and evaluate our range of solutions in light of the resolution that we seek. Learning concerns our appetite for knowledge, wherever we can gain it. Those of us who have a healthy respect for learning will always have the educational advantage.

We are always learning in one form or another. We are provided opportunities for learning nearly every day of our lives through the various experiences that we are afforded. Education is nothing more than learning a lesson that has been provided to us so that we can build character, gain wisdom and be better decision makers than we were before.

For example, we must ascertain lessons from such experiences as these: what lesson did we learn from our last failed relationship or marriage; what lesson did we learn from our last failed business venture or financial debacle; the last job or friend we lost; the last clash with our teen over his or her latest mate choice; that test we failed or that bad grade we received last term.

If we find it easy to create excuses like, "I'm a lousy spouse or friend" or "I'm dumb about that," we have completely missed the point of the lesson we've been provided. When we learn from our experiences, our responses are more like these: I need to be more open about my feelings or sensitive to my partners needs. I should not select a partner based solely on physical appearance or sexual performance. I need to take my job more seriously. I need to study more seriously; perhaps use a tutor and so on. When we respect learning, we always look for the lesson from our experiences whether we think of those experiences as good or bad.

There are many ways where we can gain an education. There are also numerous places where we can gain the knowledge we require so that we can create a fruitful quality of life. Having a broad range of knowledge is helpful for enjoying a multiplicity of pleasures in life.

However, a specialized knowledge of an area of life, about which we are absolutely passionate, can create the path to success in life that most of us seek. Whatever our preference, it is our level of respect, for knowledge, that will be the vehicle that allows us to realize our life dreams. Consider the many options in acquiring an education:

> **Formal Education** – This is the regular classroom style of education through which most of us grew up. We threw paper wads, passed notes (nowadays text), hated some teachers and loved others and played dirty tricks on our classmates and tried to get out of doing class assignments and homework. If we weren't able to go to college, right after high school, the biggest change is that, in the world of work, the people who teach us, earn a lot more money and have a lot less responsibility.
>
> **Informal Education** – This area of education is generally concerns all of the other ways we gather and learn new knowledge. Regardless of where we find ourselves in life, opportunities for specialized learning abound. Most informal education takes place while we are transitioning to a new phase of

our lives. This kind of education is often acquired out of necessity for some life-changing endeavor like new job training, home care for a loved one, pre-business ownership, on-going learning, military training and so on. They are these:

Coaching – This is adaptive learning. Suppose we are an eight-year veteran of our field. We have recently changed employers. Today, we find ourselves in a new workplace with a new employer. Our industry knowledge is solid; however, we must be taught updated information regarding the paperwork, policies and procedures that our new employer requires. We will be coupled with a competent, experienced coworker from that company who will teach us and document that we understand what we need to, so that we can, soon, work independently in our new workplace.

Counseling – This is also the type of education we receive from our physician, social worker, psychologist or other professional so that we can care for ourselves or a loved one regarding a particular situation. This is also the kind of education our insurance agent, investment advisor, attorney and other kind of consultants must provide to us so that they can sell to us or work with us to achieve a particular goal.

Training – This type of education may take place in the workplace or an employer-sponsored educational facility so that we can become an efficient and effective employee. Here, generally, we learn by doing or imitating our coworkers until what they are doing begins to make sense to us. Training actually involves repackaging our formal education and prior work experience so that it can be used for a new purpose.

Life Experience – This also known as "the school of hard knocks" because no one offers us any help that we don't request. Everyone presumes that we know what we are doing (as though we have a realistic master plan); and if we don't, too bad for us. If we have a respect for education and learn well from our mistakes, this is a worthwhile way to gain knowledge. It will divide the serious and committed learners from the excuse-making and undisciplined "want to-be" learners.

The best illustration of this is that of going into business. This life-experience education is one that separates successful business owners from the naïve employees who want a free ride on the backs of other employees. As employees, we learn a great deal about ourselves as workers when we attempt to go into business as owners.

We quickly learn that employee training, sick days, personal days, laziness, lateness, benefits, recruiting and advertising all cost money. Those, of us, who aren't serious about learning, soon find that we have no place in business ownership. We often return to the labor market as employees with a renewed respect for our employers.

Self-education – This is the pinnacle of learning and it can take place anywhere: in a formal or informal setting, at work or on our own time. This is when we take an active role in our own learning and personal development; we don't leave the responsibility of learning to anyone else.

We study until we can explain what we have learned in our own words with passion and conviction. We learn our subject so thoroughly that we can point out deficiencies in the teaching quality of our teachers or professors and we can spot inconsistencies in the various text books from which we gather our information.

Many of us develop ourselves for complete career changes by going to the library and studying all materials that we can find on the new field we desire to study. Although no diploma will be attained or awarded, self education is among the most solid forms of education that anyone could possibly attain.

Functional Education – This is learning for the express purpose of applying the knowledge immediately for our own protection. It is acquired on an 'as-needed' basis. For those of us who have sent our children to college, we know a great deal more about the college financial business now than when our student was in junior high school.

We became an expert because we had to in order work things out for our family. If we would do the same thing regarding automobile engine repair, we could stop being concerned about an auto mechanic ever over charging us compared to quality of service that he or she renders.

When we become knowledgeable about our home, we will be confident in hiring contractors (plumbers, electricians, roofers, HVAC and installers of all kinds); we would become confident that we are getting the best quality products and services for our money. We would ask better questions and be familiar with our options. In some cases, we may find that we might want to handle the work ourselves. Our functional education approach can pay off immediately!

Embracing a functional education is quite necessary before we can begin to take full responsibility for every area of our life. In short, we learn according to our need and apply our knowledge accordingly. With a functional education, we can experiment with a collage of methodologies until we find the right combination of options and solutions that fit our life.

Our perception of education is important to adjust if we are to begin to accept responsibility for each area of our lives. We have the ability to learn as much as we want to improve our own life and the lives of those to whom are the closest. As we build our functional education from gathering information based on facts, science, history, logic, and reason, we will move quickly to building the life changing wisdom that only life experience can provide.

Gain a Financial Education

A significant reason why we find our lives are in a state of emergency is that so many of us lack an understanding of the importance of financial fitness. Many of us come from backgrounds where we weren't taught financial literacy, basic banking knowledge, investment strategies and financial planning.

This section is about money. Money is a fact of life on earth. Money is neutral; there is nothing inherently good or bad about it. The same money that one person hordes and uses accomplish selfish goals can be used to build safe housing for the poor to finance a new business venture that would eventually employ hundreds or thousands of people. (Wattles, 1976)

Believe it or not, the richest people do not have all of the wealth. They do influence where the vast majority of it is invested because so many people refuse to accept financial responsibility for their own lives. That is right; they literally give away their financial responsibilities to people they don't know.

They give this responsibility to their employers, financial institutions, government institutions, insurance companies, financial planners and so on. These same people are actually surprised when their employers announce, one day, that they are decreasing the workforce. Worse still, the pension fund is not solvent because their employer used the funds for collateral on a risky financial venture that did not work out well. (Clason, 1926)

Even when we do gain a significant sum of money, we waste it. Did you know that the average multi-million dollar lottery winner is usually financially broke within about seven years of taking possession of funds? Look how many former professional athletes, many of whom have signed several multi-million dollar contracts throughout their career, have virtually nothing, financially, to show for their superior athletic mastery. (Eker, 2005)

Many second-generation business owners literally bankrupt well established, high quality family-owned businesses within a few short years of taking over as principals. They usually do not internalize and practice the sound financial principles on which the business was built.

So what is the common denominator here? The greatest difference between people who have amassed great wealth and those mentioned above is the financial mentality each group. Rich people invest money and poor people spend money. I use to enjoy giving my students a financial exercise that never failed to prove this point. See how you do with it.

Here is the situation: We win sixty million dollars in a lottery. We can receive the full value over a 26-year period or we can take the "present value" of your winnings now in one lump sum of 29 million dollars. Which do we take?

Once we have made our choice, I would ask, what would we purchase with our winnings? What kind of lifestyle would we have? Where would we travel? What is the quality of our accommodations? Describe our social life? How would we entertain in at home? What kind of cars would we own?

The room would become highly energetic; filled with chatter about all of the possibilities that some much extra money could bring to their lives. We would keep track of the spending until all of the dreams of everyone in the classroom were fulfilled. We would then total the combined costs to fulfill the common dream of the class. The total for the home, cars, vacations, clothes, social life and miscellaneous expenses usually totaled about 5.6 million dollars.

At this point, there would be complete silence – we could hear a pin drop. Everyone in the class has now demonstrated conclusively that after our dreams are completely fulfilled, we have no idea of what to do with the remaining money. I repeated this exercise for about ten years with adults. They results were typically the same.

Whenever I would ask what we should do with the remainder of the money, the very last suggestion that would ever be made was to invest the money. Even then, no one could agree on exactly how that should be done. I did this well after the groundbreaking investment authority, Robert Kiosaky published his famous book, "Rich Dad Poor Dad."

Each day, we have the opportunity to make the decision to accept full responsibility for the situations, direction and condition of our life. Since we do not know what will befall us next year or even tomorrow, each day we put off this crucial decision, the further we push ourselves away from a life of fulfillment of our own creation. Our financial education is just another area for which we can choose to accept full responsibility.

The Good Ole Days

Life was so much easier when we lived with our parents. We had no bills, free food each day and a roof over our head. Many of us had virtually an unlimited use of a car. Our social lives were filled with school activities, parties, concerts, running with our friends and maybe a cushy part-time job to pay for dating expenses. Life was great. Our future was bright and promising; all those speakers at our graduation ceremony said so!

We all start out with the same apparent opportunities for a happy life. As we progress along in our respective worlds, we discover that our knowledge of survival and prospects for success varies considerably.

When we look at life based on our high school experiences and classmates, especially those who seemed to have answers for virtually everything, we could reason away all of our future problems and rationalize success strategies for every facet of our lives. As we look back, we see just how solid that knowledge was when it had to stand the test of real life.

Real-life situations quickly separated the best prepared from those who merely talked a good game. Real-life situations filtered out the procrastinators from those who were proactive. Likewise, the superficial were quickly distinguished from those who were serious about their lives.

If we came from an environment and a family that did not prepare us well for life on our own, this was a particularly traumatic time for us. If we did not take full responsibility for our life condition and prepare appropriately, we found ourselves reeling after graduation. We may have felt, at some point that we may not recover from this trauma for the rest of our lives.

Most of us realized that we had to grow up quickly so we made decisions like securing gainful employment in a hastily chosen career path, enlisting in military service or trying our hand at higher education. Before long, we found ourselves in adult circumstances like a marriage, growing debt and under-employment situations.

The complexity of these circumstances were further complicated by the realization that our mate selection, career choice, higher education major and decision to have children could have been better thought out. It was at this point where we made our life altering decisions.

Despite the repetition of hearing for most of our lives that we "should not," we make self-damaging choices like choosing to smoke, excessive use of over-the-counter drugs and ever-increasing alcohol consumption as a way of escaping our stressful situations. Even worse, others, of us, chose to compromise our characters and values by turning to criminal activities and lifestyles to make ends meet.

This was a particularly self-damaging option in light of the amazing technological advancements made in the law enforcement industry. If we view such advances in the context of the impact of public opinion on world politics, it was difficult to expect that any clear-thinking person would, remotely, consider such options; that is our clue that there was more to this mystery.

Imagine this situation: we don't have as much money (disposable income) as we believe that we should have (acquired from gainful employment that we don't enjoy). Add a stressful mate relationship at home with someone we are struggling to understand and still getting to know. If there are children in the home, this only increases the pressure for suitable provisions. It is possible that many of us don't have to imagine this scenario because we have been living it.

Purely from frustration and pressures from work, home and the developing primary relationship, it is easy to develop obstacles to being fully responsible for our life circumstances. We begin to procrastinate on bill paying as none of the options are pleasant. We begin complaining about our employment at home and about our home situation in the workplace.

Then we begin buying into the mentality that allows for gossip and rumors. We eventually find ourselves becoming more interested in the lives of other people than our own. Consider how much attention we give to lives of celebrities compared with how much we give our own. They are living their dreams while we are adding, daily, to our own misery.

Our primary relationship issues seem to escalate. Our children seem to develop more issues. Our overall health seems to ebb from good health periodically. If we don't consciously focus our attention on one area over another, we seem to lose total perspective. Still, we often develop self-esteem and self-image issues. We often begin to look and feel much older than our age because of the stresses in our lives.

We also start viewing our own lives, as well as the lives of our loved ones, in the most limited perspectives. Worse still, we start teaching these unhealthy views we have, of our lives, to our children. Ideas that the rich are to blame for our problems; that certain races of people are the root cause of the problems; that marriage is a bad institution; that you can't get ahead by playing fair and following the law and so on. (McWhorter, 2000)

The life choices that we make determine how far up (or down) on the economic ladder we position ourselves. How easy is it to lose prospective, at this point? Under these circumstances, our family support systems and our social influences are critical to our sanity and our physical well being. If we somehow damage these in the process, we only add to our self destruction.

With the above situation as a foundation, let us see how this scenario can increase in negativity. If we have family and friends who appear to be getting through life with some comfort, we are more likely to adopt those methodologies that seem to be working. So, we bring on the cigarettes (along with the jokes), alcohol and drugs (legal and illegal).

If "plausible," part-time criminal activities (like shoplifting, auto theft, trafficking, prostitution, workplace/business scams and so on) are a part of the perceived solution, then we find it difficult to resist, especially if we have a mentor who is a family member or someone we regard as a friend that encourages us to move our lives in this direction.

Before we realize it, we have created a tremendous web of difficulties we would have to overcome if we are to make the decision to take responsibility and turn our lives into something infinitely positive. Even at this point, when we have an apparent mountain of difficulties to surmount, it is still worth choosing to make the decision to accept full responsibility for the condition of our life and resolve to take charge and change it, permanently, for the best.

If this sounds like our lives now, don't be discouraged. There are hundreds of thousands of people who started out in worse situations and who turned their lives in a positive direction, prospered and made many positive contributions to their society. We can too!

Just because our life isn't where we want it right now, doesn't mean we can't "clean it up." Embracing a solid respect for learning is a great first step. We can resolve to continue our education every day. Instead of sharing our unsolicited opinions so much, why not spend at least half of our conversation time asking questions and listening, attentively, for any new wisdom that we can add to our own. We can spend more time seeking educational content when we choose to view television or surf the internet.

Public television stations spend a great deal of effort to keep its public, objectively, well informed on social, political, environmental and quality-of-life issues. They also feature regular concerts and in-depth interviews of the world's most popular celebrities. Also, the quality of the nature and historical programming is unrivaled.

Additionally, scheduled at convenient times through the week are course programming that features teaching in the area of mathematics, chemistry, science, geography and various arts like: sketching, painting, sculpting, language and music lessons. The entertainment programming is family friendly and often international in scope. I realize that many of us are saying to ourselves like, 'when will I ever need to learn this stuff now.'

Such thoughts are the immature ramblings from our days as an under-achieving student when we were children. Who else thinks this way? If we are parents, we should learn the above-mentioned subjects. We might actually be able to help our children with their homework or educate them about options on where they could take their senior trip.

When we schedule our spare-time activities, keep in mind that there are always expositions and shows scheduled at the local convention center. Public home building supply stores feature regular courses on home repair and building projects. When we check at our local library, we can find numerous local groups of special interests groups who meet regularly to exchange information and ideas on modeling projects, collecting, nature interests, business development, community improvement, inventions and so on.

We must take the initiative in furthering our learning. Just as no one is going to knock on our door to offer us a great job, no one is going to knock on our door to find out if we want to do anything to improve the condition of our life. It is our responsibility to get out there and make it happen; it always has been.

Let's allow ourselves to develop a superior respect for learning in every phase of our lives. At the very worst, we will become more gifted conversationists, establish healthier relationships, broaden our range of interests and enjoy greater social experiences. We can use self-education to change the direction of our lives.

Keep a Distance Regarding Foolish People

Not everyone appreciates the value of learning. Many of us simply choose not to learn from our experiences (especially our mistakes) and we shun education in any form. If we are serious about accepting full responsibility for the condition of our life with the intention of taking control of our life and making it a positive and productive existence, it is in our best interest to keep such people out of our personal life, at all costs.

If we keep company with people who, routinely and carelessly, engage in stupid and foolish behavior, stupid and foolish circumstances will eventually over take our lives. Any progress we would have made would be wasted.

As we examine the people we spend our time with in our life, we can identify the foolish people by their thinking and their behavior. The richest and wisest man in recorded history, King Solomon, wrote down the wisdom he gained from his life experiences, for his sons, so that their successes in life would not be impeded.

As an indicator of his wealth, it is rumored to have taken over 7000 loaves of bread to feed his many servants for just one meal of the day. He owned 12,000 horses with horsemen and 1,400 chariots. He is rumored to have had 700 wives and 300 concubines. He credited his wisdom as being responsible for his ability to amass such great wealth. Regularly, people from surrounding nations came to hear Solomon expound on his wisdom. (Scott, 2006)

King Solomon identified foolish people this way. They are people, who:

- **Despise wisdom, instruction and wise counsel** – They do not appreciate it when we give them helpful information for their own benefit. They want to do things their way even when they know that they are wrong. Control is more important than doing the right thing or doing things correctly.
- **Hate correction** – They don't like to be told when they have made a mistake. They would rather make excuses and blame others for the troubles they bring rather than to accept responsibility for their choices and make things right, in life.

- **Take no delight in understanding** – They make little or no effort to see how information, outside of what they know, can be useful to them. When we observe them closely, it actually appears that they are trying to misunderstand or miss the point of what is being communicated regarding their shortcomings. It will seem pointless to keep explaining the same information to them.
- **Whose mouth is their destruction** – The majority of their problems stem from something they said. They seem to thrive on rumors, drama and gossip. They don't seem to learn from their negative experiences because they keep repeating them.
- **They answer a matter before they hear about it** – They express their opinions and reach a conclusion before they examine all available information on the matter. Outside input is either not welcome or not taken seriously. Explaining a problem that is on their horizon will not reach their ears because they will refuse to acknowledge it.
- **They hide their hatred by lying and slandering others** – They smile in the faces of the people they don't like and attempt to set them up for destruction behind their backs. Often, these are people in influential positions directly or indirectly. They will recruit naïve and gullible people, as pawns, to do their "dirty work" for them. Through these pawns, they will execute poorly thought out acts of deceit, manipulation and scandal against those whom they secretly despise.
- **They do evil as a sport** – They lie, cheat, manipulate, gossip to anyone who will hear them, in an effort to improve their own image and to get their own way. They enjoy creating situations that put others in an unfavorable light or at a serious disadvantage simply for their own entertainment. They enjoy taking "cheap shots" at people who mean them no harm. They thrive on fear mongering, intimidation and creating chaos for others.
- **Their words are hasty; their mouths spout folly (recklessness)** – They are not diligent in their efforts to gain the truth, be honest or to justify fair treatment. They will often try to out talk us by resorting to verbal attacks, talking faster, raising their voice and changing subjects quickly without giving us an opportunity to respond. This is done to confuse and disorient us. When we stoop to their level by arguing with them, we will appear to be just as foolish. When we allow ourselves to be engaged in such behavior, observers cannot see a difference between us and the foolish ones. That is the aim of the foolish.

As we examine King Solomon's wisdom for identifying foolish people, certain people who we know are coming into our thoughts. We can give them the benefit of our doubt by talking with them about our decision to change our life and accept full responsibility for the condition of our life.

We could see if we can gain their support. They might not be so foolish after all. We can ask them to think it through and to feel free to make some suggestions, to us, on how we might improve our life. Then, wait a week or so and ask them if they have any suggestions for how we can approach taking control of the direction of our life.

If they have no idea what we are talking about, we might have classified them correctly. When we remind them of our decision to accept full responsibility for our life, see if they make up excuses and make a promise to deal with it in the future. They may never bring it up again. If this is the case with our friend or family member, we must move forward on our own and allow them the serenity and security of the world they have come to value.

We have to commit to bringing people into our world who can relate to where we intend to take our life. Make sure that they are doing the same. The people with whom we surround ourselves will make all the difference in our endeavor to improve the quality of our life to a positive and productive condition.

In the recipe, for success in life, education (respect for learning) is a most critical component. It is through education that we learn to grasp the most important concepts that improve the quality of life for each of us in the most basic areas like, how we can become financially prosperous, rear children to be responsible and productive adults, improve our personal relationships as well as those relationships with family and friends.

Whenever we choose to educate ourselves in each of these areas, commit to mastering the knowledge. Also, we can study the lives of those who practice their mastery so that we might benefit from their wisdom and advice. A positive education, however we might attain it is always an excellent idea.

We will never be worse off for knowing new things. Our peril comes when we make poor decisions about how to use what we learn. Always seek to do good and right for all people who are concerned. Our lives will improve in unforeseen and unexpected ways, always.

Chapter 4

True Love comes from God, and love is demonstrated through character.

— Philemon Laida

The Essence of Our Character

In order to make important progress in improving the condition of our lives, it is necessary to be honest about what kind of person we believe ourselves to be. In the first chapter, we were asked about whom we are; sort of a personality check. The reason was so that we could accurately assess the condition of our overall life condition – physically, emotionally, mentally, socially and spiritually. After we examined each of these aspects of ourselves, we could then develop some idea of where we wanted to begin in revamping our life condition.

Here, we are concerned with our personal character profile. When we examine this area of ourselves, we can uncover specific reasons why our lives are where they are. Let's begin with the negative and self-damaging characteristics in our personality.

Some of us like to cut corners; cheat a little here and there. Sometimes we tell little lies; distort the truth a bit and bend laws for our convenience. Often, we allow ourselves to support ideas like, "what a person doesn't know won't hurt them." or "I get what I want, even at the expense of others (with no thought of fair compensation)."

Some of us will cheat a friend or confidant if circumstances are such that they would never find out about the deception. It can be entertaining to engage in spreading gossip, negative and damaging rumors that have are not based in facts. We sometimes allow ourselves to think the worst about someone, who we don't know well, because of what someone else thinks and told us.

What We Believe

Our character shapes what we believe about various areas of our lives and ourselves. Let's observe our current life situation. It is a summation of what we believe. It is not necessarily a reflection of what we think or say. It is, without a doubt, the sum total of what we actually believe about ourselves, our living arrangement, our income, our social situation, our employment situation and so on.

This isn't another endorsement of the law of attraction nor is it an attempt to condemn ourselves for the areas of our life that do not work for us. Nothing, under our control, exists in our life that doesn't support our beliefs, whether we are proud of them or embarrassed by them.

Let's observe ourselves. As an example, let's start with our home. We might live in house, condominium, apartment, mobile home or a trailer. The market value of our home really doesn't matter. What does matter is our mentality about our home. Our mentality is reflected in our home environment. If our home is sloppy, cluttered, disorganized and in a state of disrepair, there is a good chance that there are parallels of these qualities in our current life situations.

Let's consider our kitchen area; the place where we are responsible for preparing wholesome, nutritious, healthy foods for ourselves and our family. Note if the environment is kept clean; the used dishes washed, dried and put away in a timely fashion; the condition of the floor; the insides of our refrigerator and oven. The conditions of these various areas of our home are literally reflections of our beliefs about what is acceptable for us in our life.

We can do this with any area of our life: our wardrobe and grooming, mode of transportation, social skills, public conduct, commitment to education, trend of employment choices, respect for the law, respect for other people, respect for animals, respect for the natural environment and so on. These all add up to what we believe about ourselves.

More to the point, the standards that we establish for ourselves, based on our beliefs, are public indicators about how we treat ourselves as well as how we will allow ourselves to be treated by others. These include family, friends, neighbors, acquaintances, employers, customers, co-workers, public officials and so on. All of these are manifestations of our character.

Character Influences

So many of us trust, virtually everything, we read in our news outlets, view on our televisions and hear on our radios as being fact. We tend to care only about matters that we are told that we should care about. We view certain influential figures in our life experience as virtually unquestionable. We must always be on guard about the information that we receive through such channels. (Williams, 1988)

Many influential people will create the illusion of possessing positive character qualities as a way to maintain the strength of their influence. Too many of us will trust such an image without question. That is why so many of us feel deceived and manipulated when we learn the truth of a situation. Some of us might even consider ourselves to be gullible or naïve.

There is nothing wrong with trusting influential people who support our positions when they are of good character. Unfortunately, so often, we find that these same people are really not imbued with the good character that they project. We find, time and again, that they are willing participants who routinely suppress important information, facts and details from the public, as a way to shield those, who they serve, the most powerful and influential, from public scrutiny. (Smallstorm, 2007)

There is a great deal wrong with accepting information that is given to us at face value without asking questions, investigating and verifying that the information as presented is accurate. We also must make it a rule to routinely verify the background of the presenters of such information as well.

A solid understanding of positive character qualities will help us to form a basis by which we can measure our own core character and that of others. By strengthening our overall character make up, we can repair and heal damaged relationships, prevent misunderstandings, promote harmonious social interaction, and intelligently resolve difficult situations, so that no one else feels cheated or victimized. The character areas that I find most appropriate to identify for this purpose are these:

> **Trustworthiness** – We practice being reliable by keeping our word as well as our promises. We must be honest in all of our dealings in all situations. Be loyal to those who care for us and stand up for causes that are good and positive for all people.
>
> **Ethics** – This characteristic is concerned with practicing a proper etiquette (conduct) that is positive and acceptable in all situations. We also practice morally correct behavior even when it appears that we do not have to do so. We must treat other people who are in a position of disadvantage with fairness and dignity. If we are unable to be of personal assistance to someone in need, we can still help them by providing information, opportunities and education to referrals, networking and organizations that can be of assistance.
>
> **Respectfulness** – This is treating others the way *they* would like to be treated. That means being tolerant of the differences in other people as well as being considerate of them and their needs. We should not threaten, hit or hurt anyone if we can help it at all. We must use language that shows the person, who we are addressing, is important. As often as possible, we must try to be polite: use the words 'please' and 'thank you' often in our interactions. Finally, we must value learning as much as society values sex and money.
>
> **Responsibility** – As the title of this book implies, we must be fully accountable for the circumstances our choices create. We should execute our duties at work, home or elsewhere in a timely and high quality manner. Further, we are to control our temper, language, body and word choices; we must discipline ourselves. It is important that we think matters through before we speak or take action on them.
>
> If we are in a leadership position, we must serve our subordinates, unselfishly and generously, by providing for their needs. Good character is the cornerstone of solid leadership. If we are in a subordinate position as an

employee or member, then it is our responsibility to support leadership that is fair, positive and productive so that it is effective and efficient.

We must be accountable for our learning efforts regardless of how strong or weak. We will pay our debts as we agreed (even if it now seems pretty unfair). As a parent, we are required to rear our children in matters of love, health, education, social skills, self-esteem and proper attitude. In our workplace or in our volunteer efforts, we must demonstrate a strong work ethic (that is to do it right the first time).

Integrity – This is where we build and maintain a good reputation. We deal with our anger in a peaceful and constructive way. We deal with the anger, insults and disagreements we receive from others peacefully. When dealing with challenges, be accurate, thorough and solution-oriented. Do not participate in gossip spreading, using profanity or language that makes other people feel uncomfortable. Of course, we must strive to be positive and productive in our lifestyle as well.

Fairness – We must remember, as we were taught as children, to share and take turns. Opportunities to learn, help, grow and create are everywhere but we must be open-minded so that we will recognize these opportunities. We must maintain an unbiased mentality in examining new information, ideas and concepts. We should never take advantage of others even when we could without anyone else becoming aware. We should never, carelessly, place blame on others or uphold double standards. We must be open to allowing second chances for those who demonstrate an "earnest" desire for such an opportunity.

Caring – Be kind by showing compassion and expressing thankfulness and gratitude openly. Forgive others as they request, after they apologize and atone for their transgressions. We must help those who are in need as our abilities and discretionary resources permit.

Citizenship – Commit to being a good neighbor (or friend, student, patron, visitor, participant, acquaintance, member and so on). Be cooperative and helpful in positive matters of community interest. We should vote, religiously, when we are of age. We must stay informed about our immediate, national and world environment from a variety of different sources.

Beware of "Experts"

These are people who are highly credible, noted authorities on a given subject who dispense advice, wisdom or helpful counsel, on issues of great public concern, for the benefit of the public at large. Their credibility and quality of knowledge is virtually unquestioned because of the reputation they have built for themselves. Consider the "Nader" example:

In 1971, there was a world-wide oil crisis according to the oil producing nations, oil industry moguls and world government leaders. In America, the average family annual income was $10,600 and the price of a gallon of gasoline was 40 cents. Their message to the world was that the earth is quickly running out of oil and so we must raise gasoline prices and ration purchases to retard demand. Their answer was to create an oil embargo in 1973. The citizens of nations that were the most dependent on gasoline powered transportation were near a state of panic. Then, an 'expert' surfaced.

A lawyer from Connecticut, Ralph Nader, who had become an advocate for public safety and general welfare, was addressing a federal congressional House-Senate economic subcommittee to verify the federal government's accuracy of claims that there was a world-wide oil (gasoline) shortage, regarding the oil crises and subsequent oil embargo issue. His presentation was passionate and fact filled. The most quoted statement, throughout the world community, that was gleaned from that presentation was this: "The world [earth] is literally drowning in oil." (Associated Press (Washington), 1974)

Like magic, the oil crisis and subsequent oil embargo issue evaporated in a matter of days; however, gas prices were still increased to 55 cents per gallon. With one quote from an expert, the efforts of the most powerful people of the world, to influence what its consumers believed about their economic futures, were crushed. Public opinion on this matter has been a significant political force since.

This is what an expert is expected to be — a responsible person of integrity and good character. The expert should be ethical and have pure motives when dispensing information for the public's benefit. Nader acted selflessly in serving and respecting trust that the international public had placed in him. His research was thorough, credible and unchallenged.

Suppose that on that day, Nader chose to deliver quite a different message. Suppose that he chose to align himself with the world leaders and oil industry influences for personal gain. That would have changed oil pricing strategies throughout the world up through today.

No one, publicly, would have been the wiser and Nader could have still enjoyed the benefits of his current status. His character, ethics and integrity, especially in this matter, is what distinguishes him as a genuine expert.

In our quest to find solutions in our lives, we will discover as many self-proclaimed experts as there are subject areas that we choose to investigate. Most will be educated, knowledgeable and have a desire to assist us in some way. What we will have to determine is the purity of their motives; their true agenda for rendering help.

We must determine if they have an ulterior motive or hidden agenda. We must be willing to discover for ourselves, with whom are they aligned industrially, politically, socially and academically. We must be willing to determine conclusively if they are steering us in a particular direction over another for any selfish reasons.

Note: Please do not confuse honest business people with these 'experts' although some may actually be both.

Whatever an "expert' tells us, either in person or through the media, it is important that we realize that there is more information that should be gathered. Also, some messages that we receive from television advertisements will be presented anonymously often referring us to an information source. Whatever the case, if it arouses any kind of suspicion in us, here are some things we will need to learn:

- **Begin with the expert** – Check credentials, affiliations, reputation and background. Next, gauge their sincerity and motives: Find out for which endorsements is this person being paid to support and by whom.
- **Examine the messages** – Study what is actually being said, as well as what is not being said. Discover if certain important aspects of the subject area are intentionally being avoided regarding the subject matter. Figure out, to whom are these messages being directed – all people or a select group? Whom does this message enrich? Is there any ambiguity in this message – can it mean more than one thing to one or more audiences? We must be on guard and willing to always investigate to gain clarification.
- **Notice the timing** – Does the timeliness and form of delivery of this message conveniently validate the position of a particular industry, political group or segment of the population (by the way, this is a double edged sword so we should be careful in our assessment and subsequent action). We must pay attention.

If we learn that there is real deception and manipulation of public trust being perpetrated, it is our personal responsibility to expose this fact, to everyone that we know, by whatever creative means we may devise. People who demonstrate questionable character by misusing their wealth and influence to manipulate the public's trust must be exposed and discredited. In this way, we are able to make important contributions to the improvement of honest and well-intentioned people everywhere.

Regardless of where our investigations take us, there is always a lesson to be learned and knowledge to be added to our own. There is something else to add to this subject. Please don't confuse a 'spokesperson' with an 'expert.' Here is the difference:

> *Spokesperson* – This is a person who is hired by an organization to present a message or a position on behalf of the organization. This spokesperson is often a gifted presenter regarding the subject matter at hand. This person

may be a celebrity from the entertainment industry, sports industry or a public figure in politics or some other walk of life. The fact that they are being paid doesn't diminish the seriousness or importance of their message. Still, we should apply the above-stated considerations in making our decision regarding the worth of their information for our personal adaptation of their message.

Expert – This person is usually an educated, experienced, veteran of a particular field or industry. An expert's testimony should be unbiased and it should not support any particular industry, political agenda or constituency. They are not necessarily honorable people. They are not necessarily interested in dispensing information that is in our best interest. In many cases, they are only trying to further the objectives of those who may not have our best interest in mind. We must investigate them to determine this for ourselves. The crucial components will be that person's reputation, educational credentials, character and documented motivations.

Here is a popular scenario that illustrates how experts may not have our best interests at heart. There are countless other examples that can be used but this one has almost become routine within mainstream radio and television programming.

Many people, in their search for ways to improve the quality of their health have found that herbal supplements hold a great deal of promise for attaining and maintaining the quality of health that they desire, instead of synthetic (pharmaceutical) treatments.

There are simple and effective herbal remedies and treatments that have been documented for controlling blood pressure, acid reflux, blood circulation issues, attention deficit issues, symptoms of Alzheimer's and Parkinson's disease, thyroid conditions, kidney issues, skin disorders and so on.

Millions of people use these treatments to attain the successful results that they desire without the side effects that often come with pharmaceutical treatments. (Kloss, 1972)

Of course there are "experts" who rush to discredit and discourage consumers from using these treatments, remedies, strategies and methodologies that are time-tested as being effective in cultures around the world for centuries.

Their message usually is generously sprinkled with statements designed to imply that you should doubt their effectiveness or arouse suspicion about the industry agendas like these:

- "We have no evidence that these supplements are safe to consume"
- "We do not know enough about these remedies"

- "There are cases where people have had very bad experiences with these herbs"
- "We can't recommend these for use to treat real medical conditions"

Of course, the above statements are intentionally ambiguous in nature. They are all untrue. Collectively, there is a great deal of, well documented, information available from the herbal supplements industry. These statements are design to instill fear in us, because the above-statements are intentionally vague, as though there are some deep, dark secrets that are being withheld. Anyone who is deemed an expert and who uses such tactics should arouse a great deal of suspicion in each of us.

When someone who is supposedly an expert uses such statements as described above, the first question that we have to ask is, who is, "We?" Whenever an "expert" rushes to discredit an entire industry, that has demonstrated exemplary standards of ethics and integrity in policing their industry, we must become suspicious of that expert's motives. Seek these answers:

- Find out, to which industry this expert has been most closely aligned over the last two decades.
- Find out which financial ties that "expert" has to the discrediting organization.
- Identify the political ties that the "expert" has to the discrediting organization.
- Uncover the "expert's" specific area of expertise and determine how qualified he or she might be to render an informed opinion about a competing industry.
- Indentify the public good that this "expert" has personally delivered in the past.
- Besides the general public, find out who else has benefited from this "expert's" opinions and goodwill.

Of course, there are many other questions that we could ask but it is important to at least investigate thoroughly when an expert chooses to take an "all or nothing" approach in rendering opinions. Here are some additional matters to consider in this particular example:

➢ Since these experts are so concerned with what is best for the health of public in general, why aren't these same experts speaking out about the known harmful side effects of the prescription drugs that are glamorized through the media?
➢ Why aren't these same 'experts' speaking up about the lack of nutritional foods served by so much of the fast food industry?
➢ If these experts openly admit that they "do not know much" about the products on which they have volunteered their comments, why are they commenting at all?

We could continue but the point is made. All experts do not share the ethics and integrity that Ralph Nader demonstrated in 1973 regarding the oil embargo issue. In one of my favorite comedies, the main character, Joe Banks, who was trying to find answers for his life, eventually comes to this realization: "There are certain doors that you have to walk through alone." Well, accepting responsibility for our life condition and doing something about it is one of those doors. (Halsey, 1990)

There is another area around this topic that requires clarification. It is the perception that intelligence and status implies good character. Nothing could be further from the truth. There is no substitute for good character. A person of good character is welcome and valued in all situations and circumstances. To the naïve person, there is no apparent difference between the behavior of an intellectually gifted person and a person of good character. So let's explore those differences.

An intellectually gifted person could be a corporate business executive, great inventor, an entertainment or sports celebrity. This person may have amassed great wealth and be a high profile public figure. This does not necessarily mean that the business executive would demonstrate good character by caring as much about his employees' financial fitness and welfare as his own.

It does not mean that the inventor would necessarily be committed to only creating inventions for the benefit of the public good over more divisive inventions that would lead to greater profitability for him or herself. It does not mean that the superstars would be as concerned with setting a good public example for their fans as they would be to satisfy their own ego-driven desires.

An intellectually gifted person could be a person of great public influence like a politician, public educator, religious or military leader. It does not necessarily imply that that he or she would never misuse or abuse that influence for personal advantage.

If a mistake is made that requires someone to accept full responsibility and perhaps relinquish a coveted position, would they do so without being pressured? Would those who occupy such prestigious positions admit their mistake or pass the blame? The answer lies in the quality of each person's character, not their intellectual abilities nor the position each occupies.

Although it is reasonable to expect that people who occupy such positions would want to prove worthy of the public's, and their employees' trust in all aspects, the credentials of these individual have nothing to do with the quality of their character. Unless he or she consciously commits to living a life marked by good character, we should not presume that they, necessarily, value such qualities. If they do value good character qualities, it would show in how they approach and execute their tasks and duties in their personal and professional lives.

Decide Who We Are

This is a question about us; how we express those unique and special traits, qualities, talents and abilities that make up our personality. What excites us? What holds our attention? What kinds of things make us burst with laughter? What melts our heart? What brings tears to our eyes?

Which kinds of friends do we value? What kind of work do we enjoy? How do we like to socialize? What do we consider a great time? What kind of entertainment do we enjoy? How do we like to relax at the end of a long day? How do we go about making decisions and solving problems?

How many people will give all of the same answers that we would? Yet, until we answer these and many other questions about ourselves, this chapter will only be of minimal value to us.

The subject of this book is taking responsibility for the condition of our lives. Nearly everyone I have ever approached about this subject (from a cross-section of backgrounds, income levels, education levels and so on) has replied about how responsible he or she is. Each person seems eager to share why he or she believes that other people are "so irresponsible" as a parent, employee, spouse, boss, mate, business owner, friend, political leader, religious leader and so on.

It is easy to point out shortcomings of others with whom we are acquainted whether in person or through the mass media. Yet nearly everyone I've engaged in the above discussions will eventually allude to personal challenges as though they are helpless to do anything about them.

They usually conclude their comments with statements like, "...but that is what the doctor said, so what can I do about it?"; ...that is just what marriage is after _ years, no one is really happy after that much time.";"...so I will never be able to lose any weight."; "because of those statistics, I will be alone for the rest of my life.";" I am just an honest person so I will never get ahead."

These responses have led me to the following question: What do we believe about ourselves as individuals? It is amazing, to me, what we generally believe about ourselves. It is absolutely astounding as to why we believe what we do. Can we improve our health? Can our financial situation improve? Will we rationalize the difficulties in our relationships as unsolvable? Will we ever be happy? Most of us know that all of these are possible. (Hunt, 1989) So where do we get the idea that it is not always possible in our lives?

When we conclude viewing of the television news, or finish reading the newspaper, are we satisfied that we have received all necessary information on the subjects covered? When our physician announces his diagnosis of his examination and confers with us about the treatment, is that all we need to know? When we leave our marriage counselor or therapist, is there anything more that can be done? Our child's teacher insists that our son or daughter just isn't cut out for this subject, is that the final word on the subject?

The fact of the matter is that most of us engage in "irresponsible" behavior. Consider the following two questions: What do you stand for? What do you believe? I've heard answers like, "Human Rights, Animal Rights, Smoker's Rights, and Rights of the Unborn, Justice for All, Freedom, Quality Education or The Environment." While it is obvious that each of these individual is interested in the subject each stated, it appeared that each only had a superficial understanding of what he or she said was important.

Where we stand, regarding such matters is an indication of the quality of our core character. If our character profile is replete with double standards, discriminatory ideas (based on privilege), convenient exceptions (in our favor), exclusionary positions (based on any person's non-criminal background or geography), we may want to examine these areas further as clues to problem areas in our world. Let's look at a few examples.

- If we truly stand for respect for human life, we have no choice but to respect all human life (including those of the worst offenders, international enemies, as well as the unborn without exception)
- If we believe that children deserve a good home and supportive environment, we must believe and enforce that for all children, without exception. This means that we must stand firmly against wars that would create orphans and put innocent children is harm's way unless we are willing to provide for them ourselves.
- If we believe that God loves and blesses his creations, then our only position, and wish, can be 'God bless us all,' with no one, anywhere excluded.
- If we believe in a clean environment for our family and friends to enjoy, then we must practice that mentality for all people, everywhere, without exception.
- If we believe that everyone should consume healthy food and have access to clean water, then we must only produce these for everyone, throughout the Earth, regardless of profit incentives.

We may have trouble with committing to any one of these positions without exceptions and conditions. When we do not commit to these positions, we are being hypocritical. We are creating double standards and the discriminatory positions that none of us would want held against us personally. As people, when we allow such fluidity to concern our character, we set ourselves of up for social, political, legal, moral and ethical conflict on every level. It is important that we solidify our positions of personal character as a way of providing societal stability throughout the world.

Consider that when we explore character issues individually and collectively, we cannot change the rules or the definitions of any of the character qualities. For example, "Honor" in the context of being a person of integrity is the same in all serious situations and circumstances for all who internalize this character quality.

It does not change when we are at a sporting event, in a bar or defending our child of accusations of wrong doing by witnessing school personnel. It does not change when our spouse admits infidelity in our relationship nor in the workplace when your coworker attempts to gain your support through dishonest dealings to have another coworker dismissed.

The repercussions for moral wrong doing are always severe to those of us who do wrong. Those who we have wronged may not be present to witness those repercussions but the price must still be paid. It might manifest in our bodies as a health issue, within our relationships, in our children's behavior or some other form. It will be taxing and not worth the corner-cutting behavior that set it all in motion. (Carmen Herra, 2009)

Once we decide who we are from the perspective of our character, we are all free to enjoy life, to the fullest, and expect all of the good that the quality and level of character that we are internalizing will yield. By clarifying our character profile, we are eradicating any fear and uncertainty that would have concerned us before. When we know where we stand and why we stand there, justice in life will be ours for all of our dealing from this time forward. Of course, our passed decisions will still be reconciled, accordingly so we must be patient.

Chapter 5

"Accept responsibility for your life. Know that it is you, who will get you where you want to go, no one else."

— Les Brown

We Are Never Too Young To Accept Responsibility

If you are under eighteen years of age, I thank you for spending your time and attention on this section.

We hear adults say, all the time, how tough it is growing up these days. If we think they are out of touch with reality for making these statements, we are probably right, for the most part. This is the only time we have to grow into adulthood and it is no big deal to us.

What we must understand is that our parents and other adults who tell us such things because they did not have nearly as many life choices in front of them as we do at our age. They cannot imagine that anyone could be smart enough to actually be able to handle such heavy loads of information at one time because they, themselves, are struggling with it right now.

This is what I mean. Adults did not have cell phones, sophisticated portable video games, mp3 players, portable DVD players, laptop computers, debit cards, email, a "texting" mentality and an instant messaging mentality. The music adults listened to was slow enough and clear enough to understand every word the artist sung (the truth is that a lot of the singers back then had serious speech impediments and parents weren't really sure what they were saying).

What our parents actually mean is that singers, before the 1990's never packed more than 125 words per minute into a recording. Today's music, for example packs around 220 words per minute into a recording using the gifted articulations of the artists and some technological enhancements.

Our parents could barely think that many words per minute and those in our generation routinely imitate the most gifted rap artists with minimal effort. Just imagine how many passwords and pin numbers we all have to know just to use the internet to retrieve information and make purchases. This is second nature to us but adults struggle with it every day.

This is what our parents are talking about. Now add these to the current social issues that we all must consider:

Violence – The number of portrayals of violent behavior on television, in movies and video games that minors are exposed to is several hundred times greater that it was when our parents were our age.

Sex Issues – The adult sexual images, suggestions, jokes and conversations on billboards, in magazines, advertisements, daytime television, primetime (8pm to 11pm) television viewing, in store displays at the mall, which many of us purchase to wear at school, have increased exponentially since our parents were this age. Advertisers use any tactics that are available to get our attention so that they can tell us about new products and services they want us to know about.

Language – There appears to be a relaxing of what is considered proper social protocol as there is excessive profane language that we are exposed to in the various mass media (television, radio, music, movies and on the internet) over what our parents experienced at a similar age.

Lifestyle – Lifestyle options are presented to us with less and less bias. Most of our parents want us to add to the family line at some point of our adulthood. They know that if we choose a gay lifestyle, for example, they may not get those grandchildren. That is why we hear all those "family values" arguments in political circles and at our place of worship. We can just promise them some grandchildren, at some point, so they will get off our back (we have to keep our word, though; you know, good character and all that!).

Health – Health issues are another deep concern that our parents harbor. Not only do we consume excessive amounts of "fast foods" that have virtually no nutritional benefit to our growing bodies, we playfully pursue habits and substances that they, our parents, know will bring physical ruin to our body (as well as any career and relationship progress that we make) in our early adult years. We should make the effort to learn about good nutrition and follow the rules.

Behavior – Finally, there are the maturity issues that imply responsible behavior. Many of us won't even do our school work in favor spending long hours online and/or with our video games. Since many more of us refuse to keep our bedrooms clean and we complain about helping with household chores, our parents are scared to death to trust us with decisions like sexual involvement, choosing a mate, rearing children and [our poorly thought out] career choices.

Our parents are constantly examining our behavior for outward signs of inner progress of our adult development. Our involvement in religious organizations, athletics, scouting or advance placement academic gives them cause to be hopeful.

However, nothing can signal our maturity better than accepting responsibility for our own growth and development in all areas of our life and making decisions based on good character principles and the valued input of responsible adults who are serious about our success in life.

Perhaps we can understand why our parents stay so stress out over whom and what we may become. Our parents are trying to teach us, as they learn life's harsh and difficult lessons, regarding employment, money, relationships, social involvement and so on. So many parents are trying so hard to give us the best life they can afford.

Yet, our appreciation shows up in the form of, "buy me this" or "I want that" and "why can we have this…" or "I never get to do…" all the way to, "if you loved me, you would let me…" and "everybody else gets to go…" Does any of this seem familiar? We now understand how our parents are seeing our life. Let's deal with the realities that we actually face as minors.

The truth of the matter is that no generation before us, has had to negotiate so many life choices and technological changes. The generation, before us, has not fared very well as a result of dealing with so many of the same choices and changes. Employers have reported that so many new, young entrants to the work force are careless, sloppy and irresponsible in their work habits.

Law enforcement officials report that young law breakers seem to view criminal life with some prestigious reverence. The welfare roles, again, are swelling with youthful recipients who simply did not foresee the consequences of our poor mate choices and decisions to enter parenthood with no reliable means of support for our new families.

If we have parents who are trying to teach us to steer clear of these trappings, we are among the most fortunate in our generation. Many more, of us, have no clue what lies ahead for us. Many of our generation believe that if we make it through high school, that we can make it to the next goal that we set. This is a grave mistake. Here is why.

If we show up at high school and make a believable effort to do our work and not cause any trouble, there is a very strong likely hood that we will at least graduate on time regardless of our skill level. After all, school officials can document our attendance, effort and conduct. They have virtually no legal reason to prevent us from graduating. There may be some issues with our teachers about our performance quality, but that doesn't show up on our diploma.

Everyone who has come before us (employers, military recruiters, college recruiters and etc) knows that also. We are virtually viewed by everyone else as a gamble. We may or may not be worth the faith that someone chooses to place in us. Our educational standards are relatively low and teaching methodologies used today are highly inefficient.

We may have noticed, in the field of professional athletics, there is a great deal of emphasis being put forth, by the drafting organizations, to find talented athletes who make it a priority to stay out of trouble with the police. They want to improve their odds of making a good investment in that person.

That is why we will find employers who want us to take a drug test, do a background check, and take an aptitude test before they move forward with the hiring process. If we don't pass, we have to stay with our parents because we will have no means of supporting ourselves – this really scares our parents.

If any of us are beginning to feel a bit worthless, that is good. As magnificent as we are as a collection of intelligent characteristics, talents and abilities, we will actually be measured, in this world, by how productive we are to everyone else. In short, we are evaluated not by what we can provide for ourselves but what we can contribute to society, businesses and institutions of our fellow human beings.

Even pets are productive in this way. They are loyal, entertaining companions who, in exchange, are compensated with food, shelter and a loving home. We must, at least, be this productive to someone in order for our lives to move forward. If we are no better prepared in life than this, we could place the blame, conveniently, on our parents but that would be really bad form, especially if we know in our heart that they really tried to do right by us. So what now?

We may say to ourselves, "but I really do have sorry parents; what can I do?" Yes, we may really have parents who were, woefully, under prepared to rear us. That is why I decided to write this book. If we have a dysfunctional family situation and we are fully aware that our friends are far better off than we are, then we are reading the right book.

We may very well be a victim of poor parenting or virtually no parenting. Unfortunately, this is a fast-growing trend. We might have had to grow up faster than the rest of our school mates. We have to choose between positive or negative growth, or depending on our environment, some combination of these.

Positive growth means that we think for ourselves and we are creating a life that puts our self respect first. We are focusing on doing things that further our ability to do well in our school work and create solid friendships with people who think and behave the same way that we do.

We steer away from negative thinking and criminal mentality, behavior and acts. We believe that we deserve the best that life has to offer and we are willing to work hard to have the life that we want without it costing us our dignity, self respect or jeopardizing our futures. We also do not want to infringe upon anyone else's freedom or privileges to pursue a positive and productive future.

Negative growth means that we have developed a predator mentality. This is never good because it means that we are willing to get whatever we want at another person's expense. Predators, by definition, only prey on those who are physically, emotionally and mentally weaker than they are. They are basically cheap-shot artists.

This may include lying, using, cheating or stealing from others. Negative growth means that we are willing to put our self respect aside, to make whatever personal gains that will further our own agenda without regard to how others might be adversely affected. These gains will dissipate from us at the worst possible time.

Negative growth means that we will give no thought to about how our decisions and actions will affect our future, immediate or long term. We show no regard for adults and other authority figures. We also have no respect for the wisdom that they may choose to impart to us for the benefit of our own development and wellbeing. We trust no one and no one trusts us. This is a losing strategy in life because we all need good friends, a good reputation and good character. Negative growth destroys each of these.

Combination growth means that we are allowing others to influence what we think is important and valuable but we will still make the final decisions. Being accepted by others and winning their approval is more important to us, than keeping our self respect intact. We will do what will keep us popular.

We may or may not respect adults and other authority figures; it really depends on what we can get out of it. We are never really sure whom we can trust, so we let our influences make such decisions. We don't really stand for anything and we will rarely stand up for any worthwhile position. Often, we will appear to be directionless and malleable. We are weak people, at best.

Let's examine our recent life pattern; if we haven't chosen a purely positive growth pattern, it is not too late. Please understand that it is entirely worth whatever sacrifices we believe that we will have to make. Of course, in time, we will attract others who are more in line with our new thinking. Each day, move toward positive growth.

Regardless of where we are now, we cannot succumb to pressure from those whose life experience is no greater than ours. We must steer important decisions that we have to make about our future to someone who is older, wiser and who we can trust; we should start with the teachers that we have come to hate. Once we share our dilemma with them, they will understand us better. Conversely, as they share their wisdom with us, we will understand them better. In the end, we might develop a profound respect for one another.

Each day, we must work on making changes that will further our chances of having a successful and fulfilling adult life, complete with the wealth, health and quality that we want. If the main problem, at this stage of our life, involves parenting problems and it is clear that things will not get better any time soon, then we must still take responsibility and control of the situation. This is not an impossible task. We still have a practical option available to us.

We can get some new parents! We don't have to change residences or make any other physical changes. The only thing we need to change is our mentality – the way we think. Our friends' parents are already pretty well occupied so we can just allow them to be our advisors when things get really complicated. Let's see...parents...parents... We might try those who have already, successfully, reared their children to adulthood. We see them all the time. They are the older couples in our community; those quiet, happy, drama-free, older couples in the nieghborhood! They might be looking for something to do.

If we don't have a speaking relationship with any of them, we can fix that with a quick introduction and a sad, forlorn look in our eyes that says, "Be my parents, please!" If we already do have a speaking relationship, then we should consider bringing up the idea the next time we see them, while they are out. Ask to meet with them later to discuss a 'personal matter.' Their curiosity will almost guarantee that they will say "yes." **Note:** Nosiness increases with age.

When we meet with them, it is important that we are completely honest about what we want from them. Good parents understand and appreciate that we are motivated enough to create a promising future for ourselves and that we are taking the initiative to make it happen. If they can assist us at all, they will.

Since we are asking them for their time and energy, offer to do some chores (yes, chores) around their home in exchange for their wisdom and generosity. We need only to meet with them once or twice each week and we could do it by phone as well. Still make the offer to help whenever they have a need. We can always invite our friends to help us if we are assigned a monumental task.

If we do not know any older couples who might be able to help us in this way, then we must be resourceful. We can check with the leaders of our community like police officers (yes, them), firefighters (they have a lot of free time), parole officers (better to talk with them now), postal carriers (they seem to know who is available and when), community business owners and places of religious worship.

We must explain, clearly, what it is that we want to accomplish and ask these leaders to assist us in locating some happily married couples who have adult children and who might be interested in talking with us about being our surrogate parents. Most of us would be surprised to see how eager everyone is to help us.

Expect there to be conditions attached. Generally, we may be requested to check in so many times each week, learn something new or work a part-time job or something else. Accept those conditions or arrangements so long as they don't violate any moral, social standards or laws like cigarette, alcohol, prescription drug (or other drug), or sex-related favors. We must watch for evidence of good character before we make a final commitment.

We may have to meet and discuss what we want to do with many couples before we find a comfortable fit but it will be worth our time. We may actually choose more than one set of surrogate parents. If we can handle it, we should go for it. The more positive resources we can develop for ourselves, the better for us.

Also, we must trust our surrogate parents to point out things, in life, for which we must be prepared. Remember, they have made their share of mistakes, as anyone has. When they give us guidance and counsel, it is often because they see that we are about to make a serious mistake in action or judgment that will come back to haunt us at the worst possible time in our adult life. Scrutinize their advice closely and follow it when in doubt.

Our surrogate parents may also take it upon themselves to teach us concepts and ideas that would have helped them if they knew them at our age. We must be cooperative and let them help us all they want. They may also want to share some life enhancing interests with us like art and music appreciation, a special love of the outdoors (nature), fishing, farming, horseback riding, military history, business success or craft making.

It will depend on whom we choose and their unique background. In making our final selection for surrogate parents, we must let the standards of good character be our measuring system. We are already cultivating a great deal of community respect by just making this effort to connect with responsible adults who are willing to accept the responsibility to help us with their guidance and knowledge of the world.

If, for any reason, our selected parent choices are not able to assist us, we can thank them, sincerely, for considering our request and politely excuse ourselves from their home. Their reasons for not being in a position to help us will probably have nothing to do with us. Those reasons may be personal. For example, we may remind them of a son or daughter they lost to an accident or illness or some other tragedy.

Also, since many people are victims of serious corporate corruption and mismanagement, economic neglect from politicians or natural disasters, many of these people may have no retirement savings and must work long hours or more than one job to make ends meet. They simply would not have the time to help us effectively. So don't take it personally. Life can be tough at any age, for anyone. This is why we must take responsibility for our lives at the earliest possible time in our life.

Once we have handled our parenting issues, it is time to deal with our everyday issues. The first thing to do after we have changed our mental state to a purely positive one is to decide to treat ourselves with the respect that is consistent with our [new] mentality. Because we treat ourselves with the appropriate respect does not mean that we treat others with any less respect. Follow the rule that if we can't find anything kind to say to or about anyone, then say nothing. This rule will serve us well throughout our lives.

When it comes to our classes at school, we should get to class on time and never leave early unless we have a real emergency. Develop strong study habits; again, they will serve us well throughout our life. We must study our subject material and be ready for class each day.

We must be prepared, always, to have at least two questions about the class material to ask our teacher each day. Just for fun, we can try to stump our teacher each day. That way, we keep our teachers on their toes. We will increase their interest in being prepared for class and we, single-handedly, increase the quality of learning in our school all without effecting funding or local political involvement.

Socially, we must treat our classmates with respect and dignity, even when it is clear that some of them do not deserve it. We will not let them be able to name us as a reason why things went wrong in their life later on. Do not attend scheduled after-school fights. We will hear all the details later if we want. In general, try to stay away from crowds all together. We will attract friends who treat themselves the way we treat ourselves and others. We can be sure that they will appreciate our wisdom and mentality.

Never worry about ending a friendship with anyone. We will not lose friends because we have chosen to upgrade our mentality and thinking. Our friends and associates will take one of two courses of action: They will either, 1) choose to upgrade their standards with us and support our efforts as best they can or 2) they will quietly begin to drift away from us by opting to find others who share our previous mentality.

They will, in effect, take themselves out of our life. However, they will continue to watch us and note our progress. They will check in with us periodically to see how we are faring. They will use us as a resource when they attempt such a transformation at some point in the future. Be there for them.

When we find that someone wants to date us and who we know has no self respect and shows no respect for anyone else, we simply do not date him or her. We cannot help those persons by dating them. We are nothing more than a conquest to them.

By dating them, we will only temporarily boost his or her ego and social standing. At the same time, we may be ruining our ability to attract the kind of potential mates into our life who we truly desire. Remember, whether we realize it or not, there is always someone, who is interested in us, who is watching and taking notes about us. They do not always reveal themselves right away. Never forget this.

When it comes to our health, apply the same purely-positive mentality. If we have a choice between consuming some fast food, with virtually no nutritional value to our body, or some fresh fruits and vegetables, we can make the choice that shows that we value and respect ourselves. We must get a fair share of exercise each day by walking or taking a part-time job where we do physical work. It won't be long before we notice the change in the quality of our health and our physical appearance.

The early stages, of this transformation, are the most difficult because we are, virtually, alone. No one knows what we desire for ourselves until we bring it to fruition. After a few months, our life's direction will be obvious to all who observe us; but in the beginning, expect to be alone. Only we can build this foundation and only we will get the credit for our transformation.

The discipline we develop, through our transformation, will serve as a reminder for the rest of our life that we can accomplish anything we choose. We can reflect upon what we have accomplished when we approach greater challenges later in life. Think of this transformative phase of our life as the foundation for every great thing we do in our life. No matter how things appear to be going, never get discouraged and never quit. We can take a break, if we must, but never quit. We will develop a great deal of character and wisdom on this journey. We will do just fine.

Our Reputation and Public Image

An area that I must address is our public image. I don't mean so much around our friends in this case, although that is important. I am more concerned here with our public, out-of-school conduct. I have enjoyed many of the advantages of the inner-city like traveling on public transportation for many years (as many city dwellers do), frequenting libraries and so on. Some of the kindest people I know, I have met on a city bus, in a library or at a grocery store. Of course, I have also met some other very interesting personalities of which I had limited experience.

Many of those people who I have enjoyed engaging in intellectual jaunts were professional people who held highly responsible positions in corporations and in the community. Many are very influential in deciding who gets hired for summer employment, internships and co-operative educational positions. These are kind, decent, law-abiding citizens who are highly sympathetic to those who come from backgrounds categorized as disadvantage. I can remember countless incidents when groups of high school students would board a bus when we were enjoying polite conversation.

Within seconds, the entire bus became filled with loud, profanity-laced exchanges of name calling, sexual harassment accompanied with rude and threatening behavior among the students. This kind of behavior became so common at one point, that the bus drivers would not permit certain students to board their buses.

This of course caused the students to be late because they have to wait for the next bus. Through the years, as I came to recognize many of these students, I watched how many of these students were hired for summer employment; none were ever hired by the bus-riding professionals with whom I became familiar.

Eventually, I came to know some of these students when they enrolled in the local college where I taught. To my surprise, I found that many of them turned out to be very bright and showed a great deal of educational promise. Their social skills, however, still left much to be desired. I could only imagine how much further they might have progressed in life had someone taught them the importance of building a good reputation and public image in the community before they became teen aged.

As I would frequent various business establishments, I would recognize others of those high school students who apparently opted for employment after high school. Their mentality had not changed. Their appearance and attitude, both, were extremely unprofessional. For example, they would engage in personal phone calls while waiting on customers or treat their customers like they were an inconvenience as opposed to a valued source of income for their establishment.

It was clear that no one had impressed upon them the importance of summer employment or a first employment opportunity. They continued to build an unpopular reputation by appearing to be uncooperative, unappreciative and a poor promotion choice in the workplace. They were also, always the first to complain about unfair work conditions and discrimination at work.

If we have not had our first summer employment opportunity or first job, it is important that we treat it with the highest importance that we can and that means preparation. We should get as much advice as we are able from adults who would like to see us do well. Our friends' parents, our grandparents, adults at our place of worship are all good choices if they have reputations for being good, responsible people.

If they advise us to change any part of our appearance like our hair color, take out a piercing, or cover a tattoo, do it. It is all right to ask why; they will tell us. They will advise us about our on-the-job conduct, punctuality and work ethic. Take notes and apply their advice accordingly. We want to build a good reputation as an employee from our first job.

Even if we do not agree with what we are being told, do it anyway just to prove them wrong. In every case that I can recall, the employee, who followed the wisdom of experienced and successful people, was promoted, paid more money and asked to return the following year.

It should come as no surprise that the "nobody's-going-to-change-me" employees were never rehired in the following years. Of course, they had to find a job the next summer and convince someone new to give them "a chance." This was just the beginning of their enrollment in the "school of hard knocks."

We can choose to take responsibility for the condition of our life right now. We simply decide what kind of life we want to lead and what kind reputation we want. Then, we decide what kind of home and mate we want. We make decisions about the friendships that we want to establish, as well as those we do not want.

We must figure out in what industry we would like to make our employment contributions and at what level. Now, we can decide that we are going to achieve it, no matter what the obstacles. We would do well to write it down and remind ourselves every day. Next, we find as many people as we can to help us and, in return, we must be willing to help them in reaching some area of their goals whenever we can.

Finally, we must never allow anyone to work harder than we do, when we ask them to assist us in reaching our life goals. Consider the following scenario.

A serious situation develops where dedicated fighters are needed to do battle. The leader, who stands to benefit greatly from a victory, approaches us and convinces us that this battle is worth our involvement and any sacrifice we make. Imagine following that leader into battle and when things get tough, the leader goes somewhere to have a cool drink to watch the battle and relax while we and the other combatants continue fighting, furiously, for the victory.

Once we observe our leader's behavior and obvious lack of commitment to the cause that he or she so passionately convinced us to support, we may not be so eager to continue with our service and support. As people who accept full responsibility for our lives, we are also leaders and role models. We lead the charge in every phase of our lives.

The better we lead the more help we will attract for our benefit. Conversely, whenever we are asked to assist someone else in achieving their goals, we are to never work harder than the person we are helping, to reach his or her goals. It is their responsibility to lead in every area of their lives. Think it through and adhere to it.

If our lives aren't going in a positive direction, then we must seize control of it. If our family is involved in excessive and unnecessary legal entanglements and we do not have the role models in our life that we need to help us to reach our goals, we must consider accepting full responsibility for the condition of our lives. Once we commit to this, our lives will never be the same.

Chapter 6

"Take care of your body. It's the only place you have to live."

– Jim Rohn

Become Obsessed With Wellness

When we think about our health, different issues come to mind for each of us. For some of us, we immediately think of the condition of our back or our blood pressure. Our cholesterol level is uppermost in mind for others. It is possible that, others of us are harboring thoughts of the possibility of cancer or some other serious condition. We might think of any of these or something that we perceive to be much worse. It is worth considering how such thoughts affect our mental, emotional and spiritual health. (Anderson M., 2008)

For many of us, there is no need to panic. We just visit our doctor, share our concerns and after a few diagnostic tests, everything will be all right. Ideally, for many of us, we simply ingest whichever pharmaceutical pills that our doctor prescribes and our health issues disappear.

In recent years, however, many of us are finding that our health concerns do not necessarily 'disappear' but rather become 'managed' so long as we continue the regimen of prescriptions that are prescribed for each of the health issues that our doctor uncovers.

Over a period of years, many of us have come to find that we have developed a weekly or, in some cases, a daily schedule of pill ingestion and we have accumulated several pills to manage our various health concerns. Even though, this can become a very expensive burden, we convince ourselves that we are better off because we are enjoying a healthier quality of life.

As we age, many of us have convinced ourselves that having annoying aches, pains, ever-dulling eyesight and hearing, wrinkles, graying hair, age spots, unsightly weight increases or decreases and increasingly poor health are simply facts of life that must be accepted, with dignity and grace, as immutable and inevitable.

Those of us, who accept this mentality, tend to find that our quality of life becomes consistently less fulfilling. We convince ourselves that we do not want to participate in physical activities during outdoor family outings and at local recreation centers because of our age. Eventually, we add household chores and significantly reduced activity in our intimate lives to our list activities that we can no longer enjoy.

Over time, we begin to long for our youthful selves. We convince ourselves that we were so much more than we are today. We tell ourselves that if we had another chance at having a fully functioning, healthy body, we would take a different road to good health for the rest of our lives.

Few of us, who are in this frame of mind, realize that we can have a dramatically different and improved state of health right now. Most of us, who have taken this road in healthcare, understand that we have given virtually all responsibility for our state of health, to someone else, for the balance of our lives. We have, passively, participated in a systematic reduction in the quality of our own state of wellness.

To illustrate, let us return to an earlier time in our lives, for a moment, when we had whole and vibrant health. We might have been teenagers or young adults. Let's think of a time when we were full of vibrant health and were highly active in every area of our lives. We looked good and felt great virtually all of the time. Focus, for a few minutes, on when we had our first health issue from this point.

If we found that we had back or joint pain, did we also notice that there was a significant increase in our weight at that time? If so, did we bother to share that fact with our doctor or did we just complain about wanting relief from the pain? If we found that we had experienced an increase in headaches, anxiety, mood swings and so on, did we note a change, in recent years, of our daily diet or our day-to-day responsibilities? If so, did we disclose that fact to our healthcare provider?

Doctors can only work with the information that we provide to them about our health. That is why they interview us about our health concerns before they examine us. If we choose not to disclose important information like we have reduced virtually all physical exercise in recent years, our doctor might not make the connection to the significant increase in our physical weight gain.

If we choose not to disclose the fact that we, as a family, have adopted a fast food diet for ourselves over the last year, our doctor might not make the connection that we, and the rest of our family, might be suffering from malnutrition and that our health issues might be connected to this fact.

This is a good time to state the point of this chapter. This is it: Whenever we visit our physician, whatever the diagnosis, it is our responsibility to make a full recovery – not our doctor's (and the assigned support team); the full responsibility is our own.

Think of it this way: whose life and family will be adversely affected if we don't fully recover – ours or our doctor's? How often do we find that physicians are discovered wandering the streets at night, unable to sleep or function because of our failing health? Doesn't it make sense that the person most affected by poor health, should be the most concerned? Consider how empowering it is to choose to accept full responsibility for the state of your health at all times.

As an exercise, let's do it! Imagine, just for this exercise, that we now have assumed full responsibility for our own health. We have access to all of the information that we will ever need and we have all decision making authority. Some us feel a bit giddy with power, already! Others of us are somewhat nervous because we are thinking, "well I'm not a doctor, what do I know?" Well, let's see what we do know.

Now that we're in charge, what quality of health do we prefer: poor or great? When would we like to feel good: once and a while or all of the time? Do we want our appearance to be weak and sickly or vibrant and beautiful? Do we want our state of mind to be unstable and clueless or focused and confident? Do we want our emotions to be numb and distant or loving and compassionate? Do we want our bodies to be filled with aches and pains or bursting with strength and vitality?

It appears that we do, in fact, know quite a bit about what we desire about our state of health. As we study the answers that we want about our health, it is clear that, when we have a choice, no one wants compromised or managed illness. In all circumstances, we want cures – total wellness. For the vast majority of people suffering from various health concerns, this isn't just a pleasant dream, it is a real possibility, when we adjust our thinking.

I'm not a doctor either and, like you, I have the highest respect for their knowledge of how the physical body is constructed and operates. The fact remains that if we are diagnosed with a serious medical condition, we are going to feel the pain of this condition, our physician will not. It is like having a tooth ache – our dentist tells us that there are no openings today but there is an opening the first thing tomorrow morning.

Sure, our dentist can appreciate what we must be going through but our dentist will enjoy his (or her) meal and family time this evening and get an uninterrupted night of sleep. What about us? Many of us will tough it out and take that morning appointment. Others of us will go to an emergency dental facility instead. In either case, we must take full responsibility for our condition and make the decisions that support our desired outcome.

Conversely, when our physician pronounces us to be well and "fit as a fiddle" but we still do not feel the way we are use to feeling, should we leave it at that? Whatever our action, we are ultimately responsible. Perhaps, all of our vital signs are in the normal range. It is important to note here that we are more than physical beings. It is possible that our food diet contains ingredients that might be adversely affecting our emotions or mental state. It is also possible that we could be reacting to the pressure of a stressful situation in some other area of our life.

Through recent research, we now know that it is possible that various stresses could lead to physical illness. Whatever the answer, we are responsible for investigating it so that we can learn the answers for ourselves. It is usually not a bad idea to also discuss our findings with our physician to get his or her "informed" opinion. Just keep foremost in mind that the condition of our health is still ultimately our responsibility, regardless. (Anderson G., 1995)

When we discuss our health, we must do so in greater terms than our physical health. In truth, our state of health reaches beyond our physical state and includes our emotional, mental, intellectual, social and spiritual states as well. As human creatures, we exist on many levels and each level has its developmental and maintenance requirements. (Toy, 2009) Consider the following:

> **Physically** – Our physical bodies need a nutritionally balanced diet of fruits, vegetables, grains, proteins, various minerals and complex carbohydrates. Our bodies do not require the ingredients found in processed foods, fast foods, candies, bakery items, frozen meals and all micro-waved foods (as microwaves completely destroy the nutritional integrity of our foods). Notice that we never hear or see the words "nutritious" and "delicious" in the same sentence when microwaved foods are advertised. (Newell, 2010)
>
> Further, our bodies require clean drinking water, fruit and vegetable juices. Our bodies do not require the ingredients found in most alcoholic beverages, soft drinks, caffeinated drinks and other processed sugared drinks (often created for children).
>
> Our physical bodies also require basic exercise, playtime, quiet rest periods and periodic positive physical contact (like hugs, kisses and caresses, at the very least).
>
> **Emotionally** – We require seeing beautiful and happy images. We require hearing kind, encouraging words and music that evokes our many positive moods. We also need to hear the many sounds of nature like the sounds of bird singing, falling rain, woodland creatures in their natural habitat, river water running and the ocean waves crashing. We require the enjoyment of smelling of flowers, food cooking and smells that denote cleanliness.
>
> Additionally, we each have a need to give and receive love, experience compassion, affection and connection to and with other living creatures (people, animals, plants and so on).
>
> **Mentally** – We require verbal contact and exercises that help us develop problem assessment, decision making and problem solving skills. We also require exercises that assist us in developing various areas of motor skills so that we can participate in athletic endeavors, music making, building projects, computer work, household chores, craft making, personal creations and personal maintenance.
>
> **Intellectually** – We require stimulating conversation that encourages rational, creative, linear, integrative thinking and reasoning skills. We require challenges that provide us opportunities for various areas of character development like becoming trustworthy, responsible, ethical, caring and considerate of others, learning and practicing discipline, empathy and integrity.

Socially – We require periodic contact with others with whom we can learn fair play, team building, compassion for others, sharing, competition and opportunities for verbal engagement and development of a sense of humor. Here, we learn the art of acceptance of others as well as being accepted so that we build and enjoy stable bonding relationships and experiences.

Spiritually – We require learning about the planet on which we live as well as the universe where we find ourselves. We require opportunities to explore the mysteries of natural occurrences like lightning and thunderstorms, earthquakes, hurricanes and tornados. We must explore the mysteries of life cycles in the insect, plant and animal kingdoms as well as the natural rejuvenating process of our planet.

We must study the movement of our solar system and our galaxy and how it impacts our existence. We have to explore the natural conclusions concerning other life forms, in other areas of the universe and those (possibly) existing in other dimensions, as we are able to conceive, so that we can make sense of the single originating source of all that we experience.

So our health far exceeds that of our physical bodies. It encompasses a great deal more than we consider at first thought. Still, we are ultimately responsible for our own development in each of these areas. It creates a fuller, higher quality community within the human family.

As we choose to develop each of these aspects of our health, we become more versatile and competent in our roles, as a parent, as a wage earner, as a friend, community contributor, as a mate and as a fulfilled individual.

Basic Care of Our Physical Self

Taking basic care of ourselves appears, at first, to be an obvious matter. We cannot enjoy good health, proper growth and maturity if we neglect competent care of ourselves. For a variety of reasons, we all do not receive the same information concerning the proper quality and care of our physical bodies.

I am not aware of any one definite source of healthcare information to which everyone would have equal access. This one, definitive source of basic health information would be a wonderful starting point for the world community to give each of us and our families the best chance at enjoying life-long, consistently good health.

If we consider a randomly chosen group of elementary school children, we can observe marked differences in quality of hygiene, nutritional variances, respect for cleanliness, physical fitness and states of good health. Since all of the health habits that these children observed were taught to them by their parents, it is a direct reflection of what the parents understand regarding human wellness. Since the human anatomy is such a magnificent and complex organism, we must give it the highest consideration when we discuss its care and maintenance.

Our skin is the largest organ that the human body has and it protects the body. It contains cells, sweat glands, pores, nerves and blood vessels. It protects our muscles, organs and various systems from harmful contaminants, maintains proper fluid balance as well as extreme temperature changes in our environment. About 300 to 400 thousand skin cells die and dry out on the surface of our skin daily.

Our skin's primary purpose is to expel toxins, pollutants and other impurities, from the body, by sweating through the pores of the skin. If we have excess pollutants in our body, our skin will develop blemishes, dark areas, acne and unpleasant odors.

This is our skin's signal to us that we need to make some positive changes in our diet, fluids we drink and our skin care regimen. Below are the basic things that we all will need to do to keep our bodies operating in good condition on the inside and outside.

- ✓ **Wash** – The skin that covers our bodies requires constant cleaning through washing with soap and water. The water should be clean and drinkable and contain no contaminants. Our soap should be vegetable-based and only contain ingredients that are easily digestible within our body (herbs, oils and fragrances).

    Even though we do not eat the soap, it is absorbed through our skin into our bloodstream to mix with the fluids within our bodies. Any 'preservatives' or processed ingredients (sodium lauryl sulphate, petroleum, animal fat, triclosan [a pesticide] and carcinogens like formaldehyde) contained in soap will poison our body.

    Eventually, the residual accumulation of these poisons will create or promote illness in our body, in the form of allergies, immune system damage, breathing difficulties, vision problems, liver damage, blood pressure issues, skin rashes and cancer. (Siegel-Maier, 2009)

    Also, we must secure the proper washing tools that do not damage our skin but will remove the dead skin cells from our skin surface. We must do our research now that we are committing to being fully responsible. Our loved ones as well as our own health is at stake.

- ✓ **Hydrate** – Our bodies are approximately 78 percent fluid. With this in mind, we must pay close attention to keeping our bodies properly hydrated by drinking clean distilled or preferably spring water. It does wonders for the appearance of our skin complexion. Most of us are chronically dehydrated and many of the health issues that we discover can be directly related to our level of dehydration.

For example, a lack of water, in our body, will cause us to feel fatigue or occasional dizziness at some point in our day. Proper hydration will ease our back pain and the pain we experience from arthritis. Dehydration causes us to experience short-term memory loss and to lose focus when we require it most. (Amy Jamieson-Petonic, 1995)

Water is great for all of our internal organs and it is capable of reducing our risk in developing many different cancers. Most credible authorities recommend that we all drink 8 to 10 8-ounce cups of water each day. (Extreme Nutrition Ltd., 2009)

✓ **Cleanse** – Just as the outside of our bodies require daily cleaning with soap and clean water, our internal body must be cleansed too. We refer to this procedure as, "Internal Body Cleansing."

Toxins, pollutants and poisons are collectively considered to be "toxic wastes." These harmful molecules can be found in great abundance in our air, drinking water, food supply, as well as in pharmaceutical drugs. Many of these pollutants are manufactured chemicals that are use to aid in the production of commodities that we purchase and value as a society. We call them "Modern Toxins."

These include pesticides used on crops, additives used in processed foods, synthetic hormones to make cows, pigs and chickens to grow unnaturally large (quickly), additives in fuel, chemicals used to make packaging for fast food containers, household cleaning products and so on. These also include heavy metal pollutants like cadmium, copper, lead and mercury.

Toxic chemicals also wreak havoc on our environment, poisoning our lakes, oceans, soil, and as a consequence, our bodies. *"Since our bodies are not able to process or eliminate these "modern" toxins, they become stored in our glands, tissues and cells. What results is eventual "self-poisoning."* (Berry, 1997)

Poisons in our bodies are the result of poor digestion and elimination (*Autointoxication or Self-Poisoning*) when we consume excessive "junk foods" like candy, desserts, fast food, soft drinks, deep-fried foods, vending machine snacks and so on. When we smoke and drink alcohol, we further complicate our body's natural process of digestion and elimination. Prescription drugs and the use of excessive facial make up only add to the body's burden of self-purification. The symptoms of Autointoxication are these:

- Allergy or intolerance to certain foods
- Bad breath and foul-smelling gas and stools
- Constipation, diarrhea, sluggish elimination, irregular bowel movements

- Frequent congestion, colds, viruses
- Flatulence and frequent intestinal disorders
- Frequent headaches for no apparent reason
- General aches and pains that migrate from one place to another
- Intolerance to fatty foods
- Low energy; loss of vitality
- Lower back pain
- Lowered resistance to infections
- Needing to sleep a long time
- Pain in your liver or gall bladder
- Premenstrual syndrome (PMS), breast soreness, vaginal infections
- Skin problems, rashes, boils, pimples, acne

According to Dr. Linda Berry, a chiropractor and clinical nutritionist, the symptoms of self-poisoning are summarized this way:

"If you experience any of the above-listed symptoms, you may be experiencing autointoxication (a process whereby you are poisoned by substances produced by your own body as a result of inadequate digestion and elimination), and therefore you might want to consider some type of internal cleansing program. (Berry, 1997)

✓ **Fuel** – Having the proper nutrition can make all the difference in the world in how we feel each day. Researchers are rethinking their support of the 'Standard American Diet (SAD)' in favor of a 'High Nutrient Dense (HND)' diet. Researchers have found that it is far better to eat a plant based diet with unprocessed foods that are prepared from home.

The standard American diet consists of fruits, vegetables, dairy, proteins, bread and grains. At one point, this diet was nutritionally beneficial to our bodies. However, in recent decades, food manufacturers have altered the nutritional integrity of this diet by including technologically processed foods that have rendered many of the food groups to be extremely unhealthy and not at all beneficial.

They include such non-nutritional substances as hydrogenated oil, high fructose corn syrup, phytic acid, acrylamide, sodium nitrate, monosodium and glutamate which are devoid of basic vitamins and minerals. (Aitken, 2007)

The HND diet contains more than mere vitamins and minerals. It contains foods that provide our bodies with sufficient amounts of "phytochemicals" that are "essential for proper functioning of the immune system and to enable our body's detoxification and cellular repair mechanisms that protect us from chronic diseases," according to Dr. Joel Fuhrman, M.D. renowned speaker and author of human nutritional research. (Dr. Joel Fuhrman, 2008)

These healthy HND foods are vegetables that include but are not limited to, asparagus, bell peppers, cabbage, celery, eggplant, green beans, leeks, mustard greens, potatoes, spinach, sweet potatoes, turnip greens, avocados, broccoli, carrots, cucumbers, garlic, mushrooms, onions and squash. (Deanna M. Minich, 2009)

- ✓ **Grooming** – There is no substitute for proper hygiene. Aside from bathing our bodies, at least once each day, with vegetable-based soaps and clean water, we must also tend to the details of cleaning our physical selves. This includes brushing our teeth, tending to our responsibility of maintaining fresh breath, maintaining clean hair, using deodorant when and where we need it, cleaning our ears, cleaning our finger and toe nails daily, washing our hands before preparing or eating food and keeping our faces free of soilure (food, mucus, body fluid stains) and so on.

  Most of us find it embarrassing to point out to someone that they have food wedged in their unbrushed teeth, have debris in the corners of their eye from when they were asleep or dried saliva in the corners of their mouths. It is even worse to be the person who greets other people all day with such an offensive appearance.

  Such distractions can detract from our ability to be taken seriously in our workplace, at school, while doing business in various establishments and during our social interactions. We can commit to good grooming and checking our appearance periodically throughout our day. We can also alert our friends to please tell us if they should notice anything that is out of order with our appearance at any time.

- ✓ **Exercise** – Though many of us do not like to do it, daily exercise is a very good habit to adopt. When we begin an exercise regimen, our bodies tend to hurt, sometimes very much, depending on how much we exercise our first time. This is normal for anyone at first. Our bodies will hurt for about the first two weeks of regular exercise whether we are engaging in callisthenic exercises like 'jumping jacks, lunges, sit ups and pushups; aerobic exercises like walking, running, dance, jumping rope, swimming or cycling; stretching for flexibility; martial arts training or weight lifting.

  It just doesn't matter. For the first two weeks, our body is going to ache. Further, it will appear to ache even more when we begin our exercises each time. This is a conditioning period for our body. For those of us who have had to adjust to a new physical responsibility on our workplace or within our family, the physical ache to our body is the same and it will last for about two weeks. If we want better health, we must accept it and tough it out.

At the conclusion of that two week period, if we have been faithful to our goal of continuous exercise (despite the pain), we will notice that we have a great deal more energy and strength. As we increase our exercise routines to more intense levels, we will find it to be more empowering than painful. At this point, we are well on our way to dramatically improved fitness, along with all of the health benefits that accompany it.

When we choose to employ the services of personal certified trainer, we can be sure that our trainer is aware of the pain we will endure during the first two weeks. They will deliver the results we desire with as little discomfort as, humanly, possible.

Remember, that if we are employing the services of a trainer, we are paying, not only for that trainer's knowledge of health and fitness, but for our trainer's iron will for us to succeed. However, our will to succeed should supersede our trainer's desire for our success.

Whether we use a trainer or go at it on our own, be sure to get a check up from a qualified physician before implementing an exercise regimen. We should begin at a tension and intensity that is challenging but still comfortable for us.

In subsequent workouts, match or exceed what we accomplished in the first day of exercise. Also, drink plenty of spring water before, during and after exercising. Eat lots of leafy green (uncooked) vegetables, fruits and healthy meals. A protein supplement will lessen some of the periodic muscle pain. Allow for sufficient sleep.

- ✓ **Stabilize** – We must keep our body temperature in a comfortable range as often as possible. This simply means that we dress for the weather regardless of where we live. If we live in a warmer climate but choose to go to an air conditioned facility like a library or movie cinema, we should bring the appropriate clothing to compensate for the change in atmosphere so that it does not shock our body.

  For those of us who live in a climate that includes seasonal changes every three months, we must be prepared for these extreme changes to our body. We want to keep our body as comfortable and stable, temperature wise as we are able.

- ✓ **Fortify** – Enhance our health with body-strengthening strategies that will improve its immunity especially during changes of season, when airborne illnesses are most likely; against bacteria and virus transmission.

  There is a great deal of research that supports that food supplements (herbal, vitamin, mineral, whole food) in both powder and liquid forms have had tremendously positive health benefits in boosting our immune system, stimulating brain activity, inducing sleep, regulating blood-sugar balance, detoxifying our digestive system, improving our food absorption efficiency and so on.

Food supplements can be beneficial to us at different stages of life. For example, if we are pregnant, as children, as senior citizens, teens with irregular eating habits, as vegetarians, as athletes and so on. (Gina Kemp, 2011)

There are several other options we have available to us in keeping our physical body strong and healthy. We might invest some time learning about our body's subtle energy system. It is quite fascinating and we can learn a great deal about how excessive use of wireless devices can affect our emotions and mentality. We can also learn about ways to naturally reduce tension and stress. (Dale, 2009)

- ✓ **Contact** – The last area that we can concern ourselves with is the importance of physical contact and stimulation. We all need to experience being touched by someone else daily. It can be a handshake, a fist bump, a high five slap or a simple hug. We also need and benefit greatly from the physical affection that is unique to our pets.

    It is through physical contact that we communicate our emotions. We share our feelings of joy, happiness, compassion, frustration and gratitude through our touch. We also are able to receive messages from others that they are supporting us, loving us, empathize with us and so on.

    It is through our sense of touch that we maintain relationship and strengthen our bonds with others. With gentle caresses, hand holding and light massage we demonstrate reassurance, faith and confidence in others. We must never neglect this area of our physical care nor should we down play its importance in contributing to our overall well-being. (Keltner, 2010)

Basic care of our physical body is just one area of improving and maintaining good health. Be aware that the condition of our skin and the function of our various organs and systems are solid indicators of our physical state of health. Let's always pay attention to what our body is telling us.

Our Amazing Emotional Faculty

When we think of our emotions, we think of the state of our feelings; our mood. Our mood is affected by our emotional faculty. We may feel hopeful and encouraged at one moment. Then, suddenly, our mood changes to that of feeling discouraged and doubtful. The reason that we experience these abrupt changes is that we allow our thinking to be affected by negative ideas that we tell ourselves. Often our hormone levels can intensify these changes as anyone who observes teenagers can attest.

According to Dr. Candace B. Pert, a researcher of human emotions, our emotions are based in our physical internal chemistry. Once we choose our emotional state, consciously or unconsciously, our body chemistry will form the molecular structures in our blood stream, that will instruct our brains how we are to feel: happy, surprised, sad, worried, pessimistic, angry, loving, compassionate and so on.

It appears that our body will create an internal potion for our every emotion. We just have to choose it. It is as basic as 'energy follows our thoughts. The emotion that we choose will stay with us until we choose a different one. When we prolong our entrenchment in a particular emotion, it creates a mood. (Candace B. Pert, 1997)

Our emotional faculty is a highly sensitive energy sensor. Although the energy is quite subtle, it is not affected by time and space. It senses intelligent (living) electromagnetic energy. It senses its disposition, frequency, charge and intensity.

> Our disposition is the state or type of emotion we are experiencing. This involves the many emotions like: acceptance, affection, aggression, ambivalence, anger, compassion, doubt, despair, disgust, empathy, envy, embarrassment, euphoria, excitement, fear, forgiveness, frustration, guilt, gratitude, grief, happiness, hate, hope, horror, hostility, jealousy, loneliness, longing, love, pity, pleasure, rage, regret, remorse, sadness, shame, suffering, surprise and sympathy.
>
> The frequency of our emotion is the natural address location on the electromagnetic wave spectrum where human beings register emotions. This electromagnetic spectrum is consistently present throughout the universe. Because of the discovery of this electromagnetic wave spectrum, we have used its various frequencies for radio and television transmissions.
>
> We use other frequencies on this spectrum x-ray, microwave and short wave technology. We detect some frequency ranges as visible light as we see in its natural progression in the rainbow. On a different area of the spectrum, we can detect with our ears as the audible sounds that are responsible for the universal music scale. The area, where human emotions register, is extremely high on the spectrum.
>
> The charge, of our emotional impulses is determined by the direction of our intensity – it will be positive, neutral or negative.
>
> The intensity of our emotional impulses concerns the speed of our emotional vibratory rate (the faster the speed, the higher the intensity). It will range from low to extreme. (Sereda, 2009)

Our emotional faculty can locate its object at an instant. It controls all of the information exchanges that concern our emotional impulses. The information that our emotional faculty gathers for us must be interpreted by our mental faculty so that we may make sense of what we are receiving. This interpretation gives us our feelings which are a physical manifestation and subsequent expression of the disposition we are experiencing. Our mental faculty does this function for our entire being.

Our intuition (gut feeling) is our involuntary use of our emotional faculty. We get a sense of something changing in our world that may be affecting someone about whom we care deeply. It is not clear exactly who it is or what is changing. Often this sense of change creates a deep feeling of concern that may affect our mood.

Our mood is our chosen perspective with which we decide to view our world. It can be positive or negative. We may say or think things like, "I have a feeling something good is going to happen today," or "something is wrong." Since this feeling is unqualified by our mental faculty, it creates a great deal of uncertainty for us.

Consider the connection between a mother and her child. The child is playing with friends in a different residential neighborhood. All is well and the mother is at ease because she knows the family and neighborhood where the child is playing. The child darts into the street to retrieve a ball and the driver of an approaching car that just drove into the neighborhood slows down as the child does this.

The child retrieves the ball and is startled to find a slowing car so close but the child is never in any real danger. The mother will sense this "impulse of surprise" that her child is experiencing. The mother may or may not call to check on the child.

So why did the mother sense that her child was startled without getting a clear indication about what was going on? It really depends on the interpretation of her mental faculty. If there are no recorded similar experiences in the mother's life, her mental faculty will have nothing to compare to this "impulse of surprise" that the child experienced. This impulse will remain unqualified and thus may create feelings of uncertainty that will directly affect the mother's mood.

Now, suppose that the same mother and child experience a different scenario. Suppose that the child is attacked by a large dog. If the mother has had a similar experience recorded, in her mental faculty when she was about the same age, the mother will "know instantly" what is going on with her child.

The mother's emotional faculty will immediately identify the disposition of the impulse (horror), the frequency of the impulse (that of her child), the charge of that impulse (negative) and the intensity of that impulse (extreme). Her mental faculty can and will immediately identify the impulse that her child is sending, as a familiar one based on her experiences from that age.

Our emotional faculty is able to locate and gather information from a variety of sources at any time. It does not appear to rest. This is why we experience mood swings and constant changes in our emotional states. Often, we are gathering information that appears to be meaningless to us; but it is responding to constant inquires that we are making through our thoughts. It has everything to do with what we say and think that we want.

How many times in a day have we made statements like, "I wonder whatever happened to Lisa?" Or "Where is Kevin working now?" Our emotional faculty is responding to our inquiries. It is monitoring the energy of the people with whom we are attuned regularly – our loved ones, close friends and associates. If we are a pet owner, our emotional faculty is constantly monitoring the activities of our pet. Noticed how when we sense that something is wrong with our pet only to learn later that, upon arriving at home, that our pet may be showing signs of trauma from 'something' it experienced that day?

Our emotional faculty has the ability to actively infect the emotional condition of others and then to attune it to a particular disposition. I have found no better example of this than with babies who are at least two months old. Time and again, I have been in waiting rooms, crowded buses, or other unpleasant situations with really grumpy people. No one is talking and the tension is such that virtually everyone appears to be having a bad day. Then, a young mother makes her way into the facility with a baby slung over her shoulder.

After the mother finds a place to sit or stand and stops moving, without fail, the wide-eyed infant will raise its head to see what is going on and who needs some love. The baby makes eye contact with one person at a time and smiles. Those hard-hearted, stone-faced, miserable people, who look as though they haven't smiled in years, are moved by their melted hearts to return the loving and non-judgmental smile that the baby gave, so freely, to them. The emotional energy in the place warms immediately; people begin to smile at one another and even engage in brief chatter.

So what else does our emotional faculty do for us? If we pay attention to it, it does a great deal for us. It reads the energy of creatures in the plant and animal kingdoms. Both plants and animals respond to the workings of our emotional faculty. It reads the energy in certain locations. Nearly all of us have entered a room only to mistakenly interrupt people in conflict. We immediately sense the angry disposition, negative charge and intensely high emotions. It also reads the energy of people we have just met.

We have all met someone and had the feeling that something just wasn't 'right' with this person. We may have sensed, "coldness" or an "emptiness" in this person's personality. We aren't sure how we feel about this person. The information our emotional faculty has brought to our mental faculty to interpret simply does not register because there is nothing in our personality and experience bank that is like what our emotional faculty has found in this person. As we get to know this person better, we may learn that some tragic experience has damaged this person in some way that shows up in the emotional impulses.

Sometimes we have the exact opposite experience. We like this new person, instantly. Sometimes we feel a deep unexplainable attraction that defies explanation. There is usually nothing visual about the person that would explain this apparent chemistry. As we get to know this person, we often learn that we have a great deal in common with him or her. Our emotional faculty working in concert with our mental faculty brings this information to us.

We can all relate to the winning feelings we get when we are playing family-evening board games or in athletic competition. We notice that, mentally, we are laughing, joking and taunting our opponents and they are doing the same with us. Clearly, we are not mentally focused even though we are enjoying our winning streak. We are, however, emotionally focused. The next time we are in this winning "zone," we can note how we are feeling as opposed to what we are thinking.

Of course, we are feeling good but think about what more is going on inside of us. Notice that nothing seems to dampen our thoughts. Also, notice that nothing seems to fully occupy our attention. Notice that distractions don't seem to bother us; we don't need quiet and stillness. We must learn to duplicate what we are feeling during those moments and we will duplicate the associated winning. It is not mental as many believe, although our mental faculty does direct our actions, movements and energy that produce the winning.

Casino gamblers know well how their 'luck' seems to change when the house sends a "cooler (a bad-luck person)" to cool the hot streak of the winning player. The winning gambler seems confounded by this phenomenon and, even worse, he usually feels powerless to overpower this person.

The gambler will try to think winning thoughts, repeating positive mantras and so on but nothing works. The Cooler already understands that there is nothing mental going on. The Cooler is attuning the winning player with emotions of insecurity, fear, embarrassment, doubt, loneliness, sadness, despair and shame. We are just not going to overcome these feelings with mental programming. We must master our feelings.

Dogs, horses and dolphins are each prone to emotional attunement. With a look or a gesture, they can positively change the rhythm of our day. We regard them as very intelligent creatures yet we can only prove that they understand simple commands. Emotionally, these creatures are masters of connection.

They seem to understand how we are feeling and they respond in kind. If we are intent in wallowing in our sorrows, out of support, they will wallow with us. When it is time to end it, notice that they will do things to distract us and that cause us to feel happy, surprised, compassionate or humorous.

At one time or another, most of us have been in the presence of someone who was absolutely bursting with joyous or happy feelings. Perhaps this person had good news to share or just had a very positive life-changing experience. Whatever the situation, we probably found ourselves unexplainably excited and happy as well. Our friend or loved one's emotional faculty infected our emotional faculty and attuned it to a comparable intensity.

Our emotions must be controlled and managed with great discipline. If they are not, they will be an uncontrollable source of negative stress which will lead to unhealthy mental and physical manifestations like baseless worries, anxiety, fearfulness, depression, pessimistic thoughts and feelings of powerlessness. Our emotional faculty is fascinating to explore; we must learn all that we can. Our emotional health is at stake.

Our Mental Faculty

Remember the first time our parents asked us something like, "Have you lost your mind?" I was very young at the time and I didn't even know that I had one to lose, at the time. We may ascertain from this statement that I started 'messing up' rather early in my life.

Instead of being insulted or ashamed about what I must have done, I became fascinated with the question. I spent the better part of my life trying to figure out the answer. Through research and lots of experimentation this is what I found.

Mind is Eternal consciousness. It is literally a part of every entity, everywhere. It is even in entities that we do not necessarily consider living, the way we understand it. For example, water, rocks and earth all have consciousness and they all respond to the creative instructions, directions and commands of Eternal Intelligence.

Mind is aware of itself; it is active and responsive. Mind is responsive to the energy of Love, Truth (Law) and Life. Our mental faculty is our mind. It is our personalized manifestation of Eternal consciousness that was gifted to us at birth; it came with us as part of our package upon entering this physical existence. (Fersen, 1923)

Think of our mental faculty as containing both a broadcasting and tuning component, a sender and receiver respectively. Eternal consciousness is a vast vacuum of creative thought energy. Similar to the way our airwaves are filled with television, radio and other communication signals. Our mind's eye is the mental venue through which our mental faculty interprets creative thought energy that we gather, send to or receive from others. This interpretation process is imagination.

Our mental faculty uses imagination to communicate creative Eternal thoughts through energy to, from and among one another. Our mental faculty uses imagination to interpret energy sensations gathered through our five physical senses: sight, sound, smell, taste and touch. Our mental faculty uses imagination to interpret intelligent electromagnetic energy that we receive through our emotional faculty.

Our mental faculty uses imagination to aid us in acquiring meaningful information from a variety of thinking tasks like learning, reading, problem solving, assessing, resting, listening, talking, studying, exercising, meditating, visioning, dreaming and reminiscing. (Stone, 1976)

Thinking is our mental response to information presented to us as a question, supposition, challenge or circumstance or some combination of these, that requires processing (assessing, analyzing and understanding), evaluating (examining and comparing) and resolution (deciding, reviewing and concluding) that results in experience on the part of the person responding.

Our mental faculty is a supreme recording device. It literally stores information about every facet of our lives (and I literally mean "lives"). It stores physiological information about our anatomy from the moment of conception. It stores every sound, smell, feeling, touch, image, experience that we have ever had in eternal memory storage. This eternal memory storage is called, "The Akashic Record." It has the ability to retrieve any of this information, at any time for examination and review. Amazing? There is much more that it does. (Barty, 2008)

Our mental faculty also can retrieve information from other conscious matter. This means that we can gather ideas, concepts and information from other minds regardless of the content we seek. Our mental faculty has the ability to communicate with these other minds at any time. When we choose to communicate with any creature, they can understand us, not through our words but through our intentions, images and desires. (Murphy, The Amazing Laws of Cosmic Mind Power, 1965)

I love watching children at the zoo bargaining with the many animals to come closer so they can get a better view of them. When the animals respond, the parents usually seem surprised. The children know intuitively, as do the zoo employees that the animals do understand our intentions, images and desires for them. When I go to the zoo, I love to demonstrate this to family and friends. It has never failed.

Plant owners know well that plants will respond to our intentions and desires. That is why some people are branded with the mantle of having a "green thumb." There is no great secret. Simply treat the plants the way you would want to be treated if you were a plant, with their spectrum of concerns. This is all the work of our mental faculty. Bee keepers and etymologists understand this as well.

The great American educator, scientist, botanist and inventor, George Washington Carver, understood the concepts of Eternal mind and its proper use quite well. Although, he was a tireless researcher and scientist, like all of us, he would become frustrated and perplexed by the lack of information he was able to logically uncover about his subject matter.

Carver is famous for admitting that, during these moments, he would actually talk to his peanuts (and other subject matter) and ask them quite honestly, "Why did God make you; what good are you to us? Show me how you can make our lives better." Below are some of his famous quotes. (Kremer, 1991)

"When I was young, I said to God, god, tell me the mystery of the universe. But God answered, that knowledge is for me alone. So I said, god, tell me the mystery of the peanut. Then God said, well, George, that's more nearly your size." GW Carver. "If you love it enough, anything will talk with you". GW Carver.

Carver is credited with discovering "three hundred uses for peanuts and hundreds more uses for soybeans, pecans and sweet potatoes. Among the listed items that he suggested to southern farmers to help them economically were his recipes and improvements to/for: adhesives, axle grease, bleach, buttermilk, chili sauce, fuel briquettes, ink, instant coffee, linoleum, mayonnaise, meat tenderizer, metal polish, paper, plastic, pavement, shaving cream, shoe polish, synthetic rubber, talcum powder and wood stain.

We can choose to study Eternal life energy for ourselves and further educate ourselves about the mystery of Mind. It is present everywhere and in all dimensions. It affects all of us, as it does everything. Many of us have a natural propensity to access this Eternal mind. We are creative, dominant, right-brained thinking artists, musicians, dancers and so on. Anyone can learn to access it, along with the Laws that govern it. It is a life-changing step toward permanent independence for all levels of life. We can no longer allow fear to prevent us from exploring these completely empowering phenomena.

Solidifying Our Spiritual Health

Our spirit is a real part of our living being. It is active in our life and it has been since our conception. Our spirit affects our physical, mental and emotional well being directly. Indirectly, it affects our relationships at every level and our ability to learn, grow and develop into fulfilled, productive people.

The last and most underappreciated area of our health is that of our spiritual health. Many of us associate this area of our lives with our religious denomination or how often we frequent our place of worship. Although what we are taught at our place of worship will affect our spiritual lives in some way, this area of our health is much more involved. Our religion is the actual practice of the doctrine for which our denomination stands. It is the duty of our faith to develop a personal relationship with the personality of the Eternal Supreme Being.

So our spiritual health is not our religion; it is not the acts and deeds that we do; it is not the beautiful artwork that depicts sacred images nor is it the idea of haunted places, ghosts, angels, guides, demons, trolls or unicorns. Our spiritual health involves learning about the Eternal Spiritual Intelligence that created and designed all life, worlds and the dimensions of existence.

Eternal Intelligence rules the creation, development and manifestation processes of matter, ideas, concepts and circumstances onto our physical world. It is the same living intelligence that arranges "chance" circumstances so that pets find loving homes, people become friends, mates have an opportunity to meet and get to know one another, and seekers of knowledge find answers and solutions to their important concerns in life.

Eternal Intelligence brings knowledge, options and wisdom to us though our dreams (both daytime visions and while we sleep), imagination, thoughts, actions, observations, study and research. It brings enthusiasm, humor, beauty, motivation, passion, creativity, love, appreciation and gratitude to us in our quiet moments of solitude. It infuses our imaginations with life-changing ideas, insights, concepts, opinions and world views.

Spiritual health concerns our ability to make full use of the Eternal Intelligence in our lives. This means learning the laws that the Eternal Spiritual Intelligence follows to rule the numerous processes unfolding throughout the universe (the most popular laws of Eternal Spiritual Intelligence are the laws of attraction, karma, love, success and cause and effect but there are literally dozens more). Unlike the personality of the Supreme Being, the Eternal Spiritual Intelligence is impersonal. We can make use of it just as the Supreme Being does. That is right. We can learn to use the power of the Eternal Spiritual Intelligence to create and bring into existence what we want in our lives.

Spiritual Intelligence has laws that govern its behavior, actions and use. A classic analogy of Eternal Spiritual Intelligence is that of having an environment of fertile soil, water and light. One person may choose to plant an apple seed, another may choose to plant a cotton seed and someone else may choose to plant a peach seed. As long as we have a favorable climate, all three plants will sprout and grow to maturity. So long as we follow the rules: apply the appropriate amount of water, light in a favorable climate. We each followed the rules for growing our plants and we were successful.

Now, think of the soil as the Eternal Spiritual Intelligence; did it care what kind of seed we each chose to plant? Of course, it does not. The seed is our desire; what we want to bring into our lives. The water is analogous to the actions we make to nourish the seed. The light is what we learned about caring for the object of our desire (the information or knowledge). The climate is our mentality; it must be suitable for growing our ideas, concepts and desires to manifestation so a positive and productive attitude is ideal.

Spiritual Intelligence is important to grasp as, it is the intelligence that underlies all intelligences in any form. It travels in a spiral pattern. Just study the constellations, the growth patterns of creations in the waters and the fastest traveling fowl. Watch water as it drains from your sink, tub or pool. Spiritual Intelligence has the power of attraction as well as the ability to repel.

Spiritual Intelligence is conscious, electro-magnetic energy. It is always active and it will assume the personality, will and direction of whoever uses it. That means that Spiritual Intelligence does not care who we are or what we want. If we follow its rules, it will yield what we desire. So if we are a negative person, who wants negative things, it will attract those things to us according to our enthusiasm of our desire. If our life is fraught with misery, pain and negativity, guess how we have been using Eternal Spiritual Intelligence, whether we realized it or not?

Obviously, it is best to use Eternal Spiritual Intelligence for positive and productive purposes only. It will continuously yield what we desire as we continue to refine our ability to follow the laws. Regardless of who we are and what we desire, if we are serious about accepting full responsibility for the condition of our lives, we must tend to the development of our spiritual health.

It is important to remind each of us here, that there will be those who will try to convince us that we are wasting our time by putting our efforts into understanding this area of our being. Some of us only trust what we can see, hear, smell, tastes and touch. In short, our insecurities have taught some of us that if something does not have a physical manifestation, we should not believe that it exist at all. They will want us to support them in this mentality, even when we know better.

We must look closely at the condition of the lives of those who are trying to discourage us. If we want our lives to be better than their life is, remember that Eternal Spiritual Intelligence only gives us what we want when we follow the rules (laws). All of the most noted historical figures that we studied in school (or should have), solidified their spiritual health in this same way. Simply do what they did and develop a circle of friends who are traveling along, on the same path.

For every great public figure that we can name, from any time period in world history, in addition to the important contributions for which he or she is remembered, we will find that each one was a student of spiritual laws in his or her own right. They learned and followed the same spiritual laws that are available to us, for our personal use, right now. Each followed the spiritual laws and found their ways to greatness. We can do exactly the same.

Our Social Development

We are all social beings by nature. Some of us are decidedly more social than others. We socialize in a multiplicity of ways and with varying frequency. The experience of socialization is mutual and interactive. In other words, as we give of ourselves, we expect to receive the same in return. For example, if we choose to share ourselves, we expect some form of acceptance or validation in return.

Our social spectrum includes humans, animals, plants and inanimate objects. Often our focus is on more than just making contact with others for the sake of communication. Often we have objectives of learning, observing, sharing, acquiring, recruiting, bonding, mating and playing. Regardless of the specific reasons why we socialize, we still must do so for our own overall growth and development.

It is important that our social encounters always be positive and enriching. With each social encounter, we become better people in one way or another. When social encounters cease being positive and enriching, these encounters become damaging to us. The more negative encounters we have, the less we develop.

Consider a four-year old who plays with other children, who are physically abusive. If the four-year old was taught not to socialize that way, he or she may become withdrawn and grow apprehensive about the socialization process. The same is true of a child whose first encounter with a dog results in a painful bite from the dog. That child may not ever want a dog as a pet.

These negative experiences can affect us at any point in our lives. When we have too many of these negative social encounters, we become shy in those categories of encounters. Consider a shy teen who doesn't dance well and is insecure about dancing with others, unless others intervene and either teach the teen or demonstrate that they don't dance well either, that teen may shy away from these types of social encounters.

Many of us find ourselves with some social deficiencies at some point in our lives. The easiest examples come from our dating habits. There are literally thousands of single people, who are looking for a mate, who walk by each other every day in communities throughout the world.

Throughout the week, we pack into social establishments with the hope of meeting someone with whom we might find compatibility and contentment. Then, we just stare at one another while sipping drinks and listening to loud music. How many negative social encounters must we have had to create this level of socialization?

The same thing can be seen when a new employee comes to work at a well populated workplace. The stares are quite focused on the new employee. What are we all thinking about this new person? Be among the first to extend a hand in friendship. We might want to welcome that person the way that we would like to be welcomed in a strange, new workplace.

Are we that new employee or are we one of those staring with intense curiosity? What are we waiting to happen? Are we going to be the first to welcome this new person into the workplace fold? Will we wait for this new person to approach us? Let's always take a proactive approach and be among the first employees to extend a welcoming hand.

It is never too late to develop or improve qualities in ourselves that make us more socially or personally comfortable around others. Many of us go through our lives without any thought of upgrading our social skills or knowledge about improving our ability to socialize with a broader circle of people. Let's always look for opportunities to come together. Be an honorable leader in bringing people together despite any differences that we may have with one another. Commonalities that bring people together are work, sports, causes, music, disaster, education, illness and values.

Reasons to Share

Socially, we are proud people. We like to appear that we are always in control and that nothing rattles us. When everything is going well, there is nothing wrong with establishing and maintaining a cool exterior. It is actually great; a lot of fun. When the flows of harmony in our lives change, too many of us shun the opportunity to share our concerns with those who care most about us. This leads to isolation and unnecessary suffering in silence. Our burdens are always lighter when we share them.

When things aren't going our way, we must understand that our children, spouse, family, friends, coworkers are all empathetically supporting us when we are dealing with such uncomfortable, or even devastating, circumstances in our lives. They are cheering for our healthy emergence from the challenges we face. They are waiting to talk with us; for us to tell them how they can help us. They are eager to be a positive resource of support for us.

When we turn to alcohol, tobacco, overeating or any other self-damaging behavior, we are basically signaling to those who hold us in highest regard that we do not believe that we can count on them to help us through our crisis.

We are not even allowing them an opportunity to share their wisdom and words of encouragement with us. When we do not share what we are experiencing with our closest family members and friends, we cheat them out of an opportunity to grow closer to us; to share our burden and understand us better.

Most of us are surprised when we learn that someone we know has committed suicide. We feel a sense of loss that is different than when we discover that someone, who we care about, has lost his or her life because of an unforeseen set of circumstances that resulted in an accident. When someone commits suicide, we begin searching for indicators, in our most recent encounters with this person that would qualify as a 'cry for help.'

We find ourselves feeling clueless as to why someone we know would do such a thing. Then, we torture ourselves with questions about why this person did not turn to us, or anyone else, for help. We ask ourselves what could be so burdensome that ending his or her life would be an acceptable solution. Finally, we petition other survivors to share their burdens; to 'come and talk with us about whatever is bothering you.'

When we exclude our friends and coworkers from our grieving, we are refusing them their wealth of support for us, which comes from a diverse cross-section of life experiences. Our solitude does not help us and it does not help anyone else. We must open up and give others a chance to share our heavier burdens. When we open up and share what we are feeling and thinking, we accelerate the healing process and minimize our grieving period.

Reduce Stress to Improve Our Health

We probably have heard of and had experience with some form of stress at some point of our lives. Stress has become a "one-size-fits-all" term to describe the unseen obstacles that side track us from enjoying our day, job, relationships or life. Stress has been a convenient excuse for why we engage in self-damaging behavior. We allow stress to take away our good health; usually without a fight or any resistance from us.

Stress is anything that affects the normal, natural operation of any system, organ or function of our being. For example, if we are walking around with a 150-pound adult riding on our back, we are physically stressed. If we did not have that adult hitching a ride on our back, we would be walking at our normal pace, completely unencumbered.

If we are trying to read, in a room with very dim light, the lack of light is stressing our reading efforts. If we are attempting to hold a conversation over loud music, the music is creating stress on our ability to communicate. These are exaggerated examples because sometimes, we do not like to identify stress in our lives. If we did, we might feel the need to do something about it.

Stress can be negative or positive. That's right. In the above examples, this is how the positive and negative nature of stress will affect each situation. If we are carrying a 150-pound stranger from an accident scene to a place where we can get help, it may take all of our strength.

It is negative stress because we are trying to do a good thing and we may not be physically up to the task. If the person on our back is someone we love deeply, we will ignore the stress that is put on our body because we will be preoccupied with keeping them encouraged. This is positive stress because the reward for us is to keep our loved one in our life at all costs.

Stress can be physical, emotional, mental, social, academic, spiritual, intellectual and in a variety of other areas of our lives. When we have more bills than money to pay them, we often put pressure on ourselves mentally and emotionally. We tell ourselves negative things (thus creating negative stress) that we allow to dominate our thinking. This causes damage to our self esteem, self image and our self concept. We start getting headaches, muscle aches (especially in our back), joint aches and we develop trouble sleeping.

At this point, our negative stress begins to manifest through the largest organ we have, our skin. It begins to blister, boil and hive. Soon our normal bodily functions aren't so normal. We develop digestive and urinary troubles. Our stomach, kidneys, liver and spleen begin showing signs of inconsistent operation.

Our health troubles only create additional negative stress for us. We try to find comfort in the processed foods that tastes most pleasurable to us. This further complicates our health issues. Our negatively stressed bodies are now receiving considerably fewer nutrient-rich foods. We experience chaos in our circulatory and nervous systems, which affect our entire being.

We aren't able to concentrate or calm down. Hey, maybe tobacco and alcohol will help (stop laughing and agreeing, I am trying to make a serious point here!). Even the tobacco and alcohol create negative stress in the form of cancer and liver disease respectively.

If we do not feel good at any point of the day or night, we are experiencing negative stress in one form or another. This is the best reason to learn about the proper operation of our body, emotions, mind and spirit. Once we do learn what our bodies need to operate at peak efficiency, without artificial and unnatural stimulants, we will enjoy the health of our youth, when our energy level seemed boundless and when we looked our best on a regular basis. We want to get rid of negative stress all together, though.

Ideally, we want to infuse our lives with positive stress. Positive stress is usually a motivator. Great entertainers are under a great deal of pressure to deliver great performances night after night. Imagine if we knew that there were tens of thousands of our adoring fans paying top admission to pack great auditoriums just see and hear us perform.

That is a great deal of pressure. Few up-and-coming entertainers would run away from this kind of pressure because it is overwhelmingly positive. The better we perform, the more we solidify our fan loyalty and we are becoming wealthy in the process.

Positive stress is what motivates artists, athletes and musicians to practice the same motions, pieces and routines until we establish our targeted level of proficiency. It is what motivates serious students to study complex subject matter until they master it. Positive stress creates the challenge that keeps mates, family and friends close through the decades.

Positive stress is often a goal set from a vision, of the reward to be gained at some point. Let us say we want to put aside 125 dollars a week for a year. If we can save 75 dollars each week to go into our mutual fund and 50 dollars into our savings account, we will have the down payment for the house we want and we can take a nice vacation with our savings. Though this requires discipline and sacrifice, the reward itself, creates positive stress.

It can also take the form of a win-win wager. For example, since my credit card bills and your student loan bills are about the same total, let's wager that whoever pays his or her debt off first gets a home-cooked meal for a month from the other. We can be creative in how we bring positive stress situations into our lives and the lives of our family and friends. If it is positive stress that simultaneously solves important issues, definitely do it.

The greatest and most accomplished achievers throughout history have used stress, positively, to motivate themselves to reach certain goals they believed were important. Any of us can do it. We simply must make a commitment to ourselves to accept full responsibility for the condition of our lives. Then, create positive stress situations that solve negative issues that we want to eliminate from our lives, permanently.

Creating Our Personal Health Management System

We understand the importance of our health and that it spans many levels and dimensions. The best way to manage the full range of our health concerns is to create our own personal health management system.

If this seems like an unreasonable idea, name three people who care more about us being in perfect health more than we, ourselves, do. Perhaps, we could think of just one person who would switch places with us so that we would enjoy decidedly better health. Not so unreasonable after all.

Actually, that is an individual decision that will be different for literally everyone. There is no "one-size-fits-all" health program. That is why we must cover this extremely important subject. There is a combination, of strategies, methodologies, remedies and solutions, that is perfect for us, personally but only we can define it and it probably will not work for anyone else. So where should we begin? How can we begin assimilating the information that we need, to create this personally customized program?

We must begin by establishing a battery of general information about ourselves like what fitness level do we want, what diet will give us the healthiest quality of life, our consumption of liquids each day, our social and recreational plan, how often that we should visit our doctor for a checkup and so on. We will also need to include our educational, mental, emotional and spiritual goals as well.
This is an "organismic" approach to our wellness. It simply means that we are addressing the health concerns and well-being of our entire being. This is important because each of the areas, of our health, as discussed earlier, is inter-related.

We should be creative about how we design our personal health plan. We can create our personal health plan using a chart, journal, file, map, story board, visioning board, mind movie or some other way that makes sense to us. Whatever we do, we must include all areas of our health.

It is also helpful to establish performance standards in each category. For example, we may want to establish and maintain a basic level of physical strength and endurance, stress level, weight range, activity level, social interaction, recreation exposure, mental stimulation, emotional development and so on.

Remember, this plan does not have to make sense or work for anyone else; it must make perfect sense for us, personally. We have the freedom to make whatever adjustments we need to make, whenever we want, as our experience with our plan dictates.

With that in mind, we are free to experiment as much as we want. If we ever do develop a health issue that we may want our doctor to diagnose, we have several tools to consider already at our disposal that we can use to correct any imbalances that may develop.

We must be creative in securing our solutions. For example, if we desire more humor in our life, we might use a joke-of-the-day calendar or subscribe to a service that sends humorous messages to us each day. We could include more comedic entertainment in our life in the form of movies, television viewing or occasional comedy club visits. We could create a weekly humor night and include the whole family.

We have to experiment to find what works for us. We can do this in every area of our life from our physical to spiritual self. This may take some time, so we must be patient with ourselves; it is worth our faithful effort. Eventually, we will come to some areas of our being where we have a serious shortage of information at our disposal. This brings us to the next phase of our personal healthcare management system.

We will need resources to continue our work in creating a high-quality, high-powered personal healthcare management system that is custom fit to our needs, personally. We must create a Health Resource Bank (HRB). It is exactly what it appears. We assemble a personal team of professionals to act as information resources when it concerns any area of our health.

As a basic HRB, We might have a nucleus of these specialized professions:

1) **Medical** – These professionals specialize in traumatic, surgical and pharmaceutical treatments. They tend to have the most current diagnostic equipment for identifying advanced illnesses. In terms of the detailed operation of the human body is concerned, professionals in this area tend to be among the best educated and most rigorously tested. We should have at least two medical doctors at our disposal.
2) **Chiropractic** – These professionals specialize in non-surgical correction of the muscular-skeletal structure as well as excellent advisors of non-pharmaceutical and non-invasive healing protocols.

3) **Dental** – These professionals specialize in the area of facial care especially the mouth cavity.
4) **Nutritional** – These professionals specialize in various phases of diet management.
5) **Herbal** – These professionals specialize in natural healing remedies from animal, plant and mineral sources. Never hesitate to consult with them regarding health and dietary issues.
6) **Fitness** – The professionals range from exercise physiologists to certified trainers and specialize in muscle and joint fitness and flexibility.
7) **Psychological** – It is important to have competent, objective and responsible people with whom we can talk openly about virtually anything without judgment. They do not have to be paid and well educated professionals but it would help if we could work something like that out with them. They must be people who we trust to provide wise counsel when we need it. In this category, we should have at least five (5) people of different backgrounds, genders, and experience levels.

We must keep updated information for each person in our HRB. List each person and their specific area of specialization. Include multiple contacts information as well. It is important to indicate here, that there are many online sources of information that have many areas of specialized knowledge. We can research these as well. Never be afraid to make contact by phone or email.

These people will make time for us. We must also bear in mind that these are business people so at some point, they will expect to be compensated for their effort to serve us. Characteristically, these professionals are in the habit of delivering an extremely high quality of service for a comparatively reasonable rate.

We can set up our standards and guidelines that are consistent with how we would like to meet our life goals. For example, we may decide that we would like to lead a vegetarian lifestyle with no intense exercise regimen. We may want to create a nutrition-based plan as the foundation for our health program. We must create what works for us in light of the wellness goals that we establish and choose to maintain.
Never have just one source of information each category. For each of the above categories, have a minimum of two professionals. We should have as many more as we desire for each category. Remember, this is about them providing high quality information for us.

They do not have to agree with one another but they do need to explain their positions to us in a way that helps us decide what the best course of action for us is based on the guidelines that we have set for ourselves.

We must access as many points of view as we can with regard to every concern. If we have trouble with depression, headaches, allergies or sleeping at night, we should find out what the professionals in each of our resource categories can tell us regarding this problem area, from their own perspective.

The cause could be related to our diet, workday stresses or from the ingredients in the cleaning products we are using in our home. We must get all the information that we can. The answers will be different for each of us as we each have different patterns, routines, diets and outlets for our lives.

Our Personal Health Plan

The creation of a comprehensive personal and/or family health plan is the best investment that any of us can make in ourselves and those who are within our household. There is no insurance company, government entity or business agency that knows the specifics of our personal care needs as intimately as we do.

None of them are as personally concerned with the quality of our wellness the way we are, ourselves. To date, these various organizations have only been able to engineer general plan guidelines in an attempt to have us to choose the 'best fit' for our situation. By taking this step, we can help them to serve us better by taking an active role in our own health management.

In addition, they charge us a great deal of money to administer these plans that seek to simply manage our various illnesses, not cure our sickness. Many of us have been in managed illness situations for decades without once considering that we could take responsibility for our lack of health and find a solution on our own that might absolutely cure our condition.

When we create our own personal health plan, for ourselves and our families, as illustrated before, our goal is not to prolong sickness by managing it; our goal is to create perpetually excellent health under all circumstances.

This is a very real possibility too! Consider how we have been taught to approach our personal healthcare, to this point in our lives. We rely on over-the-counter pharmaceutical products for allergies, common colds, flu symptoms, headaches, dental pain, annoying aches and pains throughout our bodies.

When these solutions eventually fail, we contact our physician, who, after a very basic interview, prescribes for us a more potent pharmaceutical product. This more potent product usually is not designed to cure what is ailing us, it is designed to desensitize the nerve endings that tell our bodies that there is a problem in that area; thereby, relieving us of the pain we feel, only.

Obviously, this solution, in itself, has great value to most of us, in the short run. Yet the trouble, in our body, that is creating the pain issues persists. We know, intuitively, that the pain will return at some point. We know that we must eventually settle on a solution. We could take higher doses of the product that dulls the pain. That is simply an extension of the short-term solution.

We have been taught to manage our illness, not cure it. When we are unable to delay the onset of the now increasing pain (our body is intensifying its message to us that there is now a full blown crisis), we contact our physician.

At this point, this is the best idea. Our physician is extremely well educated about the how our body operates, how to diagnose irregularities within our bodies and what will happen to us, if our body is not relieved of the issue(s) that is causing us so much discomfort.

This wealth of information that our physicians provide, to us, is extremely valuable, especially to those of us who have chosen to take full responsibility for our state of physical health. We can take the recommendations of our physician and weigh them against the opinions of other healthcare experts who specialize in successful health solutions for a broad range of conditions. (Ausubel, 1987)

These healthcare experts are doctors, therapists, technologists and counselors who, for one reason or another, have also chosen to take full responsibility for their state of physical health. Their personal stories are quite compelling as many of them are survivors of "terminal" illnesses of many descriptions. (Desai, 2004)

These healthcare experts have found their way into their chosen disciplines because of their experiences of years with managed illness protocols. They discovered solutions to illnesses that have frustrated the mainstream medical community for several decades and they are eager to bring those creative solutions to the rest of the world. (Gimbel, 1994)

These healthcare experts specialize in a variety of important areas that are important to our health like nutrition, chiropractic medicine, naturopathic medicine, massage therapy, acupuncture, herbal medicines, speech and hearing pathology, substance abuse, psychology, homeopathy, iridology, psychoanology, nephropathy, energy medicine, occupational therapy, sound therapy, aromatherapy, integrative medicine, internal cleansing, breath and energetics, color therapy, mineral and crystals, regression analysis, life coaching, magnet therapy, meditation, reconnective therapy, sexual therapy, reflexology, release therapy, spiritual therapy, exercise physiologists and so on.

Finding a starting point to such a vast array of available solutions can be a daunting task. The best place to begin would be with an established chiropractic physician or wellness physician. These two healthcare disciplines tend to be at the hub of these many highly valuable healthcare solutions. Professionals in these two categories can narrow our search to the best options for our research based on our medical physician's diagnosis.

The costs for any of these services are quite affordable and their solutions have a tremendous history of success. From there, we can educate ourselves about the healthiest, non-invasive, least painful and most effective solutions in curing our illness so that we may continue building our lives, while enjoying the highest state of health that we can imagine.

Whether we create our personal health plan on a posted chart in our home, in a notebook at our bedside, on our computer or smart phone, it is important that we take this important step in safe-guarding our health. Health industry, political, workplace and economic influences, demand that each of us take a dramatically more responsible role in improving and maintaining our own good health.

We are able to do more than just manage our unhealthy conditions. We have the ability to work, actively, toward the consistent attainment of wholeness and perfect health for ourselves and our families. Because of advances in health and wellness technologies, the concept of excellent health well into our retirement years is neither a dream nor the result of naïve thinking anymore. It is, very much, a reality that is well within the reach of anyone who genuinely desires it.

It is worth mentioning here that no one is going to knock on our door at home and beg us to consider any opportunity that will make our lives better. Employers won't do it; educators will not do it; nor will any physician or attorney do it. If we do not have the strength of personal concern, for ourselves to seek solutions, that make our lives better, for ourselves, then we are demonstrating a profound dereliction of our responsibility to ourselves and loved ones. The answers are available and it costs nothing to find them to evaluate them for ourselves.

Chapter 7

"Do what you love. When you love your work, you become the best worker in the world."

-- *Uri Geller*

Embrace and Respect Work

A good friend of mine, Geronimo, and I were enjoying a day at the 'Taste of Chicago' a few years ago. We were taking a break, from sampling the many fine food items that were being sold, when we spotted some portable horse stables. As we walked closer, we discovered that these were the famous Clydesdale [breed] horses that were the mascots for an international beer brewery. We marveled over the size of these large and powerful Scottish work horses.

The handlers were busy grooming these magnificent animals. They brushed, picked and braided each horse's mane and tail. Even their teeth were in excellent condition. Geronimo, a retired, international horse racing jockey from Peru, turned to me and said, "These horses are treated better than people!" I agreed, as we laughed about it. "Well, they have great jobs and they make a lot of money," I added. That is the point of this section.

Work is honorable. It builds character. It gives us practice to become proficient. It allows us an opportunity to learn and accomplish. It provides each of us an opportunity to pull our own weight in life. It gives us respect. It provides us an opportunity to manage our money and acquire assets. It justifies us as deserving a good meal and a good night of sleep.

It allows us a say as to what goes on in the home where we bring and share our earnings. It allows each of us an opportunity to save and invest our earnings for a better life. Work provides us an opportunity to be a good example to our children, extended family members and friends. Employment, in any legal form, is a good thing. Unfortunately, there are still some of us who do not respect work, at all.

We accept a job with an employer and complain that we don't like the work. We don't want to follow the rules. We call in sick when we are not and complain about our employer's benefit package. We steal from the supply cabinet and take excessive coffee and cigarette breaks.

Then, we complain about how much we are being paid to do our job. We complain about business decisions that make the business stronger but inconvenience us personally. We rarely make serious suggestions to improve our workplace in the areas of productivity, performance quality and profitability.

Work is not always easy. Sometimes it is stress filled. Sometimes we choose the wrong job, wrong employer or, worse yet, the wrong career. It happens. Nothing

about it feels right but we have gotten use to it. We have become familiar enough, with our line of work that we learn to cope. We are not happy.
We don't earn enough and the hours are terrible. We miss time with the family and, more important, time for ourselves. We feel trapped as though there is no easy solution to changing our workplace circumstances. We feel powerless; no one understands, believes or hears us. That is our responsibility.

There are still others, of us, who have so little respect for employment that we consistently find reasons to be terminated from our places of employment. When we are not employed, we attempt to convince our family and friends that there is no work to be attained. If there are obviously jobs that are available locally, we pretend that no one will hire us.

If an aggressive employer pursues us out of sheer desperation, we make up excuses like we are not physically able to do the work or the work conditions are too severe for us. If those excuses aren't acceptable, we complain that the job does not pay enough or that the hours are all wrong and we don't have time for that. We are looking for the easiest possible road to basic living, with as little inconveniences as possible.

When we choose not to respect employment, what we are, in effect, saying is that we would rather have someone else provide for us, as though we are children. We want the respect of being a responsible adult with all the privileges that come with it but without the actual responsibility of earning our way.

We would rather be a financial burden to our mate, extended family, friends and society in general, instead of a community contributor. Often, we will propose the idea of enrolling onto some sort of government assistance program as a life success strategy. When we are healthy and allow ourselves to think this way, we become a person who is to be avoided at all costs. We are openly choosing to embrace irresponsibility.

We can never allow ourselves to think this way once we have committed to accept full responsibility for our life condition. If we continue our association with someone who openly embraces irresponsibility, that person will sabotage every stage of our progress, until we finally give up the notion of having a better life and settle for where we have been, along with the misery and frustration that it brings.

If, on the other hand, someone in our life and perhaps our home is making the commitment to accept full responsibility for his or her life condition just as we are, then, we both will need some help if keeping gainful employment has been an area of struggle in the past. Even when we do respect employment, finding the right employment fit, can be a challenge, in and of itself.

Make Your Resume Useful

The first area is our "Employment Objective;" the first heading of our resume. Using a customized Employment Objective will distinguish our resume from all others from the beginning. It does not narrow our choices but it does clarify the circumstance where we know that we would be a great fit in the workplace.

It should cover the level of job (entry, supervisory, management, administrative, etc) we are interested in securing. It should also cover the environment (office, outside, retail, warehouse, manufacturing, etc.) and industry (transportation, hospitality, medical, law enforcement, food service, finance, etc.) where we are comfortable working. We can indicate the kind of employer (progressive, established, small business, corporate, franchise, etc.) for which we would be most comfortable working.

Next, we can indicate at least one significant contribution (dependability, responsible, high performance, loyalty, creativity, etc.) we are interested in making to that employer and how we would expect that employer to reciprocate (promotional opportunities, large bonuses, relocation, etc.) our contribution. Now, here is the challenge that makes most of us cringe. Do all of the above in one sentence. Yes, it can be done. Here are three examples of an Employment Objective:

1) "I am interested in securing an entry level position with an established employer in the medical industry that rewards its most dependable employees with education opportunities that lead to advances in salary."
2) "I am interested in securing a supervisory position with an expanding law enforcement concern that values creative contributions from its employees, demonstrated through opportunities for promotion."
3) "I want to secure an administrative position with an established financial institution that rewards its most loyal employees with periodic pay increases."

We should never copy these onto our resume, word for word, as each person's employment objective will be different depending on our personal wants and talent level. We can simply create one for our resume that is unique for us and one that states our expectations realistically. Believe it or not, we do not have to lie on a resume to secure the position that we want. The truth is often the most powerful contribution that we can make.

Next, we include a "Summary of Qualifications" section. This section should include our skills, important personality traits, workplace abilities and any special talents (or inclinations). First, it is important to explain the difference for each, as many of us jumble them together quite randomly. That makes for a very sloppy presentation. So here are the differences:

A "skill" is learned. It may have been learned in school like typing or on the job like car audio installation. It may have been learned in home like basic cooking or tailoring, or from volunteer opportunities like event management or interior decoration. Wherever we acquired the skill, it is ours. It is applicable wherever we choose to use it; even in the workplace. So let's keep our skills listed in the same area.

Personality traits are unique, to us, as individuals. Examples of personality traits are a good sense of humor, a pleasant disposition, being inquisitive, detail oriented, being responsible (or irresponsible), being trustworthy (or untrustworthy), friendly (or unfriendly) and being empathetic. Some personality traits are highly desired in the workplace by employers. As we might suppose, most are positive.

We must decide what our best personality traits are and then choose the ones that our perspective employer might value in the employment position that we want to attain. If we are unsure if some are suitable to be placed on a resume, we can leave them off and mention them in the interview if we think they might help us there.

Workplace abilities are work-related challenges that we have mastered from experience that we can bring to our new employer. These workplace abilities include such experiences as managing a certain number of employees in an operation such as in a kitchen or manufacturing environment.

These abilities can also include such experiences as managing a retail establishment or a building project. We need not have been officially designated as a supervisor or manager to have done the work and understand the nuances involved. Employers value those who can take over an operation with just a few days of training. Personality traits and abilities should occupy the same area.

Each of these listings, skills, traits and abilities with related experiences should be confined in the "Qualifications" section.

The last area is in the "Employment" section. Under each job we have done, we waste space detailing what our duties were. If we worked at a retail establishment, the person with whom we are interviewing would know what that work entails or they should not be interviewing us.

Instead, our space would be better used by listing our 'accomplishments' for that position. Employers are only interested in hiring us because they want to find out what we did in our last job that makes us deserving of a better one.

What better way to demonstrate this than to explain how we came up with a way to increase employee productivity which yielded a seven percent increase in monthly profits. Maybe we found a more efficient way to process orders or developed a more effective marketing strategy that increased traffic into our establishment.

If we were doing the hiring, would we want someone who just shows up (maybe on time) and does as little as possible until it is time to go home or someone who is genuinely interested in making the workplace a great place to work by creating an environment where people want to come and give their best by working together? That is the perspective that we want to focus our accomplishments.

We can simply place ourselves on the other side of the interview desk. We do not need to lie or mislead. We can be honest about what we want from our employer as well as what we intend to contribute to our employer.

It is possible that we are in an industry that does not pay well, for the lifestyle that we desire, especially at the lower positions. That is something we must cover with our interviewer in the interview. If our sincerity is genuine, our employer will find a way for us to earn more money at that establishment based on the contributions that we are willing to make. In the short term, we may have to supplement our income with a second employment opportunity.

If we must find a second employment opportunity to supplement our income temporarily, we should be sure to share that in our interview. In this way, we are not misleading our second employer about our future availability. Surprisingly, employers tend to be very receptive about having extra people to plug into the weaker areas of the work schedules. We can find opportunities that complement our full-time employment. For example, if we sit all day, find a second opportunity where we are up and about, perhaps getting some much-needed exercise in the process.

Embrace second employment opportunities as a way of learning about a whole new industry about which we have always been curious. Among the places where we can test out new industries for secondary part-time and temporary opportunities are in the area of hospitality (hotels, car rental, airline), food service, janitorial and sanitation, night clubs, retail, call centers, transportation services and safety and security. We can gain a tremendous appreciation for those who work in these industries, full time, for their life work. We can meet some of finest and often the most creative people in our area.

We will meet others, who like ourselves, are accepting full responsibility for their life condition and taking control of their destiny. We can swap stories, solutions and strategies. Each person will be at a different place on his or her own path. Expect to make wonderful new friendships. By the way, this is a benefit that those who do not respect employment will never enjoy.

We can respect employment, not only for what it can do for us but, for what it allows us to do for ourselves in changing our life to the most positive and productive state possible. It allows us to support our local, state and national economy. It gives us a justified voice in community and political matters. By the way, when things do not go our way with certain law enforcement officials, many of us tend to want to use our taxpayer status to bully them.

This is wrong and not the intent of this chapter. The local police do not appreciate the, "I pay your salary" bit from taxpayers. We call them to deal with situations that most of us want nothing to do with. Let them do the work they were trained to do and give them a pass on this one. Good police officers, who are of good character, are worth their weight in gold; let's appreciate them for that.

We must secure the employment situation that supports our commitment to accept full responsibility for our life condition. Constructing the right resume is a good first step. As the employment coaches will counsel, we should dress appropriately, be well groomed, clean up our language (no slang or profanity), be on time and be prepared to interview, intelligently.

Interviewers can sense sincerity just as they can sense a scam. Our intentions must be pure and honorable. If we are serious about accepting responsibility for our life situation, our intentions will be evident to our employment interviewer.

A Few Interview Tips

Now that we have improved our resume, we must be properly prepared for the interview process. This is an area that most of us botch because we believe that we want the position, in question, so badly. Once we get the job, oftentimes we find that we really made a bad choice.

Too many of us forget that the interviewer's responsibility is to find the best person for the position to be filled; not to reject us personally. If we keep this in mind and cooperate accordingly, the interview process is easy and comfortable. We will land fulfilling positions virtually whenever we desire, so long as the current economy will support it.

The first thing that we will cover is having the proper attitude and mode of thinking for an interview. Think of the interview process as we would a fight; a boxing match, for example; we are going to the interview to win and so is the interviewer.

The interviewer sees people like us much of the time: people who will say and do almost anything to get a job that they may not really want nor be qualified to do. We tend to think of the interviewer as a gatekeeper who wants to be charmed, coddled and entertained. This is usually not the case. Interviewers are not insecure, needy individuals who require validation to do their jobs. Just be straight with them and they will be just as candid with us.

In order to approach interviewing for a job intelligently and respectfully, we must disregard our misperceptions of interviewers and the open positions for which we are applying. It will help us to focus on four areas concerning the employment interview: Prospective, Attitude, Competence and Questions

We do not want every position that appears. We want the right fit. Let's focus on the business of intelligent and respectful interviewing. We can begin here:

Perspective – It is important that we understand the full picture in the case of the employment interview. Very little of this process is personal, for or against us. The interviewer is under pressure to hire someone who is qualified to do the job at a given pay rate. There are usually several qualified applicants.
The interviewer is next concerned with finding someone who would be a good fit in terms of personality, work ethic and character. It is so easy to ruin the workplace chemistry by adding someone who enjoys creating drama by gossiping, starting rumors and exhibiting divisive behavior.

The interviewer's next concern is to find the applicant who will stay and learn the job and become a productive and valued employee. Many applicants are just looking for money as the sole criteria for accepting a position. If another employer offers them an extra 50 cents per hour more two months later, that applicant is likely to leave. No interviewer wants to hire such a person.

The current employees would have to cover the staffing shortage created by this person's departure. The flow of work and workplace chemistry is again disrupted. The hiring process must begin again. That means the organization must spend the money to advertise the opening, interview people and train a new person. This can be quite costly; it is not an expense that most employers desire.

Next, the interviewer must consider the advancement ability of each applicant. Every employer values having people who can develop to the extent, that he or she can be promoted to a supervisory or managerial position. An applicant, who is determined to do the bare minimum to get through the workday, is usually not an asset to any organization.

If hired, that applicant is likely to be a burden to his or her coworkers, in terms of workplace performance quality. The interviewer is concerned with the applicant's demonstrated work ethic in previous work situations. If we truly believe that we are a good fit, we should position ourselves as a perpetual contributor to our workplace, operationally.

Finally, the interviewer must be concerned with the quality of each applicant's character. The selected applicant should be an asset to the company both as an employee and as a community member.

If the applicant enjoys a positive public image and reputation, it will only increase his or her appeal to be awarded the position. If the applicant has a questionable public reputation, it will definitely diminish his or her possibilities for securing the position in question.

Attitude – Here, the typical applicant is encouraged to change his or her attitude to one of contribution, of giving or serving. An applicant's attitude about his or her worthiness is extremely important. The applicant must communicate confidence, competence and professionalism.

This means dress in a professional business-like manner and be well groomed without showing tattoos and facial piercing jewelry. It is important to communicate in a professional manner with absolutely no hint of slang or profanity. The applicant should be articulate and use a familiar vocabulary (never use words if you are not certain of their meaning or the correct pronunciation).

Competence – It is important that each applicant knows exactly what is expected while occupying the position that is advertised. The advertisement is just that – an offer to negotiate for the position. Well before we attend the interview, contact the company to obtain a copy of the 'position description' (not the job posting; they are not the same) for that position.

The position description is available from the human resources department and it spells out the specific tasks, duties and responsibilities of the job. Review it carefully. We must make sure that we can perform each task and duty. We must also be certain that we can manage our position responsibilities intelligently and be able to communicate that to the interviewer.

Questions – Expect difficult questions in the interview. We are expected to sell ourselves as the ideal candidate based on everything we are able to find out about the advertised position. It is important that we are honest in our assessment of our ability to do the quality of performance demanded by the job. If we have never been required to perform at that level, we should decide if we can adapt our abilities and upgrade our performance quality, accordingly.

We have to decide if we are willing to learn to work at the required level stated, with all of the stresses and pressures that come with it. Once the interviewer has exhausted his questions to us, we should be prepared with questions for our interviewer. It is not always clear what we should ask our interviewer.

We should develop questions that will allow us to seriously evaluate the fitness of the position that we believe that we want. The questions should center on the value of the position and those who occupy it. For example, we might formulate questions like these:

A. Is this a newly created position or one that was recently vacated? (This could be a low priority position and the last person figured it out and jumped ship)

B. Why was it created and/or what happened to the last person who occupied it? (We may have the same fate)
C. How will my work performance be evaluated? (Decide if the evaluation method is fair)
D. What kind of training can I expect to receive and for how long? (Training may be sloppy)
E. Who will do the training and is that person certified to do training? (Trainer may be inexperienced)
F. To whom will I report? (We may have several bosses and they may not always get along; we do not want to be caught in a power struggle)
G. At what times and where do we take our breaks? (Break area may be mandatory)
H. What do the workers like and dislike most about working here?

At this point, applicants are usually clueless about how to proceed. To keep things simple, I caution everyone to be honest, prepared and smart about the interview. To clarify, that means that we should construct our own resume. We do not say anything about ourselves that we cannot prove. Finally, we don't say anything that might hurt our chances to win the job.

One of my former students proved, conclusively, how demonstrating poor character and shirking responsibility can sabotage our chances for employment success. As a college student, he spent most of his energy finding ways to get out of doing his class assignments himself. He was physically attractive and he knew it.

He used his attractiveness to get his female friends to complete his school work for him. One student constructed an extremely professional looking resume for him to use in securing a cooperative educational position with a prestigious company, just prior to his graduation.

At his employment interview, he looked great. He prided himself on being a "smooth talker." As such, he assured me that his interview would "be a breeze." Apparently, it was until one of the three interviewers made an interesting observation.

One interviewer stopped the interview and called for a brief conference with the other two interviewers. Once the conference was concluded and the interview reconvened, the lead interviewer handed this student his resume. Another interviewer asked him to "read it to them."

This student never bothered to read his own resume. The information was accurate and consistent with what he had discussed during the interview. The problem came with his assurances about his ability to deliver a high-quality work performance. One of the interviewers noticed that his 'speaking' vocabulary did not match the level of vocabulary used on his resume.

This attractive young man attempted to read his resume to his interviewers as requested. He mispronounced and stumbled through it until he became frustrated with himself. He finally was forced to admit that he did not write his own resume nor did he write any of the elaborate class assignments (all 'A's') that he brought as evidence of his fitness for the position, for which he was applying. He was exposed as a 'fraud.' His professional reputation has suffered serious damage from this very preventable and careless incident.

For many of us, there just is no ideal job. More and more of us are considering some form of business ownership. Some of us have hobbies that we want to turn into profitable ventures and others, of us, desire to demonstrate our business independence through teaching, consulting, writing or some other creative endeavor.

None of it is easy because we have to work so much harder and longer each day. So many others of us cannot seem to figure out what we can do to earn any extra money. We must upgrade our thinking to fit our new commitment for being fully responsible for the condition of our lives.

There Is Always Something To Do

It so happened that I finished writing this book in the midst of an unprecedented global economic down turn. Many large companies simply could not justify hiring more employees. As a result, millions would be unemployed for the next few years.

The next best thing to do is to use our entrepreneurial spirit to create work. Anyone who grew up without getting an allowance but was encouraged to go out and 'earn' money, knows that there is always something we can do to earn money, legally.

When we are minors, in need of money, we know that we can mow lawns, clean swimming pools, garages, basements, wash cars, shovel snow during the winter, walk dogs, pet sit, babysit, stack hay, pick produce or any number of short-term chores. It is the same thing wherever we are. It may not always be "dignified work" but it is 'honest' work, nevertheless. There is always someone, who has money, who has a need.

As I look around, I found many opportunities to earn money. There are thousands of unemployed people receiving state unemployment benefits. Most are wasting their days watching television and lounging around, as their job skills dull. If this is the case for you, why not consider volunteering with organizations that need your help?

It gets unemployed workers out of the house and back into the workplace. It doesn't cost the organization anything because these individuals are receiving a regular check. What a great opportunity to keep your employment skills sharp.

Any fan of professional sports has observed how young, rich professional athletes squander their money on "wine, women and song." Many of them find themselves in unnecessary legal entanglements as a result of their reckless night time antics.

The legal fees, league fines and publicity people they have to pay off create a considerable financial burden for many of them. Why not provide these young and well intentioned celebrities the option of employing body guards, designated drivers and social coordinators for their outings. There is always something we can do to create new, legal income opportunities.

Our basic income attraction abilities are unlimited largely because of our education and programming concerning money throughout our upbringing. If we are not aware of where lucrative opportunities can be found, we will suffer financially.

It is our responsibility to research, inquire, and figure out which opportunities would be a great fit for us. We must pay attention to the economic, industrial, social and lifestyle trends of the people where we live. It is in those areas where we will find our next business opportunities.

As we uncover, issues that require simple solutions that we can solve, we can begin to develop the plans for profitable opportunities that will put money in our pockets and that can be expanded to employ other people where we reside. When all seems dismal, it is our personal responsibility to expand our awareness, broaden our thinking and engage our imaginations to develop solutions to improve our quality of life.

Some timeless business service opportunities that I have uncovered are these:
1) A labor-only moving service;
2) Grocery cart repair;
3) Small tire repair (dollies, wheelchairs, mobility carts);
4) Neighborhood clean up (apartment complexes and neglected neighborhoods);
5) Mattress recycling;
6) Computer parts repair and recycling;
7) Mailbox repair;
8) Roadside assistance service;
9) Document and Photo scanning service;
10) New business operations designer;
11) Publicity and Public Relations;
12) Exercise equipment assembly and repair;
13) Appliance Installation;
14) Assembly and installation service (home and business - furniture, sheds, etc.);
15) Event planning (including weddings and memorial services);
16) In-home cleaning service;
17) Elderly social and monitoring service;
18) Neighborhood revitalization service;
19) Basic business management (new businesses);
20) Interior building common areas cleaning service.
21) Small engine repair (landscaping equipment)
22) Wardrobe fashion specialist (private and commercial clientele)

Chapter 8

Happiness is the continuous fulfillment of our endless proliferation of desires.

– *MG Kamau*

What We Do Want Out of Life

Everyone, no matter who or where we are, wants the same thing – to be happy. Even though, each of us defines happiness subjectively, it is the truth. When we think of what, exactly, would make us happy, we burst into chatter about everything from money and material possessions to love and personal success.

If we examine each of these, subject by subject, we will find, that we know, that none of those, alone, would bring us lasting happiness. In this light, it is important that we look more closely at what we really do want out of our lives and most important, how we can get what we want.

Many of us feel that having great sums of excess money will make us happy. It is true that we would have better credit scores, more material assets and a higher standard of living. Many lottery winners and former professional athletes will attest to that. They will also attest to the fact that if we do not educate ourselves about how to manage and invest our money properly, we will eventually squander it and have nothing. That probably will not bring us happiness.

When we center our thoughts on excess cash on hand, we are presuming that those who have such cash arrangements are happy people because of the money. If this were true, there would be no divorces, suicides, self-damaging behavior or crimes of any kind among the rich. As any adult can observe, the woes of the rich are no fewer than any other segment of society, albeit money is not one of them. We have to look more closely at what 'happiness' really denotes.

From the moment of our birth, we all have desires. Immediately after our birth, I am willing to bet that most of us wanted to return to the womb of our mother. Life does go on and as infants, our desires were quite basic; we wanted to sleep, be warm, feel loved, eat when were hungry and be cleaned when we, mysteriously, found ourselves to be soiled.

That seems to make most of us happy, at that time, in our lives. However, as we grow and discover more about ourselves, our desires change. It takes more to make us happy. We want independence, choices, first-hand information and more attention, in addition to our initial basic desires.

We can see, clearly, that the desires of a 6 month infant are significantly more than a newborn infant. It follows that much more is required to make us happy as we grow and mature through life. By age 5, we are fully functioning, independent thinking and self-sufficient creatures. Happiness, at this age, is measured in gifts, treats, excursions, play and periodic parental affection. If nothing else is apparent, we can be sure that our definition of happiness is tied, directly to the complexity of our desires.

As adults, this is no less the case. The more we add to our personal development and enrich our lives, the more complex our desires become and our ultimate happiness becomes more elusive but not impossible. As we learn, we develop abilities, talents and qualities that make us more valuable.

Through our personalities, we express these magnificent changes that make us higher evolving and more actualized people. Our quest for happiness becomes an ever-evolving pursuit. This might be a clue as to why so many of us enjoy supremely fulfilling lives. Through our expanding awareness, our blossoming desires provide the fuel our ever growing happiness.

As we study the social habits of humanity, we can see that there is an ever-widening gap between those whose desires drive their happiness and those whose desires add to their misery. This does not seem to be consistent. If our desires fuel our happiness, then it seems that everyone should be happy or at least striving for happiness. Obviously, this is not the case. So, let's see what other motivations that our desires can spawn.

At some point during our growth and development, our desires that fuel our happiness, takes an unhealthy turn for some of us. That, which we learn, leads us to an awareness of what we want, as well as what we are missing. This duality of motivations allows us to identify needs as easily as we do our wants.

For example, as a child, we might become aware that we aren't receiving the same amount of attention and support from our parents as it appears that our friends are receiving from their parents. This awareness has uncovered a need that we would like to fulfill. We feel ignored or unimportant to our parents so we observe the interactions of our friends, with their parents, to see how they handle this situation.

With one friend, we observe that she is strictly obedient to her parents' desires in keeping up with household chores, homework, and proper behavior while guests are visiting the home. With another friend, we observe that he is constantly undergoing correction by his parents for making poor decisions, exhibiting bad judgment and questionable behavior.

We evaluate the respective situations of both of our friends in seeking a solution so that we can remedy our dilemma. Both have found a way to fulfill their need for greater attention from their parents. Should we decide that neither situation is an acceptable way for us to gain the additional attention we want, we may try a creative mixture of both situations.

Remember that our desires fuel our happiness. Also, what we learn often leads to a greater awareness of various needs and wants of our lives. If we decide upon a solution born of negative actions, decisions and behaviors, we will very likely gain the attention that we want but in ways that will inhibit our natural growth, development and maturity. This is important to consider when we find that our forward progress, in life, has been impeded or stopped completely.

When we become aware that certain needs are not, or have not been met in our lives, we must focus on positive ways of fulfilling those needs that will foster our positive growth, development and maturity. So long as we keep a positive perspective of our life's direction, we can focus on keeping our ever-expanding awareness, positive.

As our desires continue to proliferate, we will find positive ways to fulfill them. In this way, we can be sure to stay on a course, in our life, that encourages progressive growth, development and maturity. No matter where we are and regardless of how we define happiness, it is completely attainable in every area of our lives.

Courage and Acceptance

Some of us are so desperate to obtain the 'happiness' that we want, that we are willing to change who we are to get it. Many of us are so unhappy with ourselves that we try to convince others that we are more than what we really are. Often, we create the illusion that we are just what others expect us or desire us to be.

We purchase vehicles, clothes and homes that we can barely afford, in an effort to fit into a popular image; we decorate our bodies with tattoos, piercings and make-up so that we might be accepted by certain friends and into certain social circles. Obviously, there is nothing wrong with this if we are doing so for our own personal expression of what we believe. However, often, this is not the case.

Too often, we are more inclined to play 'follow the leader' in attaining the happiness that we desire. This is nothing more than the illusion of happiness through acceptance. Of course, the happiness that we attain, under these circumstances, is happiness dictated to us through popular media.

Such happiness will not be lasting because it is an illusion. The desire is planted within us and manipulated accordingly. Healthy desires are born from within as a result of intended personal growth. When we take the healthiest approach to finding happiness, it is always lasting.

We must be courageous in being ourselves. Everyone has a life story that is replete with mistakes, misunderstandings and setbacks. Focusing on those will never allow us to make the progress we want in our lives. Rather than hiding from our shortcomings, we can save them as lessons that we can use to help others, when we are asked. In this way, we turn our shortcomings into strengths. When we do this, we will find it easier to accept ourselves, wherever we find ourselves in life.

The basis of happiness is self acceptance. As we practice self acceptance, we build courage about who we are. We make ourselves fearless regarding the judgmental perceptions of other people. Eventually, we rid ourselves of any form of insecurity and cowardly tendencies.

As we solidify this mentality, we project an attitude that indicates that we pursue happiness in our lives with tremendous confidence and vigor. We realize that happiness, really, is just a choice because it is simply choosing to fulfill, positively, a desire that is born of an awareness of an important area of our being.

Selling Our Souls

Virtually all of us have unfulfilled desires in one or more areas of our lives. Exactly, how we go about meeting such desires, to attain the happiness that we seek, isn't always clear. For example, if we desire some new material possession, we simply manage our financial resources more efficiently until we can secure what we want.

If we are trying to win someone's respect, approval or love, the path to success, in this area, is not so easy to find. Desires that directly involve the fulfillment of desires of other people can complicate our road to happiness. Nevertheless, sometimes we can become so focused on getting what we want, from other people, that it turns into an obsession. This is an obstacle that we must avoid, at all costs.

This shift in our concentration is damaging to us because it can interfere with our creative thinking. Instead of designing, planning and executing a solution that benefits all concerned. We begin to accept the idea that it is all right to infringe upon the rights and freedoms of others.

We allow ourselves to accept the idea that it is all right to deceive, manipulate and cheat others to get what we want. This is most frequently illustrated in social politics in schools, workplaces and in places of worship when we find ourselves in pursuit of greater influence, higher positions and advantageous relationships. Because of the unpleasant consequences, this is never all right.

When we look back at times that we have observed these scenarios (or have personally been a party in such matters), we can easily identify the drama that came as a result of these power plays. The damaged parties are bent on taking revenge in one form or another.

Each bides his or her time, just waiting for an opportunity to strike. The original offending party develops a reputation for being unethical and untrustworthy. He or she becomes paranoid and chooses only the most naïve and gullible people available to befriend. The environment becomes toxic, cold and less productive. High stress, illness and misery become common characteristics of those who inhabit that environment frequently.

How positive, productive and synergistic we all could be if we would just allow ourselves to enjoy the wisdom of working together. Instead of plotting and planning against each other to satisfy our desires, we could share our concerns. We could explain that we are looking for a promotion, a career change, a new relationship or a reason to live with those that we have come to love, trust and support. People who genuinely care about us will not let us down. They will always support us to the best of their ability.

When we need help in fulfilling our desires and we share those desires, we find that many of those who care about us will put the power of their networks to use. They will ask other loving and supportive people, who they know, who might be able to assist in solving our issue.

One person may find out about an upcoming promotion that will be a great fit for us. Someone else will uncover a career opportunity that would benefit us greatly. Another person may know of a compatible person who is also looking to start a new relationship that would be a positive match for us. Others may be aware of opportunities that might highlight our value by helping others who have a place for us or need us desperately.

All of the effort we could have put into scheming and backstabbing can be avoided and a far superior situation will result for all parties concerned when we only accept positive, supportive means to find our solutions. Instead of creating enemies, we solidify our relationships and build positive history. We also place ourselves in a position to repay such kindness which provides a fulfillment within us that is beyond description. At our core, we all enjoy helping other people find happiness.

Many of us still do not understand how other people have ordered and structured their lives so that they can have the lives that they want. We convince ourselves that they are cutting corners, being unethical and deceitful. In some cases, this may be accurate. When this is the case, we still must be mindful that these people, who partake in such practices, are only cheating themselves. Their perceived happiness is only an illusion that will unravel as quickly as it was conceived.

Regardless of what others appear to be doing to attain happiness, it still has no bearing on how our lives turn out. Ultimately, only what we, ourselves, do determines the state of our own happiness. Always, we should choose the path of truthfulness, openness and cooperation with everyone who we encounter.

Far more good will come to us in the long run. Cutting corners, deceitful and manipulative practices, to get what we want, will usually get us everything but what we ultimately desire. Let's leave the drama and negative dealing to the novelists, playwrights, television and movie screenwriters where it belongs. Such activities must never consciously be allowed to be a part of our real lives.

Chapter 9

Never lose sight of the fact that the most important yardstick of your success will be how you treat other people - your family, friends, and coworkers, and even strangers you meet along the way.

First Lady, Barbara Bush

Being A Better Example Today

This chapter is about basic leadership and cultivating competent leadership qualities, especially good character. Many of us do not see ourselves as leaders for one reason or another. My purpose here is to convince each of us that, not only are we already a leader but we must accept this role and develop the qualities that will make us the best leader that we can be.

If some of us are chuckling to ourselves about now, I do understand. That should only indicate to us that we are still searching for our specific place in this world. Many of us spend the balance of our years searching for our life purpose. Tragically, many of us leave this world without ever discovering our place.

Everyone has a positive and important place in life. Figuring out that place can be quite challenging, especially with so many distractions, with which we deal each day. In our daily contact with public programming (through television, radio, magazines, internet, movies and so on), we are pressured to focus on being beautiful, exciting, witty, sexy, funny, athletic, musical, theatrical, rich, famous, daring, dramatic, smart and positively dangerous. It is difficult to be all of these and, yet, it can be even more challenging to decide which combination of these fit us, personally. The starting point for finding our ideal place in this world begins with us.

Through self-talk, self-examination, observing how people treat us, figuring out what people seem to desire from us, remember the most common questions us are asked and so on, we can begin to put together the clues that will assist us in locating our place in this world. It is important that once we identify our place that we commit to leading.

That simply means that, if we have found, for example, we seem to have an above-average ability to diagnose and repair issues concerning motor vehicles, we should not remain at that same level of competence and prominence. We can commit to educating ourselves even further. We can improve our business and communication skills to the extent that we are on course to create a significantly better way to deliver the high quality of service that is indicative of our gifts. We must strive to become the undisputed leader in our segment of the industry where we have found your place to be.

Each of us knows someone who is gifted in a particular area of service among his or her social circle. Our friend has a special gift and everyone knows it. That person might be the one we all contact when we need to have our cars serviced, computers repaired or important events arranged and managed. Clearly, this person has discovered his or her place in terms of public contributions. Unfortunately, for so many of us, we have in fact found our place in the world but we reject it. We want to see ourselves occupy a more prestigious position in life.

This need for greater public esteem is the source of a great deal of inner conflict and stress for most of us. We believe that we deserve more out of life and we look everywhere else to find it. We tug at one door of opportunity in life after another in search of our path to wealth and riches, only to have each one slam shut on us. Because we refuse to accept the magnificent gift(s) that we have been given naturally, we allow ourselves to become increasingly frustrated in life.

We are, in a sense, rejecting an important part of who we are. When we do this, we are practicing a form of self loathing. When we reject anything that is positive and up building to us, we only do damage to ourselves. We are rejecting opportunities to serve others honorably, create wealth, teach others by our example, honor our individuality, demonstrate gratitude for our gift and improve the lives of those about whom we care the most. To minimize any talent, ability or gift that we possess also minimizes who we are in life.

When we discover our unique talents, abilities and gifts, it is important that we demonstrate our appreciation for them by developing them further. We can accomplish this through education, practice and sharing. When we choose to honor these unique qualities by enhancing them, we also discover opportunities and possibilities that we never considered before. We may learn, after all, that our special quality can be enhanced to the extent that it will elevate us to the lifestyle that we ultimately dreamed.

This could never happen as long as we do nothing with our special qualities. If we have a talent for fashion, interior design or landscaping we must embrace it, develop it and share it accordingly. Doing this awakens a new appreciation for who we are individually, what we can accomplish when we focus and the possibilities we can bring to those in the world.

Consider all of the special products and services that we use for our pets, enhancing our children's' ability to learn, accessories for our motor vehicles, entertainment and recreational choices. They all began as a part of someone's individual talent, ability or gift. If those people never embraced, developed and shared these qualities, our world would be a less developed and fulfilled place. Let's examine this protocol at each stage.

When we embrace any good quality within ourselves, it becomes part of our identity. It provides us a unique place in the minds of those who know us. It allows those who know and care for us a reason to initiate conversations and tell their stories about their interactions with us. It allows all of us to dream wildly about the greatness to which we may, one day, aspire.

When we enhance our unique quality with additional education, we improve our own competence. We establish ourselves as credible authorities regarding our special area. We learn the history, present situation and forecasted future for us as members of our newly discovered discipline. We learn the latest applications, versions and processes. We renew our respect for ourselves and others of our ilk.

When we share what we know, we create connections and intensify communications. We establish a new voice, among many, in our new-found community that will shape the vision of our future. We will be provided opportunities to work together, create together and present together. Finally, we will create pathways for others, who share our unique interests, to benefit from the reliable sources and information available to date. There is no disadvantage to cultivating our uniqueness at any point of our lives.

As we embrace our new-found place in the world, we are undoubtedly serving as an example to those around us, about how we make the most of our gifts, talents, skills, as well as our life. As we become a strong and visible leader, a better example in our family, social circle and community, we add to the number of great examples that are available. Children and teens now have expanded options for their life options. We have created encouragement and hope for many who might otherwise not have any. This happens only because we choose to be a better example, today.

We Are All Role Models

Most of us who are considered to be role models have intentionally created our public image accordingly. We are happy to be the example of educational excellence, business achievement, athletic greatness, class and grace, beauty and healthfulness, sexy, sensuality and sassy in our sphere of influence.

Many role models have the vision to build upon their status and extend their influence to support important causes that are intended to benefit humanity as a whole. These might concern some area in nature conservation, human rights and well being, the selling of products, endorsing political candidates and so on.

We are generally happy to follow them because they are what, we ourselves, aspire to be – famous, rich, influential, beautiful, healthy, sexy and so on. We are happy to join them in the causes that they support because their influence with us is very strong.

There are many role models at the local level and each has his or her own unique personality that makes us all appreciate them in our own special way. In private conversations, we teach our children to respect the accomplishments and achievements of our most influential role models. In many cases, we (and we also teach our children to) emulate their work ethic, career path, life choices, behaviors and so on. This is how our society treats its role models.

So far as the rest of us are concerned, many of us have never considered that we are already role models, at least on the local level. Many of us are unintentional role models. People in our families, communities and social circles are happy to celebrate our day-to-day victories in the workplace, our place of worship, within our social networks and the like.

They support us whether we are reveling in the news of our new promotion or if we had suffered the loss of a loved one. We are role models and leaders in our chosen walk in life, whether we think of ourselves as such or not. We are exalted for the good that we do.

We are also, singled out for the lack of good that we do. For example, parents who believe the "Do as I say, not as I do" style of parenting as an intelligent way of rearing children have created a very low standard of parenting for their own children to embrace when they become parents.

Yes, parents, siblings, aunts, uncles, grandparents, cousins and family friends are all local role models. It is important that we scrutinize our decisions, behaviors and actions often especially when we are around those who are most impressionable and who hold us in high esteem.

When we exhibit self-damaging behavior in front of children and teens (like using profane language, smoking, using illegal substances, drunkenness, criminal and immoral behavior), they are interpreting this behavior as "adult behavior." Most of us know, from our own teen years, how eager children are to emulate adult behavior.

As role models who are leaders, we might consider that we should make a conscious effort to teach our children the difference between 'self-damaging behavior' and 'responsible adult behavior.' Further, we must accept responsibility for what they see, hear and learn from us, personally.

We often, irresponsibly, convey many wrong messages. The sad fact is that many of us serve as role models of what others do not want their loved ones to become. For example, if you have a reputation for cheating on your spouse or life partner, you can bet that, virtually, anyone who knows the two of you is secretly pointing to you as the kind of mate not to become.

If you are an under-achieving bully at work or in school, you can be sure that you are a frequent example, in private conversations, of what kind of person is destined to become a loser in life. We are all leaders and role models in one respect or another to someone. Let's embrace this fact and commit to being responsible in how we present ourselves in public and especially where children and teens will be in attendance.

Develop Discipline

I teach seminars in basic management. One course in particular is designed for first-time, frontline managers. It is interesting, to me, just how often I encounter people who honestly believe, that once they achieve a position of increased responsibility (like supervisor, lead, assistant manager and so on), they now have a license to tell others what to do while they (themselves) walk around or go hide and do absolutely nothing. Further, they tend to exude such confidence as though their word is law and that they are above reproach from any of their subordinates.

A position of leadership is one which requires the highest level of discipline, accountability and ultimate responsibility. Virtually, anyone can occupy a leadership position. The concern is the direction of that person's leadership. Simply occupying the position does not necessarily assure competent leadership. Leaders have taken historically profitable and well-run companies into virtual ruination because of their incompetent leadership skills. Leaders have ruined the defenses and economies of entire nations because of the direction of their leadership and their inability to make intelligent and responsible decisions.

Leaders must embrace and internalize the qualities of discipline, accountability, character and competence. A leader's focus must be to serve those who he or she represents. As a role model, celebrity or high profile public figure, our responsibilities are no different. As a star athlete, we represent those many other athletes within our chosen sport. What we do or don't do reflects, directly, on the others on our team, within our league and within our sport, at every level.

As a celebrity entertainer, our choices in life directly reflect on others within our genre of entertainment, within the entertainment industry and at every level of the discipline. Leaders who desire to be successful must establish and maintain a mentality that is positive, productive and responsible. That mentality should permeate every thought, decision and result that he or she creates for those represented.

Many years ago, on a television sports show, former Notre Dame, football coach, Lou Holtz answered a question about being such a harsh disciplinarian with the players on his winning college football teams that stayed with me over years. His response was that 'discipline is not something that you do to someone; rather it is something you do for someone.'

Such an answer registered with me as an invaluable pearl of wisdom from the mind of a genius (winning coaches seem to appear that way while their teams are winning). Nevertheless, the wisdom of this statement is timeless. We see evidence of this in music students who have mastered their chosen instrument, in accomplished athletes and entertainers, in high achieving professionals in the fields of law, medicine, engineering and so many other fields.

Discipline is what divides average from the highest achieving in virtually every walk of life. Those of us who commit to discipline will put in the extra effort, time, attention, practice, focus and concentration to bring about our desired result in achieving our relatively lofty goals that we set for ourselves. We tend to demonstrate our commitment to discipline by our actions instead of excessive talking about our intentions. (Waitley, 1984)

Those of us who are committed to discipline tend to realign our daily priorities to reflect our commitment to our intentions. Those of us who are committed to discipline tend to prepare to make great achievements by disposing of any potential distractions that we can identify before we begin our pursuit for excellence. A great leader will make his or her position clear to those whom he or she represents before assuming the leadership position. It does not matter which level of role model or leader we are, this is a critical step to any area of our success. (Giuliani, 2002)

Treasure Accountability

Leaders are not always able to deliver what they promised. Few of us are satisfied with excuses for less than ideal outcomes. It is no different with a leader. We may know, very well, reason(s) for the outcome but our respect for any leader is diminished considerably when he or she chooses to blame others instead of accepting responsibility for the ultimate results. Accepting full responsibility for the outcome is choosing to be accountable.

When we choose to be accountable, it simply means that we are choosing to look within ourselves for answers, first. We examine matters like what we promised, why we made such promises, did we take the correct approach? Did we consider all factors and variables? What might we have done incorrectly? What lessons did we learn? What could we improve upon in subsequent endeavors? Did we have the proper attitude? Were we respectful to all concerned and so on? Once a leader demonstrates accountability, he or she can accept responsibility for any outcome that was not delivered as promised.

As respected leaders, we make things right when we discover and openly admit that we were in error. As parents and role models, we set a good example for those whom we represent and lead when we are open and honest. As leaders, we become better people and a better example when we do the right things to remedy unfulfilled promises, missed deadlines, poor quality of results and so on. By doing the right things by our supporters, we teach them integrity, ethics and good character.

There are cases in leadership, where integrity, ethics and good character are not a factor in delivering results. When decisive action and quality of results are the primary drivers that mark solid leadership, we must focus on delivering outcomes that has the greatest benefits for all concerned. For example, if we want to set a good example for our children as students, we can enroll in some course work at a local institution of learning. We can appoint a study time each evening where everyone must participate. It is at this time that we can practice strong study habits while demonstrating discipline, persistence and excellence. Further, we can compare our grades for quizzes, tests and assignments to our children. They will develop a greater respect for learning because they see that it is important to us. They will be more likely to share their educational concerns with us as well.

When the concern is safety or health, whether in the home or on the job, solid leadership must be decisive and results driven. We may have to take a stand that is unpopular and that creates uncomfortable circumstances for those whom we serve. For example, certain protective clothing must be worn or a particular cleansing protocol must be mandated. Proper results are paramount in these cases.

Whenever possible, we should be the best example possible of great leadership. We must be prepared to do the right things as often as possible and be prepared to eliminate any obstacles that prevent us from achieving our goals. If interference comes from outside sources, that are intent on sabotage or counter productivity, we must be prepared to take extreme measures to change their attitudes and compel their full cooperation to be in compliance with our purpose and goals. When we lead for the express benefit of all concerned, there is no alternative strategy. Everyone must participate in the solution.

What We Bring To Others

This section concerns our impact on others as leaders and role models. Specifically, I want to deal with what we have given to or taken away from the people throughout our interactions. At some point, we have to decide that we are either going to be a positive or a negative contributor to this world. This is what summarizes our lives; our biography. This is what we account for as a person. This is our contribution to our heritage as a member of our family, community and a being who was created from the loving essence of Eternal Intelligence. This is what we chose to do with the gift that is our own life; how we chose to exercise our free will.

We all have the inherent responsibility to be mindful of the consequences of our thoughts, decisions and actions. These thoughts, decisions and actions affect more than just our intended target. If our intended target is a student at our school, we must be aware that the student probably has parents, siblings and friends. If it is our decision to help this student by being loving and supportive, we are helping everyone who is in that student's life. If our decision is to harm and humiliate that student through verbal, mental and emotional attacks, we are harming everyone in that student's life.

It has become fashionable, over the years, to be a "bad" boy or girl. It is consistently glamorized in movies, television, music videos and magazines. It is very pronounced in personal ads in newspaper and on the internet. Such portrayals are extremely popular and entertaining.

We even sport T-shirts with clever sayings that reflect our personal defiance to the political system, people who are less intellectual, societal norms and so on. These are usually witty and often very funny. It is important that we exercise our collective fantasies in a safe, secure way, through non-threatening outlets. The problem is that real-life choices are a different matter all together.

In public presentations, I often discuss 'uncomfortable' subject matter that I believe needs to be dealt with for one reason or another. This is going to be one of those discussions in this section. I do not intend to offend anyone; however, if we are all to accept responsibility for the condition of our lives, we need to be realistic in how we assess the effects of what we create. With that said, I will proceed.

If your initial thoughts, about this section, were that I was going to cover a lot of feel-good, do-the-right-things-in-this-world kind of themes, you are right. I absolutely love happy endings and outcomes. It is who I am. I am also one who likes to be objective and unbiased as often as I can stomach it. Keep that in mind as you read through from this point.

I want to discuss intentions – yours and mine. We all make mistakes, bad choices and bad decisions. In my life, I am convinced that, more often than not, people, of all backgrounds, intend to do the right things as often as we are able or permitted to do so. For example, while I was in my early twenties, I witnessed a shooting. A prostitute shot her abusive pimp at point-blank range. She emptied the gun in his face; thus, rendering him virtually unrecognizable to even his most familiar circle of associates.

I was frozen and shocked; I did not think to move or run for cover. One of my best friends, Steve, literally grabbed me and threw me to the ground and pulled me under a car for my own safety. I never took my eyes off of the prostitute. She was tall and athletic. She jumped a fence into a backyard and began to run away. She leapt over two other fences before she disappeared from my sight into an ally. As she ran away from the scene, I noticed something about her intentions.

It seems to me that if we are fleeing a crime scene, where we have just murdered someone, we would not think to do things like re-hang laundry for a line we just knock down, reposition a flower pot and move a child's bike to a back porch but she, this prostitute, did each of those things obviously realizing that it was not her place to damage the property of innocent people during her escape.

I have seen an armed robber stop his get-away car and wait while an elderly lady continued to cross the street. I have been told of many incidences of honorable behavior exhibited by people who had just committed serious crimes or who were fleeing police. I am not comfortable analyzing why people commit such serious offenses but I do want to discuss the effects of such decisions.

When I discuss our, collective, impact on others and our intentions, we often display deplorable choices that are based in ego and sexuality. We commit crimes; serious ones, most of which we will never stand legal judgment. When I use the word crime here, I do mean it literally.

It pertains to infringing upon the rights, freedoms and innocence of others. Most of those victims will never come forth to publicly accuse, yet they will carry the damage (that we do to them) with them for all of the days of their life. I will deal with one topic area at a time. Here are the areas:

Minors – Those of us, who are responsible adults, have positive intentions and who hold ourselves to the highest standards of character, make wonderful spouses, mates, parents and guardians. Our primary responsibility, outside of that as provider, is to teach our children life and survival skills. We use athletics, nature outings, travel expeditions, work projects and cultural education to accomplish these.

Children experience tremendous growth and autonomy through these years as a result of our positive influence. Children, usually, are emotionally and mentally attached to us as a result of this influence. If we are a family member, teacher, family friend, neighbor, coach, mate or some other significant person in a child's life, a trusting bond develops that appears to be virtually unbreakable. Nevertheless, many of us find creative ways to compromise these trusting bonds.

For some reason, we seem unable to fully appreciate the fact that we are role models to the children around us. Through our own efforts, we became heroes to the children in our lives. We earned this level of respect from them quite fairly. They love and respect us because of what we are to them. So, how in the world, could we possibly compromise and lose their respect? Let me count the ways:

- *Referring To One (or both) of Their Parents In Derogatory Terms* – Whether we are a divorced parent, unhappy mate or family friend, children love and depend on their parent(s) in ways that we may never fully understand. Disrespecting their parent(s), in any way, is a very bad idea. Children don't like it – even if what we say is true. The child (or children) may not openly protest against us depending on how much power they perceive us to have over them, but we will definitely lose 'respect' points. If we have convinced ourselves otherwise or we think we will buy them off, we are sadly mistaken. Don't ever joke about their parent(s), even if the truth is obvious to everyone.

- *Cheating On A Parent* – There is nothing funny about cheating. It is a sad state of affairs for all parties concerned. Both cheating partners are unhappy and unfulfilled. This, in itself, is sad enough. When we flaunt this behavior publicly, it then hurts the children who admire us and they will find such a betrayal difficult to forgive. Also, they have to hear about it at school by enduring taunts and endless gossip. This does not help them socially. It does not help them academically. It does nothing for their self esteem. It does nothing to help the family's community image. Yet, as responsible adults, we still do it.

- **Openly and Aggressively Flirting** – For some reason, when we are insecure about our fading sexiness, we feel the need to demonstrate to the minors (usually teens) that we still have 'it.' When we engage in coquetry or profane displays for intimate attention publicly, we make ourselves look quite foolish to the youth. We squander the opportunity to exemplify, to children and teens, social grace and class to attract the attention of someone in whom we might be interested. Both the boys and girls can benefit from any good example we choose to set. They don't need for us to put on an embarrassing show for them.

- **Pointing Out "Attractive" Teens To Pursue** – Most of us will not admit to having latent pedophiliac tendencies but this is exactly what we are displaying when we engage in this kind of behavior. We do not need to identify a 'hot' prospect for our teen to demonstrate an interest. What we find attractive or alluring is probably not where they are focusing their concern. Teens have sufficient hormonal activity to draw their attention to others of their age and social interest without our prompting. Let the teens deal with this. If they have any questions or concerns, they will address them with us, if we have solidified and maintained our position of respect and integrity with them.

- **Coming Home In A Drunken Or Drug-Influenced Condition** – Movies, television shows and comedians really support the humorous side of this issue. Unfortunately, we, as adults, can't seem to separate the comedy from responsible behavior. When children see us stumbling around in real life because we are inebriated, they may laugh about it in front of their friends but we are embarrassing them. We are also risking hurting ourselves or someone else if we try to drive, operate machinery, use a lighter (matches) or attempt to cook food. How much respect do we hold for people who commit serious offenses in this condition? How funny would it be if a drunk burned up our home or drove a car through our living room?

- **Using Racist, Sexist And Profane Language** – Children do not genuinely hold the prejudicial views that the teaching adults hold. You might have noticed that when two toddlers meet, they are just glad to see someone their size and age to play with. They aren't the least bit concerned about appearances, background or gender.

When we use negative language to describe the people in their school (many of whom they may regard as friends), we only encourage defiant and discretionary behavior toward ourselves. Even if the child respects us to the point that he or she accepts our biased views and mentality, we are only inviting social conflicts for the child that we 'supposedly' care about.

Eventually, our views and negative counseling will not hold up and the child will display rebellious behavior by increasing their socializing and even dating those who we have taught them to abhor. Teach them good character qualities and let the children make their own choices.

- ***Trying To Date Someone Their Age*** – This is particularly pathetic when adults fool themselves into thinking that teenagers have a deep, romantic interest in them. Teens have enough trouble with boys and girls their own age. They do not need to deal with us and our personal intimacy issues. Let's get it through our heads; we are parental figures to teens and nothing more. They want us to take them to the mall and buy them things so that they can impress the friends they know at school.

  There is nothing that a minor finds romantically attractive about gray hair, wrinkles and double chins attached to an overweight and sagging body. If ever a teen does display such an unhealthy interest, let's be the "adults" and direct them to the proper professional counseling.

- ***Forcing Sexual Intimacy On Minors*** – Many of us find it difficult to grow up when it comes to pursuing the young and attractive. Sometimes these attractive young people are still minors. Though they are physically attractive, they still have dependent and immature minds. Still, there are those of us who recklessly disregard this fact. Let's do the honorable thing and turn ourselves over to the police if we think that we might want to act on such pursuits.

  Hopefully, their parents have taught them to report us to the appropriate authorities. Aside from the legal troubles and public disgrace we are inviting, we are risking what is left of our good name. Once our reputation has been damaged in this way, it will follow us for the rest of our lives and we will never win the respect of that young person we, so selfishly, wronged.

  We are not doing the minor any favors either. Our actions are extremely damaging (physically, emotionally and mentally). That minor will be permanently damaged by our selfish need for temporary comfort. Our mental and emotional manipulation will only create feelings of mistrust and betrayal within them for us. They will carry these feelings to every relationship they have for the rest of their lives and we will always be the ones who must accept the blame for their relationship dysfunctions and failures.

- ***Verbal, Emotional And Physical Abuses*** – Some of us were never taught, as children, not to fight with someone who is physically, mentally or emotionally weaker than we are. Even as we grew into adulthood, we were never quite able to grasp the intelligence of how wrong this is. As a result, there are those of us who are limited in our ability to communicate with and get along with others.

Instead of making the choice to accept responsibility to improve our social and communication skills and resolve these issues, we resort to using fear and intimidation tactics to get along with minor(s) within our current household. Often, the minor(s) suffer for the frustrations that, we, their adult counterpart, experience at workplace, in personal relationships and within our social circle.

If we have brought someone into our home who is abusive in any of these ways, it is wise that we discontinue the association and creatively remove that person from our home, especially if we have minors in the home. If we aren't sure how to identify an abuser or someone who has abusive tendencies, see chapter 11. We must definitely get this person out of our home.

- **Teasing Minors About Their Progress Through Puberty** – Most of us have gone through an awkward stage of development while we were going through puberty. There are always a few body parts that develop ahead of others. As we look back through our collection of childhood pictures, we often do find our appearance as well as those of our friends to be quite humorous. It wasn't very funny back then because we didn't know if that was going to be the best we would ever appear or if we were going to eventually look better.

  Imagine the uncertainty a minor feels about his or her appearance. It is annoying enough when their friends tease them but their friends are experiencing the same issues so there is some equality in their ability to return any attacks. I have watched the reaction of some teasing adults when a minor points out the physical shortcomings of adults who have made fun of them. The adults don't take the teasing any better.

  Perhaps, we adults realize that we may not get any better. We clearly have our issues from childhood too. Minors usually have a great sense of humor about such matters so we can take the opportunity to share our feelings about going through our 'awkward' stage. To show respect for their self image and self esteem, why not keep any teasing on the positive and up building side. Minors love to hear how they are looking more and more like their more attractive adult relatives.

- **Teaching Minors Our Self-Damaging Habits** – Many adults brag about teaching a minor to smoke cigarettes, consume alcohol "properly" or to get 'high' off of illegal substances. These kinds of acts may, temporarily, help a minor to relate to us and it may help them to feel closer to us as an adult. As they mature through adulthood and realize the damage their bodies have endured because of our ego and childishness, eventually, they will resent us for it.

How grateful will that minor be when he or she is progressing through the justice system on a DUI charge or an illegal drug possession charge? How much will they respect us when they realize that they did not have the physical endurance to carry an injured friend to safety after an auto accident because of the toll that cigarette smoking has taken on their health? Why would we place ourselves in the position of being, indirectly responsible for the negligence of another? Minors are going to make enough mistakes and wrong decisions, on their own, without our help.

Minors have enough difficulty trying to figure out right from wrong in more complex issues. That is why they need us to be a responsible anchor in their lives that will not hurt them or steer them astray, according to our own life experience. Let's be the solid, responsible forces in their lives that they need us to be.

When we seek to make choices for ourselves, we sometimes forget that those choices affect other people or their property. We do not always consider how such choices will reflect back upon us in the future. Our choices are sometimes made to satisfy our vanity or our ego.

Those choices might be expressing what we think and feel through our acts and deeds. Our intentions are usually consistent with the expectation of our immediate outcome. The lasting good or harm of these intentions is in the long-term effect of those outcomes. We must choose our actions wisely as we remain constantly mindful of our intentions.

Parents – Many of us refuse to allow our own parents to move past their child-rearing phase of life. We spent years making fun of them, questioning their wisdom, challenging their authority and threatening to leave them. They tolerated our social experimentation (teen slang, tattoos, piercings, fashion trends, friends, mates and so on). They support(ed) us through our wrong choices and disciplined us when we choose to openly defy them. Many parents can actually identify the gray patches of hair on their own head that each offspring christened.

It is wise to seek our parents' counsel when we find ourselves out of answers at various stages in life; they know us better than anyone. Our parents usually know where we went wrong and they can tactfully communicate to us, how to get back on course, especially as it pertains to our personal crisis. Our parents wish us well and desire the best for us, always. Most of us understand that.

Yet, as the years continue, we find ourselves still insisting that our parents provide us with a place to sleep when we have disagreements with our mate, lose our jobs or our living arrangements. We expect them to rear our children when we don't feel like doing so. Many of us treat our parents like financial institutions and ATM's well into our adulthood. Once we have returned to our parents' residence, we expect them to take care of us as though we are still teenagers. Moving on, fully, from such attachments is difficult for many of us.

In many cases, we actually abuse our parents as adults. When we get ourselves into legal or financial trouble, we expect our parents to bail us out. We sometimes forget that they managed the money they earned responsibly so that they might be able to maintain their independence through their retirement years.

To drain our parents of their financial resources, that they need, is nothing short of criminal. We have the opportunity and ability to manage and invest our money responsibly right now. If our parents did it, with the added burden of providing for us, then, we can do it too.

Instead of always expecting our parents to give, materially, to us, we could just as easy ask them to guide us financially. They might ask us to cut down on our smoking and alcohol consumption and put the money in a savings account. They might tell us that we purchase too much fast food and that we could cut our expenses by cooking more meals at home and packing our lunch for work.

They might even ask us to scale back on our name-brand fashion purchases to save money. I can hear the moans and groans of discontent as we are reading this. Consider this: There are hardly better ways to show our parents that we love them, than to stay out of their home as freeloading boarders and away from their bank accounts as beggars.

Our parents have done their time for us. They have sacrificed, worried, cried, humbled themselves, served as savior, demonstrated hair-pulling patience, been our doormat, tutor, driver, mentor and friend for many years. As an adult, we can shift the responsibility for ourselves, from our parent(s), to ourselves and at least accept responsibility for our own lives. Actually, we should place ourselves in a position to be able to help our parents too, if they need us. There seems to be an evaporation of that mentality, though.

Intimates – We often compromise our own integrity by how we treat ourselves and others, who are closest to us. Some us, even in the advanced stages of adulthood, still spend our lives living off of others, as a lifestyle. Our designated hosts might be extended family members or "friends with benefits." In some cases, we live off of several people at a time. For example, we sleep in one household for food, engage in sexual relations for financial benefits in another household and still another for material comforts like plush surroundings, automobile and paid television access.

These social tactics do little to improve the positive image of anyone who chooses to engage in such a lifestyle. We damage every area of our lives when we use the people in our lives in this way. We are basically delegating the responsibility of our physical and mental well being to anyone that we can manipulate, emotionally, into championing our cause (or lack thereof). When we have made this our lifestyle for any period, we breed mistrust, contempt and dread among those who have chosen to give us an occasional helping hand.

By choosing to live off of other people, we are communicating messages that tell others that we have low self esteem, personal value and a poor self image. We are building a reputation that documents, conclusively, that we are both irresponsible and lazy. Very quickly, we become the kind of person, to whom, responsible parents do not want their children to be exposed. We also find that our base of supporters, who we identify as "friends," dwindles with each passing encounter.

When we consider what we bring to others, we have no standing when we treat others, in our lives, this way. No matter how we might attempt to convince ourselves (and perhaps others), that we are doing no real harm to anyone, one thing is clear, we are bringing nothing of lasting benefit to others. What we are taking, from the lives of others, far outweighs what we are contributing; a tremendous imbalance is created. Any imbalance, in any area of our life, is a serious matter.

Our intentions must be responsible ones if we are to improve the quality and direction of our lives. We must consider the effects of our decisions, actions and behaviors as they impact other people that we encounter. There is nothing wrong with asking for assistance when we need it. We, sometimes, must depend on the goodwill of a stranger when we are stranded away from home for a tire change, battery jump or lift to a service station. It is comforting to realize that most people will oblige us in doing the right thing under such circumstances. These acts make our lives and our world a better place.

Help Create Our Healthiest Environment

The condition of our physical, emotional, mental and spiritual health is solidly connected with the quality of our daily surroundings. It is up to us to create an atmosphere that is friendly to our overall wellbeing. That means if we are burdened with poor health, negative stress, headaches, general uneasiness, excessive noise or a weak immune system, we must accept (at least in part) the responsibility for changing the influences around us so that we are in a positive and productive environment that promotes our personal growth and enrichment. Should we come to the conclusion that we are unable to accomplish this on our own, then we must see ourselves as being gifted with an opportunity to join with others to hone our leadership, relationship or communication skills.

It is easy to allow ourselves to become angry and bitter over the circumstances that clearly are working against us. It is just as easy to convince ourselves that we are victims and powerless to do anything about it. Fortunately for us, that just isn't true. Notice that whenever we have made up our mind that we are going to accomplish something important (supporting a just cause, standing by someone through a crisis, weathering a disaster and so on), inner strength, supportive people and unfathomable opportunities seem to materialize all around us. If we haven't experienced it personally, we have witnessed this phenomenon with someone we know from our community, school, workplace or place of worship.

The fact is that we are already endowed with all the power, influence and ability to get this process started. It begins with us asking ourselves, "What can I honestly do about this situation?" Stay positive and resist all impulses to accept any negative thoughts about it. We may actually finish our day without an answer. We can stay positive and resolve to seek the counsel of many wise people, who have good character each day, until we do have the answers, plans and execution to effect the changes that we seek.

I was viewing a Public Broadcasting Station (PBS) program called, "Kilowatt Ours" by Jeff Barrie one evening not long ago that perfectly illustrated the point of this chapter. The program is a brilliantly informative and entertaining documentary about the perils of using coal as an energy resource to generate electricity.

This filmmaker takes his audience through the learning process that he and his wife underwent to learn about the effects of global warming and solutions to stop it. He included human health issues, environmental devastation, financial consequences and he emphasized personal accountability, for each of us.

Clearly, Barrie figured out entertaining, unconventional yet convincing ways to make his points without blaming big corporations or offending the sensibilities of any of his viewers. Instead, he focused on the economic benefits that homeowners, businesses and public institutions have gained by learning to embrace energy efficiency and alternative energy sources.

In his documentary, he introduces us to credible experts who share extremely useful information, as well as community leaders, who supply helpful testimony on how their businesses, schools and communities were better off for the environmental changes to which they chose to commit.

Filmmaker Barrie, was passionate about passing on his knowledge, concerns and vision. His challenge was clearly more than that of a one person undertaking. After searching his conscious, he committed to moving forward. He stayed positive and obviously sought the counsel of many wise people of good character. The result was that he created a lifestyle-changing presentation that will eventually influence millions of people around the world.

Throughout human history, people have stood up for positions that were positive and life affirming for all of humanity, often at great personal risk of damage from corrupt politicians, powerful corporations, contrary institutions and influential governments.

We have entered into an age where more and more people are organizing their efforts to bring truth to the masses. Barrie chose to make his stand in the area of "green energy" (Barrie, 2009). There are others like Annie Leonard who reveals previously obscure facts regarding corporate strategies, practices and protocol regarding marketing and manufacturing processes as it pertains to world economics, human health, employment and environment (Fox, 2009). Sofia Smallstorm, who brought to the public consciousness, previously suppressed information about a recent significant historical disaster in the city of New York that impacts our perspective about who planned the event (Smallstorm, 2007).

The efforts of these individuals have set an important precedent for the future. As more people and organizations choose to take a stand for what is ethical and right, they will escalate the mentality and consciousness of everyone in the civilized world, thus creating a more livable planet. Each of these individuals teamed with others to accept responsibility for a specific area of human consciousness, globally. They are leaders, role models and valuable experts for the entire human race. Their efforts are honorable, valuable and selfless.

Chapter 10

"An individual has not started living until he can rise above the narrow confines of his individualistic concerns to the broader concerns of all humanity."

– Martin Luther King Jr.

Our Life and Our World

Most of us are in various stages of transition on our life journey. We may be transitioning from our life in junior high school to our life in high school. From our life in high school to our life in college, military service or to a place of work, we are transitioning either to or from single life, from family life to empty nest, one career to another, one lifestyle to another and so on. These transitions are part of what is necessary for our natural, productive growth and development for our life. We are usually eager to go through such transitions with all of the promise for adventure and new experiences that they hold for us.

It is important, here, to clarify a difference between our "life" and our "world." Our life is an on-going, developmental process by which we become positive and productive influences (within our families, workplaces, social circles, communities, nations and so on) by being involved in activities, events and experiences that allow us to build good character, add wisdom and mature as people.

Our world is our personal interpretation of the people, circumstances, situations, experiences, opportunities, issues, institutions and events that we observe and perceive. For example, our life is what we create materially, in terms of lifestyle, relationships, choices in values, decisions (concerning education, home, community involvement, affiliations, associations, and occupation and so on), attitude, standards and the like.

Our world is based on our philosophy for living. For example, if we were taught by our parents to believe that our place is predestined (already determined because of who we are, how we look, where we were reared, the family who reared us and so on), we will act out that life philosophy, if we have internalized those beliefs. It does not matter what people we are around to influence us or opportunities we are afforded to exceed those expectations. Our beliefs about who we are and how we see ourselves create our world. (Bristol, 1948)

If we look around to those who we know the best, we can see numerous examples of how this plays out. We all have known people who started out in life with very little. Based on what they were taught, some found their way to unimaginable successes while others, continued with the lifestyle with which they started for the balance of their adult lives.

Some of us were taught that "you have to get [victimize] them [others] before they get you." These people accepted and played out this teaching in their lives and created a life that supports how they see the world. They are usually surrounded by others who share this life philosophy.

When we teach our children to engage in gossip, negative interactions and deceitful behavior, they usually accept such teachings because they trust us to teach them the right things. When they create an adult life filled with drama, unstable relationships and untrustworthy friends, they have simply played out the life philosophy they were taught.

Suppose we teach our children how to be excellent students, to choose good friends, to develop good character and a strong work ethic, establish and maintain solid relationships with teachers and family friends, develop good decision making skills, identify good qualities in a mate and never to make excuses for when they fall short of a goal. We might expect this child to fare reasonably well in life.

At this point, we might examine which life philosophy we were taught. Some of us were taught an illegal, street-hustling life philosophy. Some of us were taught to work the welfare system, con other people, that stealing is all right, that it is all right to trade our body for money and so on. It is important to note what kind of life we have created based on such philosophies. It is important to note how we see the world as a result of what we were taught (and accepted) when we were young.

The idea here is not to engage in blaming anyone. As parents and guardians, we generally teach what we know. Sometimes, rearing children is not what we do well. Those of us who were casualties of marginal parenting have to understand that they did the best that they knew to do, at the time. Everything else is up to us. This is why we must be willing to accept full responsibility for every area of our lives. We are the only ones who can truly decide what feels right, developmentally and directionally for our life.

Our Transition Among Worlds

Based on where we are now in life, we must decide if we are going to accept responsibility for where we are in life or are we going to continue to assign blame (an activity that no one ever respects). Wherever we are, if we choose to continue with the same philosophy, attitude and mentality that brought us to where we are, we will remain with the same life and in the same world without any possibility for having a more prosperous and fulfilling existence. (Holmes, 1948)

If we choose to accept responsibility for our current life condition and guide our life to a decidedly better destination, we must also change our accepted philosophy of life. That means that we must also change how we perceive our world, along with the way we make our decisions.

Whether we have created a dishonorable reputation, made dozens of enemies, burned tremendous numbers of bridges, ruined numerous relationships, perpetuated a poor public image, become among the most dreaded of persons because of how we have used and abused others, we can transition from the world we have created to a better and more productive one by simply changing our thinking. (Dr. Earnest Holmes, 1938)

If we have extended mental and emotional trauma as a result of incarceration or other institutionalization experiences, it is important that we accept responsibility for seeking the appropriate professional treatment and following through with it. It is not responsible for us to decide that "we can handle" the recovery, of such trauma, on our own. Eventually, the deficiencies that we did not "handle" will soon be obvious to everyone and it may create a setback in our transition to a new world, of our own creation, and our progression to the next phase of our life.

We must be honest with ourselves for what we, ultimately, want when we make this decision. We should never be ashamed to admit that we need help. Someone, who we met socially and with whom we want to have a relationship, is an irresponsible and dishonest choice for this task. We must be willing to seek the appropriate, competent professionals who can render such help. It will take some time to work through each issue and we should be prepared to expose our most vulnerable areas of ourselves mentally, emotionally, socially, spiritually and morally.

Changing our thinking must start with examining our paradigms that trigger our decision making, actions and our behavior. Our paradigms are those learned and unquestioned conclusions that we hold about how we are supposed to live our lives, from situation to situation. Examples of accepted paradigms are these: 1) It is all right to steal if we don't get caught. 2) It is all right to lie to someone if you want to protect their feelings. 3) Poor people are lazy and unintelligent. 4) Poor people are justified in victimizing those who have the most. (Bristol, 1948)

It does not take long to see how any one of us, who hold and act on such beliefs, might find ourselves in many uncomfortable positions, in life, socially, financially and legally. Yet, these are commonly held conclusions that many of us accept regarding how we should live our lives. Such ideas are usually taught to us or passed on to us from second-hand sources. As we progress through life, we usually learn through experience, that these perceptions have no basis in fact.

As parents, guardians and family friends, we are sometimes irresponsible regarding our own learning. This means that if we don't actually know an answer, we tend to attempt to deduce an answer through our sense of reason and flawed logic. Since our conclusions are usually devoid of facts and reliable information, we often arrive at shamefully irresponsible and ridiculous conclusions. We can understand how children might fall victim to this mentality. It is inexcusable when an influential parent, who is responsible for shaping the productive mind of a child, thinks and operates this way.

We can recall, in our youth, when we were curious about controversial subjects that we did not feel comfortable in discussing with our parents. We tended to ask our friends for the answers. Although our base of reliable knowledge was limited, as a group, we combined our knowledge and logically reasoned our way to our conclusions. We did this regarding such subjects as the existence of Santa Claus (Easter bunny and tooth fairy), origin of babies, sex education, how the opposite gender thinks (guys always lose this one), acceptable illegal drugs and so on. We all understand that children are doing their best to learn.

Adults, who employ this learning strategy, clearly did not pay attention in school about using the library, viewing educational documentaries or asking people whose business it is to know the correct answers. Still, with astounding regularity, we adults, many of us who are parents, arrive at our conclusions in this way. The children have the advantage over us, in this case, because they aren't consuming alcohol while they do it. Any adult who attempts to mentor children, in this way, is exhibiting grossly negligent judgment.

The result is often a collection of beliefs based in ignorance, prejudicial and stereotypical thinking and baseless fears. This way of thinking can only lead to a life of relationships, decision making, perceptions, actions and lessons learned that are highly dysfunctional. If we want our lives to improve, we must acquire a life philosophy that is based in wisdom, positive thinking and one which yields productive results in every area of our lives. (Hart, 1987)

This life philosophy will be slightly different for everyone as every one of us will have a different destination and area of comfort for our life. Depending on the paths we choose to forge our lives, we will construct a workable life philosophy that works for us as individuals. We can gather information from books, courses, teachers, experienced friends and associates and others who have a sincere desire to see us attain our most positive and productive state in our lives. Once we internalize our improved life philosophy, we will begin to notice important changes taking place that we may never have noticed before.

These changes are profound and undeniable. For example, if we find that we desire to end our use of alcohol consumption, for whatever reason we decide, virtually all of those who consumed alcohol with us, on a regular basis, will find their way out of our lives, in a matter of weeks. If we decide that we are going to be a model employee in our workplace, we will notice that those who constantly complain and do not value their jobs will find their way out of our circle of confidence, within a few weeks. We do not have to utter one word about the changes we intend to make; our actions will communicate the appropriate messages.

Conversely, we will begin to attract into our world, those who share our updated perceptions of how we want our lives to be. We will notice that others who value sobriety will find their way into our lives. We will, soon, realize that we are surrounded by people who are grateful, appreciative and most respectful of their jobs. We will find it much easier to be a most productive person in the workplace. (Fersen, 1923)

We will transition to the world that we choose by simply transforming our thoughts in positive and productive ways, based on the quality of information that we integrate into our thinking. The more sound the information that we acquire into our thinking, the more powerful our philosophy of life will be for each of us as we continue building our new world. The people who find their way into our lives, as result of our upgraded thinking, will be all of the validation that we need to signal if we are taking our lives in the correct direction as we desired.

We begin the transition from the world where we are, to the new world we are building, when we make the decision to make the change. The does not, in itself, begin the creation of the new world; it simply means that we realize that we cannot continue to thrive where we are. When we make the decision to transition to a different world, we create a myriad of new tasks, duties and responsibilities for ourselves. Creating a new world, in which we will reach our highest potential, requires a great deal of work. After the decision is made to transition, the next steps are always the same.

We must first look inward. We each must do the self reflection that will answer questions about who we are at our core; that part of ourselves that is our most innocent. It might help if we think back to what was important to us in our childhood. If we enjoyed creating music, time in nature or building things that is an excellent place to begin. We must also consider what contributions we wanted to make to the human family or world community. After we have answered these questions, it is important that we update our perspective and desires to the present while keeping in mind that, literally, all things are possible. (Price, Nothing Is Too Good To Be True, 2003)

Once we are clear as to who we are at our core and the direction that we want to take our life, we can begin the process of identifying the world we would like to create, for ourselves and into which we want to attract others. We can write notes to document this process. We must construct this world from many different dimensions – personally, socially, physically, emotionally, mentally, spiritually, educationally, and professionally and so on. In short, this world will be real in every way so we have to develop every area that we can conceive. We can begin with notes that we made for each area. More will come to mind as we venture through this development. (Rusha, 2010)

The next area that we will explore is what we believe. We can open this area completely. We can separate what we know from personal experience, from what we have accepted from second-hand knowledge from parents, teachers and friends. We will want to be very thorough in these areas. For example, what we learn from watching law enforcement dramas on television (second-hand information) may play out very differently when we are faced with similar situations in real life (personal experience). We can count on knowledge gained and lessons learned from personal experience. The rest of the untested knowledge that we have accepted as beliefs must be investigated.

Education is always important. It is most important when we measure what we believe against the confirmed facts that create the body of knowledge and wisdom that has stood the test of time and circumstances. So, we will need to do a great deal of research about what we think that we know. In this way, we will want to upgrade, consistently, our belief system to reflect our growing acquisition of sound knowledge and wisdom. As we do this, our world will continue to evolve to an increasingly superior state.

As we begin to internalize our knowledge and wisdom upon which we base our updated belief system, our world begins to take form. Our day-to-day actions dictate to those around us that we are in full transition to a new world. Without saying a word to anyone about our transition, we will find people, who share our updated beliefs, approaching us for networking, socialization and friendship.

We will notice gestures of kindness, openness and sensitivity toward and among each of us. At this point, we are in full transition to our new world. That also means that we have begun to live a new life. We must intensify the quality of our world as often as we can by finding new ways to express who we now are and where we stand, in non-threatening, respectful ways.

What To Expect Tomorrow

Making the decision to transition from our current world to a more desirable one is only the starting point. Making this decision will, immediately, make us feel better. We will have a renewed perspective on our lives and we will feel very optimistic; we should be, too. Depending on what we have made of our lives to this point, we have to understand that no one else has had the revelation that we have had regarding our life.

If we have created an unflattering reputation, that reputation is still with us. If we are not trusted by people, generally, that is still our reality. In the minds of those who have extensive experiences with us, nothing has changed. Even if we tell them that we are in the process of changing our life, we may not be taken seriously. In this case, action always communicates more effectively than words. We should keep this in mind and focus on action, not verbiage.

Our closest friends and associates are not going to perceive anything different about us until our prolonged and sustained actions indicate that we are changing. We have to create a turning point in our history. This can only be accomplished through our actions and behaviors.

When others have questions about our changing actions and behaviors, we must keep our answers short and to the point. Those, with whom we have the deepest friendships and closest bonds will accept our changes and support us completely.

Others, who are primarily interested in us for what we can do for them, or bring to their lives, will find themselves vacating those areas they occupied in our life for a new host.

Just to be prepared, we should expect this kind of activity in every area of our life, as well as from everyone in our life. Once we commit to this transition, our lives will never be the same as it was. If we embrace a proactive perspective of this process, we realize that, even though, there are not any noticeable changes that we immediately expect from others, there are preparations that we can initiate on our own.

For example, if we have openly wronged any one and not apologized or made amends for our transgressions, we can use this time to make the corrections that will begin to heal these relationships. Taking sincere and responsible action is the best way to internalize our seriousness regarding our transition.

We can do many other things for ourselves to make this pretransition period a more productive time. For example, if our new world would eventually include different surroundings or taking up residence, in a new location, we might construct a tangible representation of this change. We might consider creating a vision board. A basic vision board in nothing more than a large, cardboard poster that is divided into sections that represent important areas of our lives (i.e., home, work, health, personal, relationships, social and etc.). In each category, we place images of what we desire our lives to be collected from magazines or photographs that we have taken. We can make this vision board as basic or as elaborate as we wish. (Gawain, 1978)

If changing occupations or attaining a college education is important for our transition to our new world, we should make time to study the options that are available to us. We should look for those positions and circumstances where we can easily envision ourselves being happy and fulfilled for many years.

We should also consider the opportunities for personal growth and professional advancement that each option provides for us. We should not be afraid to plan big; we have the rest of our lives to spend taking the step toward achieving our dreams. (David J. Schwartz, 1959)

The more serious we are and the more committed we are about transitioning to and creating a new world for ourselves, the more areas we will find to consider planning. We must also keep in mind that the success we find in our life, within our newly created world, will depend to a great extent on the level and quality of effort we put into our world creation.

If we find that we are only seeing minimal improvements in our lives, it will simply be reflective of the quality of information that we have integrated into our upgraded life philosophy. It will also be reflective of the extent that we have internalized our newly-acquired knowledge and wisdom that guides our decision making, day-to-day actions and behavior. In this case, will power takes a backseat to upgraded thinking.

Take Proactive Control

When we start implementing important life changes, we focus on our vision for the future we have chosen. Without verbally claiming our aims, our decisions, actions and behavior communicate our attitude about the direction we are taking our lives. We must never be concerned with what someone "said" we intend to do. We must see to it that all who are paying attentions to us are able to say what we 'did.' To put it another way: we must allow our actions and behavior to become our primary form of communication. We can do this in the following ways:

1) **Financial Responsibility** – If we're not in the habit already, we can start paying our own way. We must be willing to pull our own weight in every situation that we encounter. If we must take up temporary residence with a friend or family member, we can walk in the door with money to cover our portion of living expenses, for the time that we occupy the premises.

    No other house guest is so welcome as the one who, upon entering the home for the first time, counts several $100 bills into the palm of the head of the household. We can also, offer to make ourselves available to help with any special projects like seasonal house cleaning, yard work or needed repairs where we might have experience or expertise.

    This will also serve as motivation for us to tend to the business of moving forward with our lives as we will begin to see the money that we distribute as an investment for the opportunity to get established in whatever environment we have chosen. We can expect a great deal of support from those whose lives we are impacting with financial relief.

    Commit to being more than just a house guest, we can find ways to become a true contributor to the household while we occupy the premises. Please note that this is not subtext for engaging in any immoral or compromising behavior with anyone in the home.

2) **Personal Responsibility** – Even if we do not have sufficient funds, on hand, to compensate for our imposition on our host(s), we can still accept the responsibility for completing several household chores and responsibilities that would surely allow the household to operate significantly more efficiently.

    In doing this, we demonstrate a strong statement about our seriousness in improving the value of our life experience. We can create a contract, verbal or written, to be completely responsible for a defined set of responsibilities around the household in exchange for a 'temporary' bed and food.

3) **Personal Service** – Every head of household wants to find ways to reduce expenses and eliminate errands wherever possible. We can make ourselves into personal servants in exchange for our food and accommodations. We can do the grocery shopping, childcare, make needed repairs around the house, with motor vehicles and bicycles, tutor the children with their school studies, and manage housekeeping responsibilities and so on. Rendering personal service is always honorable.

4) **Be An Ideal House Guest** – This simply means that we proactively do all of the above while we are in the home. When we are not inside the home, we are searching for employment or finding some other legal ways to earn extra income. We may need a place to lay our head in the future.

    No one wants a house guest (family member or otherwise) who is lazy, watches television all day, eats up the food, is a personal and financial burden and who makes virtually no contribution to the household. Such people find their supporters, increasingly and mysteriously, unavailable as the years pass.

We must take proactive control of every area of our lives. Nothing will be accomplished for us unless it is done by us, especially now that we have chosen to accept full responsibility for changing our world. So our task is a monumental, life-changing one. This is a door that we, alone, must open and penetrate. No one can accompany us in this endeavor.

There is no delegation of duties. It is our responsibility, alone, to achieve every objective and to reach every milestone. Once our new world is constructed, we can receive as many new friends, associates and acquaintances as we desire. Until then, we, ourselves, are the architect, engineer, manager, evaluator and troubleshooter in our project of creating a new world.

When Minor Things Just Go Wrong

It is very frustrating to us when things simply do not go as we have planned. It is easy for us to see it as a setback when our best plans, created with the highest intentions, do not work out. It happens to all of us at one point or another. The last thing that we want to allow ourselves to feel is discouragement. If we observe such occurrences more closely, we will often see that there is much more going on than we thought.

In life, we have many doors to choose to open and each door has its own key. Each door is the entry way to an important path of life success and fulfillment. We can open any door that we choose with the correct key for that door. If we find brilliant, beautiful keys strewn about, we might collect them and store them on a ring. Let us suppose that each key represents a specialized area of knowledge, talent, ability, skill or unique quality. When we have the correct keys, we have the freedom to open any door and as many doors as we choose.

As we journey through our lives, we encounter door after door of opportunities in life. Some doors open the pathway to wealth and riches while other doors open the pathway to health and fulfillment. Other doors open to pathways for a lifetime fame and prestige while still others open to pathways for a lifetime of loving fulfillment with a spouse, family, friends and community. The opportunities for fulfillment in life are endless. We simply must match the correct keys to the correct locks on the doors we desire to open.

Sometimes we have keys of life in our possession that we appear to have always had. We try some our keys in the doors of opportunity that appear to be desirable to us that we encounter along our journey through life. When those keys do not open the doors we want, we become angry, frustrated, discouraged and cynical about how unfair life is to us. The fact, regarding this matter, is that we just did not use the right key or we chose the wrong door of opportunity.

Through our schools, universities, libraries, online resources, teachers, mentors, on-the-job trainings, life experiences (personal, family, workplace, volunteer, community, political and so on), we have the opportunity to gather many keys of all types that will each open a door to an opportunity that will add to the fulfillment that we desire in our lives. We receive each key as we learn a new lesson in life. It then, becomes our responsibility to keep track of each key and value its power. Now, we need to identify those doors of opportunity.

We all have had to stay a little later than we want to at work from time to time or miss the bus by just a few seconds. Sometimes, we are doing the right thing in helping someone who desperately needs our help or attention that takes us a little out of way; it takes us out of our routine. Sometimes it is a flat tire or we have to give someone a ride home that takes a little longer than we want. In many cases, we are about to discover the means or road to something we have been seeking for some time.

It is important that we learn to look for the opportunities that come with the apparent disruption. Some important experience is likely to befall our path during this very time. It might be an 'unscheduled' reunion with an old friend; it might be wisdom of personal importance, to us, courtesy of a stranger; the presentation of a special opportunity of particular interest to us or any number of positive outcomes.

We must keep our eyes and ears open. Further, we must remain open to the possibility that something important for us is always coming our way. Doors of tremendous opportunity are around all the time. We must develop our ability to identify them when we encounter them.

Maybe these kinds of things happen to us all the time and nothing special comes of it. It is possible that we haven't been looking for the special importance that these irregularities are attempting to present to us. That may be why these things keep happening to us.

We may keep missing something important that we are supposed to see, experience or learn. Perhaps, we are easily distracted by little things that annoy us. If this is a problem, we must expand our awareness of what we notice to a much broader area where we occupy space.

It might be the stranger in the grocery line, with us, with whom we should have started a conversation but we were studying a gossiping employee. Perhaps, it was a new admirer, who was trying to get our attention in a crowded place, but we were just staring at the floor.

We might have been unfairly judging the fashion choice of a new business associate, who desires to help us tremendously. Perhaps, a new teacher or mentor is trying to come into our life with information that may benefit us greatly, but we are focused on projecting an image of great confidence; thus, appearing to have it all together.

Until we change our thinking and level of awareness in these situations, we cannot be sure about what we have missed. If we typically curse or react with angry remarks when minor things go wrong, we can make the decision, right now, that we are going to stop this disabling behavior. Often drivers, in rush-hour traffic will react angrily out of frustration with other drivers, without realizing that someone else may have an emergency at a nursing home or their child's daycare.

Divine Intelligence might be intervening to prevent us from getting into a tragic accident somewhere down the road or maybe, It is just preventing us from getting a traffic ticket that is meant for someone else. We do not always know the reasons for what and why things happen at the time they happen, so let's take the positive approach and expect that there is some good coming out of it for all of us, at some point.

When minor things seem to go wrong, let's give ourselves a chance by accepting that these inconveniences may have a grander significance than just creating an annoyance in our day. Let's make it a habit to look for lessons, opportunities, people or circumstances that may hold a special importance to us or for someone we care about. It is true that often times, nothing will come of these twists in our day, however, for the adventure of it all, let's stay vigilant anyway. Rarely are we prepared for pleasant surprises.

Know When To End A Matter But Never Quit

How many times have you heard someone say, "I am going to quit smoking or quit my job"? Sometimes they are referring to a habit they want to break or an employment situation that is the cause of a great deal of anguish for them. It is important to note here that "quitting" should not be confused with "ending" a matter.

I have heard women make remarks like, "I am going to quit dating him; he is just a waste of time." I have heard men declare that, 'after this night out, they are going to quit drinking (alcohol).' We understand the point but our purpose here is that it is important that we demonstrate the difference between quitting and ending our involvement in a matter.

Anyone can quit. It takes no special ability or talent. It takes no special preparation or education. Quitting is an act born of negativity and lack of commitment. It indicates a lack of good character (and especially integrity). We quit because a challenge is too difficult to surmount; we don't perceive the reward as being worth the work it takes to attain it. We quit because we don't value the opportunity presented to us.

If we make a decision to do something on a whim like build a boat, there is a very good chance that we may, in a very short time after that, quit. It wasn't well thought out. There was minimal planning and preparation. Most important to note, there was no serious commitment for follow through.

Children quit playing the sport in which dad and mom wanted them to participate. Children quit taking the music or dance lessons they were forced to study. Husbands often dispense with (quit) the courteous dating behavior once they are married. Of course, I am not stupid enough to make any comments about women here. The point here is that we quit things that we view as short term. It appears that ending a matter and quitting are the same but they are not.

Let's suppose that we are in a relationship with someone who is not fulfilling our needs. Also, we are clueless as to what that person wants from us. For all intents and purposes, the relationship is not functioning properly. At one point, we had very high expectations for this relationship.

At the beginning, we both poured everything that we could into this relationship. We were careful at every stage to move the relationship along and at a comfortable pace for both parties. It seems that we have begun to grow in different directions. After several discussions and examinations of the relationship, we both come to the conclusion that we must end it.

When we end something, it is because there is a problem that has caused us to deviate from our planned path for happiness and fulfillment. Ending is a positive adjustment to a plan for achievement. We often end something to preserve our health, sanity, reputation or financial situation (i.e. a smoking habit, those gym memberships or that MLM auto ship arrangement).

Ending requires discipline and is a reflection of good judgment and character. To end something is a demonstration of self respect and positive self image. We generally have proper justification for ending our involvement in a matter. No one just quits smoking cigarettes; we end the habit.

The reason that I want to deal with the difference between these two terms is so that you can make a clear, informed decision about whether you are really quitting or ending your involvement in a particular phase in your quest to accept full responsibility for the condition of your life and take appropriate action.

We have committed, in this section, to transitioning from our current world, which might be dysfunctional, unfulfilling, frustrating, negative and unproductive in many ways, to a world of our creation based on our introspective examination about who we are and what we want our life to mean. This is one of those rare areas of life commitment where neither quitting nor ending apply.

Crushed and Rejected

Many people have worked to, legitimately, turn their lives around. They are usually willing participants in highly structured, government-supported, community-based programs. The intentions of these programs are usually quite honorable; they openly seek to place their participants on the highest road to societal redemption.

From their participants, these programs demand constant demonstrations of good character, targeted achievement(s), measurable progress, educational preparation, an organized personal life and so on. Each participant who abides by the established guidelines and progresses through the program, as challenged, is held up as a success to all other participants who are at various stages of progress behind these honored individuals.

As each participant graduates from these "self-help" programs, depending on the participant's chosen path, he or she is fed into a formal and usually a highly supportive educational environment, business development incubator or work readiness training program.

It is from this point, that disappointment reigns most eminent. We must, realistically, decide, at this point, to accept ultimate responsibility for our personal life success as we decide for ourselves, not as the powers that be, over the program, decide for us.

The intention here is not to be pessimistic. However, real-life, without programs, can be very challenging. In addition to requiring highly honed life skills for survival, learning, personal management, resilience, persistence, commitment and discipline, we must accept ultimate responsibility for the outcome that we decide for ourselves. Often, the aims and expectations of these structured programs are relatively low in comparison to the demands of everyday life.

For example, several programs seek to prepare its participants to become competent in basic money management skills like understanding the concept of budgeting, opening a checking account, understanding which fees can be charged and why, writing checks and reconciling the monthly bank statement with personally kept records from home. In everyday life, much more is required.

Educationally, these program participants are generally encouraged to enter certificate programs that would lead to entry level employment in highly understaffed industries like healthcare, computer services, food service, retail, law enforcement and transportation. In many cases, employment in these fields may not pay for the cost of the education (loans) to attain these positions.

When we decide to enter these highly structured, self-help programs, we usually do so with great resolve. When we learn that these programs are only meant to get us started on the road to great achievement, we begin to feel frustrated.

When we, finally, secure gainful employment at an entry-level position that we might have secured without entering the program(s) from which we just graduated, we start to feel that perhaps, we just wasted our time. Obviously, that is not the case; however, when we review our net pay, it surely may seem that way.

After occupying the position for a year or two and learning all that we can, we know we are ready for a promotion to the next level. When we find that we are passed over, time and again, for the most modest promotion(s), we are told that we do not have the qualifications to do anymore than the position that we have occupied from the start. Upon being notified of this revelation, many of us feel crushed and rejected.

The reality of this matter is that, if we truly have accepted responsibility for every area of our lives, especially our employment, we cannot accept feeling "crushed and rejected" for any reason. When we consider where we started, we should be proud of our achievements to date. We also knew, intuitively, that our current job was just our starting point and nothing more. It is easy to become attached to our work environment when we enjoy our work and the people with whom we work.

It is easy to become discouraged; to feel that we want to quit. When we allow such thoughts to enter our minds, we are forgetting about our commitment to accept full responsibility for every area of our lives. This commitment does not mean that we have all of the answers that we need.

It does mean that we are willing to find the answers and integrate those answers into our updated strategy for moving our life to the destiny that we choose, without excuses. We must release the acceptance of discouragement, doom and rejection from our mentality.

Finally, we have demonstrated through our program accomplishments that we are highly teachable, flexible, persistent and adaptable. We still are this way so we can chart a new course to build upon our first level of accomplishments. We are only limited by our thinking, creativity, determination and level of discipline.

Wherever we start our career is just that. There is always a competitor who is willing to pay for our knowledge and experience but we have to be willing to prepare our resume and ourselves for the search. That means that we seek assistance from any helpful source that we are able to locate.

Accepting full responsibility for our life situation means creating and internalizing qualities that move our lives to the successful milestones that we desire. We continuously revise our plans and strategy to reflect our unquenchable desire for perpetual accomplishments and achievements that we want in our lives.

Chapter 11

"At the end of your life, you will never regret not having passed one more test, not winning one more verdict or not closing one more deal. You will regret time not spent with a husband, a friend, a child, or a parent...Cherish your human connections – your relationships with friends and family."

First Lady, Barbara Bush

Value Relationships As Great Wealth

The relationships, in our lives, are among the most precious, of valued gifts, that anyone can possess in life. No matter what else we may or may not possess (material wealth, great health, public adoration, exalted position, physical attractiveness, superior intelligence, broad influence or rare talent), our lives will still seem empty and pointless without solid, deeply-bonded relationships that we cherish. We may outgrow certain people, mentalities and behaviors but we never outgrow our natural yearning for connection with others, regardless of the form and nature of those connections. These relationships even extend to include our household pets as well.

A strong appreciation for relationships is not so natural as our need for them. As we observe the people we encounter in our schools, workplaces, places of worship, social circles and so on, we find many who are in various stages of relationship drama with spouses, lovers, friends and family members.

We can note that there is constant frustration on the part of one person in each relationship. The conflicts often center on relationship politics, manipulation issues, lack of engagement, additional parties and fulfillment problems. The common thread among these is lack of appreciation of the other person.

It is only when tragedy interrupts these conflicts that we begin to realize the importance of the relationship to us. At this point, we begin to develop an appreciation for such connections. We begin to understand the unique qualities that the other person has to share.

We make a greater effort to understand the perspective, of the world, that the other person has developed. We think of this other person in purely loving terms as we reflect on what is needed from us to create a harmonious relationship. We think, creatively, of ways to show that person that we both respect and value the relationship.

Among the best advantages about relationships is that they are healthy, enriching, educational and (like hugs) free. When are not taught an appreciation for relationships, we will destroy them with the same frequency that we can create them. We will not necessarily value one over another. In many cases, we will treat our family relationships with less respect than the other relationships in our lives.

Many of us receive very little relationship training in our youth while others seem to have a much more advanced relationship and social intelligence. These individuals eventually mature to become the human social clearinghouses for their schools, workplaces and family members and childhood community members.

Appreciation for our relationships begins with an appreciation for the people, in our lives, individually. Few of us have to be concerned about teaching children to make friends. No matter how awkward the situations, children will eventually forge some kind of friendship.

Friendship issues among children center on honoring and valuing their differences, taking turns, equitable sharing and bullying (physical, emotional, mental and social). With responsible parental and teacher intervention, we teach useful relationship skills and demonstrate them by example, through this approach, we can get the children off to a great start in their appreciation for relationships. If they are guided and taught throughout their youth, they will reap the rewards of good relationships for the balance of their lives.

In general, we must teach children to reach beyond tolerance, in their differences among one another, to proactive acceptance in establishing and developing meaningful relationships among their peers. It is important that they learn, as early as possible, that community strength is secured when everyone is an active and integral part of social diversity.

This is achieved when children are counseled against excluding anyone from their social group based on anything accept good character. They learn that all of their friends have valuable contributions to give. Each person learns to make 'a place of honor' for all others among their associations. The rewards of this approach will be especially apparent as each child progresses in school, from one grade level to the next.

Although social cliques will still develop among the students, outsiders will never see them as impenetrable, when each person knows that he or she holds a place of honor with each member. Everyone will see himself or herself as a friend of equal status regardless of the circumstances. All feelings of exclusivity will be eliminated.

For example, the student who excels academically will know that he can always sharpen his athletic skills, in pickup games, with his more athletic friends. The student from the single parent household who cannot afford music lessons can be taught and tutored by her musically gifted friends as they are available. The students who struggle academically will know that they always have a solid network of academic support among their higher achieving friends.

No one feels singled out of any particular social group. All understand their special place of worth to all others and is supported accordingly. Interactions are largely positive, supportive and even protective. If anyone does encounter any life-altering issues that create trauma, he or she has a tremendous network of supportive families who will intervene with any assistance that might be needed.

Relationship appreciation is a serious issue when it concerns gender, especially females (as teens and through adulthood). Although females are particularly gifted with solid relationship skills, among themselves prior to the onset of puberty, things change dramatically afterwards. From early in their teen years, girls are treated poorly by boys as well as other girls.

Regarding boys, despite what is considered to be socially correct and acceptable, fathers secretly want their boys to be ladies' men and nothing else. Since fathers, who were never ladies men themselves, don't exactly know how to effect this sort of result in their, usually, clueless and underachieving offspring, they usually push for volume and aggressive behavior toward girls, after their sons reach puberty.

Fathers consistently convey the same basic message: try to 'feel up' a lot of girls. Of course this does not work. These boys end up largely frustrated, rejected and even more puzzled by females than ever. Because boys are characteristically clueless and underachieving, it is not surprising that they seek to get their education about women from one another.

The usual outcome from this strategy is to study pornography wherever they can find it. This approach only furthers the perception, in adulthood, that men are either 'pigs' or 'dogs;' titles that some men eventually adopt as badges of honor. Few parents have the quality of relationship that allows them to educate their sons on the proper ways to relate to and intimately please a female, when the time comes. If we aren't able to talk with them, we can refer them to reliable sources of assistance. (Barbara De Angelis, What Women Want Men To Know, 2001)

Appreciation for male-female relationships during teen through early adult years must be a priority in teaching children to value their relationships with each other. Boys must be taught the highest respect for females, even when they do not understand them. It is just as important that this respect be internalized and practiced consistently. Parents can never allow their sons to objectify their female counterparts under any circumstances.

How girls are permitted to treat one another is even more distressing. They are cruel socially, mentally, emotionally and often physically. Girls perpetuate insecurities in one another around their self esteem, self image, self worth, personal potential, attractiveness, intelligence and lovability. Parents seem suspiciously absent when it comes to youth female socialization matters.

Perhaps, they are too tired from dealing with these 'princesses' within the household. Whatever the case, for those of us who are serious about accepting full responsibility for our lives, I wanted to include some background information that documents the magnificence of the human female in an effort to solidify my position that women deserve the best treatment that the human race can provide them, even when it appears that some of them do not deserve it.

Women's Relationship Choices

Since the beginning of our civilization, women have been an essential, integral partner in the political, business, technological, educational, healthcare, recreational and athletic development of all nations. Additionally, as mates, women have been dependable, loyal, generous and adaptable in finding ways to rear good children and strengthening family bonds.

In nearly every culture of the earth, throughout the ages, women have made these substantial contributions all while being forced to live as second class citizens: they were routinely denied proper healthcare, proper nutrition, basic education, basic human rights, safe living conditions and job training.

Women were routinely forced into a life of dependence on men. Females have been targets of various forms of random abuse, degrading entertainment, and they have tolerated indignities that their adult male perpetrators would have never accepted for themselves. In fact, men have waged wars over far less serious issues that never affected their freedom or life choices.

Infinitely intelligent, loving and creative little girls were reared to be mothers, loyal wives and tolerant adults who would be willing to do the work of men for much less pay and pretending to be less intelligent than the men for whom they might work. The men in their lives were supposed to be providers and protectors but if these men died for whatever reason, the surviving women had to suffer.

If these widows were not able to convince another man to marry them, they often became homeless. The lack of basic education, training and blocked opportunities left most women to become live-in homemakers, entertainers, beggars or prostitutes to earn enough money to provide for themselves and their family so that they would not be forced into homelessness. (Griscom, 1991)

In these modern times, few things have changed. Many female children are still being taught to eventually depend on a man for love and provisions. In the context of a marriage to a responsible man who is mature, responsible and capable of genuinely loving her and their children, there is nothing wrong with it. However, that is not what is happening.

Marginal Mate Selection Standards

Although many more women have demonstrated that they understand the importance of attaining a formal education, they are not investing much more of an effort in selecting men who are of good character. Police officers in large metropolitan areas can expect that just over 70 percent of their calls will be for domestic violence incidents. Child abuse cases perpetrated by men have shown a steady increase for decades. (Elaine Weiss, 2000)

It appears that, in general, women, around the world, are not receiving good quality relationship training from home. This means that women, generally, are not receiving wise counsel in choosing a mate nor are they being taught to be a high quality mate.

Worse still, many are still not exercising their option to be independent through education. Women are still allowing themselves to become impregnated by males who have minimal or virtually no ability to provide material support for a spouse and/or children.

Far too many women are still choosing to partner with men who are physically, mentally and emotionally abusive. Several of the males, who these women choose for mates, have no problem with living a life of crime-filled activities on a variety of levels. Their male partners are often forced to hide during daylight hours to avoid arrest by police so they convince their female counterparts that they work the night shift.

Though these women never actually see a paycheck stub, nor do they bother to verify his employment, these young women choose to respect the privacy of their chosen mates until the truth is finally evident. As a consequence, women are still suffering tremendous incidences of domestic violence, incarceration as accomplices of their mates, compromised living conditions, under employment and homelessness.

Not much has changed in terms of what many women are doing to earn money. A spokesperson for the pornography industry (which includes strip clubs, magazines, movies, internet websites, phone lines and organized prostitution) has reported the same annual message for years: that the pornography industry has yearly gross sales that are higher than the total of professional major league baseball and professional hockey combined (in America). Men only make up about 15 percent of the employees in the pornography industry.

Women around the world, despite the many opportunities that abound, are still faring far worse on average than their male counterparts in terms of quality of life. Women must commit to accepting full responsibility for the condition of their lives by raising their standards in every aspect of their lives. To do so will be a temporary inconvenience for a short time but doing so will literally improve the condition of the world in many intangible ways. (Barbara De Angelis, Secrets About Men Every Woman Should Know, 1991)

The first and most important step that women can take is to learn and embrace a boundless concept of self love and self respect. Women must actually internalize it in all areas of life. Second, each woman must learn to respect her natural beauty.

Men will always find women to be attractive but women must find a way to eliminate their vulnerability of allowing men full access into their lives based on mere flattery. Each woman will have to find much improved ways to get to know, and objectively evaluate, a potential mate's character that surpasses conventional standards.

Women are quick to demand certain qualities in their potential mates but a closer examination of such demands reveals that many women are only repeating words that they have heard from media programming or that they have read in non-fiction literature.

In the context of mate selection, few women seem able to agree on the definitions of such words and phrases as "Nice," "Good," "Honest," "Sincere," "Intelligent," "Kind," "Special," "Mr. Right," "Real Man," "Prince Charming," "White Knight," "Soul Mate" and "Other Half." This level of vagueness only invites ambiguity. No one can truly find what he or she is looking for without being clear and specific. This way, we don't mistake a mule for a pony.

Finally, women must be more thorough in evaluating the suitability of a mate. When we test drive a car or any item for purchase, we do so against a variety of real life scenarios. Women must do the same in mate selection by observing his fitness around children, pets, extended family members, friends and coworkers. Mate selection for long-term success improves as we improve our selection standards and teach what we learn to our children.

What Men Fear

There are a few more matters that we must be covered if women are to take seriously the charge of accepting full responsibility for the condition of their lives especially when it comes to mate selection and relationships. It is important for women to understand that men will have trouble sharing certain things with them if it concerns any of four categories of fears that men generally have.

We are reluctant to share issues in any of these categories because we know it can make us look weak, cowardly or powerless. It simply is not to our advantage and most of these fears are ego based. There are only a few things that men consistently fear.

When men make statements that they aren't afraid of "anything," we mean it quite literally. For the most part, it is true. We are usually not afraid of each other. We are daring and adventurous and we are not afraid of weapons or wild animals. The truth is that men aren't afraid of the things that women typically fear although we are no less vulnerable. So what do men actually fear? At the risk of betraying men everywhere and being tossed out of the "Brotherhood of Man," I will share.

There are four matters that men consistently fear; they are these:

Losing Control – Since men often take the initiative to approach the woman, we like to set the tone of the courtship that women expect to develop into a full-blown relationship. We like to position ourselves from the beginning as intelligent and successful. Most important, we want to establish ourselves as being in control. We want the final say on the entertainment schedule and social activities. Emotionally, we want to be the solid and stable foundation in the eventual relationship. Intellectually, we want to be the smart one (this is particularly pathetic but it is true). We want to lead and be respected for our leadership; even if we lead you astray. Don't worry, though; we will eventually find our way, without asking for help or directions. We do not like losing control.

Vulnerability – This involves being found out. If we have any fears, we don't want women to know about them. We don't want to appear weak or cowardly for any reason. We know that it does not inspire respect from women nor does it set a good example for our children. We are supposed to be strong, natural protectors and providers. We know that, at the very least, this is what women expect from us. No man wants to look badly in front of his woman, anytime, anywhere and for any reason. We absolutely hate being vulnerable.

Most of us do not feel vulnerable when we are encouraged to discuss our feelings about relationship matters. We are usually reluctant to do so because we know that what we have to share will probably hurt your feelings. When women have hurt feelings, men know that nothing good will come of it for us personally (see Injury below). We simply do not want to lose access to our woman's sexual intimacy, peaceful nature, giving personality or relationship trust. For these reasons, those jeans will never make you look fat.

Injury – Men actually fear injury in all forms from personal bodily injury to career and financial injury. Anything that will prevent us from enjoying the life that we find completely convenient and comfortable for us is of deep concern. We fear, deeply, being permanently maimed, losing our ability to work in our chosen profession and being sued or cut off financially. Men often feel injured when we lose our vitality, hair, teeth, virility or our personal possessions. Men do not like losing relationship privileges that we have come to value and enjoy. We are not in the habit of stirring up trouble that would jeopardize any comfort or convenience that might upset the delicate balance of our happy world.

Failure – Since technically, one cannot be a failure until he stops trying, few men will admit to such. Absolutely no man wants to be labeled as a failure in any area of his life. He wants to appear to be successful in his career, in his relationships, in his financial fitness and in his "accomplishments." If we cheat on a woman, we have failed at fidelity. We hate to admit it unless we intend to use it as a way to get out of the relationship.

If we lose money on a business idea, we have failed in business. If we miss out on a promotion or lose a position, we have failed in our employment. We do not want to talk about it. We will discuss it with you if we believe that our relationship with you will survive it or conversely, if we secretly want to get out of a relationship with you and this could be the vehicle. Examine your recent history together and the answer will be apparent.

I trust that the women who are reading this intend to use this information for good, as in building positive relationships, as opposed to using it for negative and vengeful purposes. There is enough game playing going on and none of us want our feelings hurt or manipulated.

This leads me to the next area where women seem to fall miserably short, perhaps out of ignorance, in allowing the wrong men into their lives. These wrong men can damage a woman to the extent that she may never trust herself or anyone else; thus, diminishing her chances of having a high quality and fulfilling relationship anytime in her future. These wrong men are abusive and womanizing. They are misogynists.

How to Identify An Abuser

There is no perfect test for identifying an abuser but there are many tell-tale signs that are common to identified, confirmed abusers. The problem is that many established abusers eventually learn to conceal these signs. I will cover how to get around that later. Some women think that it is a flattering concept when a man has earned the title of being a "Womanizer"; it is not.

A womanizer is a misogynist; one who "hates" women and virtually everything about them. The womanizer has learned through experience that women are particularly attracted to him over most other men. He uses his considerable ability to attract women for the express purpose of using them for sex and depleting them of any of their material resources to which he can gain access, without any thought of how his actions may affect her life. This person is often a victim of childhood abuse in one form of another. He has become a charming abuser himself.

It is important to note that abusers are not always male and that abuse can take the form of verbal, emotional, mental or spiritual, as well as physical abuse. Let's begin with some of the common traits from the profiles of known abusers (courtesy of the Broken Spirits Network).

- **Denial:** In many cases, the abuser will act as if nothing happened, in order to excuse his/her behavior. In their minds, if they do admit to their actions, it is always the fault of the victim. They justify their actions by claiming that they were provoked.
- **Abusive men and women tend to feel inadequate and depressed.** Abusive men and women generally come off to the outsider as arrogant and overly self-confident. This is, in fact, a defense mechanism they use to hide their dislike for themselves.
- **Jealousy and possessiveness:** An abuser feels jealous and over-possessive of their victim. They often demand to know their victims whereabouts at all times, get insanely jealous at the slightest hint of someone else getting any

of their victims attention, and become very hostile at the thought of losing their "property". Some people are flattered by such displays as being deeply loved by the other person. This is a very sad mistake.

- **Domination and emotional attachment:** An abuser expects complete attention and support from their girlfriend / boyfriend / wife / husband. Abusers expect and demand complete control and submission on the part of their victim. This is not a fetish or game to the abuser, it is a way of life.
- **Inability to understand or recognize their problem:** The abuser is often times, if at all, the last person to admit that they have a problem. Abusers commonly do not respond well to counseling because they are unable to understand their anger or confusion. Abusers require help from a formally educated, licensed and board certified professional. If you are a mate who believes that you can help this person on your own, you are completely wrong. If you attempt to "fix" this person, on your own, you will be deeply sorry and you will pay for it in ways that you cannot afford.
- **Alcohol and drug abuse:** Abusers tend to lean towards drugs and/or alcohol as an "escape". However, the effects of the drugs and alcohol make the attacks much more intense. Many interviewed abusers, accused of murder, use alcohol and drugs as their alibi. "I did not know what I was doing" or "I can't remember" are very common excuses. Still they are responsible because they chose to consume the mind-altering substances in the beginning.
- **Manipulation:** Abusers know how and when to make their partner feel guilty. By allowing feelings of guilt, the victim is more likely to stay and deal with the abuse rather than feel "responsible" for any harm their abuser might inflict on themselves. Suicide is frequently used as a method of manipulation. Sometimes an abuser will go as far as to cut or cause other forms of harm to himself or herself in order to keep their victim from leaving.
- **Frequent abuser:** Many abusers have previous instances of abuse documented in their pasts. Some might have even been arrested or treated for violent tendencies. However, often times, their current partner is unaware of these situations. A person who has chosen to accept full responsibility for the condition of his or her life will do the required background research to learn this information.
- **Obsessed with weapons:** Many abusers are infatuated with weapons. Many will have large stockpiles which they will brag about to others as they believe that it makes them appear to be powerful. They will collect certain weapons, spend countless hours talking about weapons, and participate in events which give them the power to use weapons. This category of abuser will seize virtually any opportunity to show off his knowledge and mastery of his weaponry.
- **Stalking:** As an undercover method of maintaining control, abusers will stalk or follow their partner from a far. Their purpose is to intimidate or frighten their victim, to prevent them from taking the initiative to leave. Overall, stalking invokes fear, without the abusers even touching their victim.

If our new mate exhibits any or some combination of these traits, it is in our best interest to proceed slowly in the courtship. If he or she becomes pushy or insistent in anyway, we might consider aborting our courtship plans with him or her.

Abusers tend to learn as much as they can about our personality so that they can develop an arsenal of weapons to use against us at some later critical point in our involvement. They will typically target our self-esteem, our self image or our psychological tendencies for systematic destruction as the penalty for defying their efforts to maintain absolute control over us. Look carefully for the following emotional and psychological attacking behavior:

- **Extremely Controlling Behavior** – Abusers will attempt to control our activities, friendships and daily travels. They will insist on knowing what we are doing, planning and thinking. They are unnecessarily possessive and will exhibit jealous tendencies regarding others in our life especially our family members.
- **Intimidating Behavior** – They will attempt to control us through non-verbal means. They will do this with facial expressions, gestures, punching walls or damaging our property. They will have no problem with resorting to bullying tactics to gain the upper hand over us. They will not hesitate to call us degrading names and use profane language to describe us, just to make us feel badly in an effort to build themselves up over us.
- **Threats** – If it will allow them to gain the upper hand, they will use threats to control us. They may threaten to hurt us, our family, friends, children or pets. If they have reason to believe that we would care enough, they will threaten to kill themselves and blame us in the suicide note left behind just to torture us.
- **Isolation** – Abusers will attempt to isolate us from the people who have most influence with us in an effort to limit our options for how we deal with them. This allows them clearer control over us and our activities. Do not be fooled into thinking that they are doing it out of love or because they need us so much; it is just a deception – a form of manipulation.
- **Economic Control** – Abusers will often use money and lifestyle to control us. We may live well and drive a nice car but we are not free to befriend who we want, attend school to improve ourselves and socialize with whomever we choose for fear of offending our abuser.
- **Children** – Abusers are not above using children to control us. They will often influence the children to think negatively about us. They will systematically teach our children to withhold love from us and/or disrespect us if we do not comply with their regimen of control over us. They will resort to verbally, emotionally and physically abusing our children simply to harass us.

A couple of decades ago, many women told me in seminars and through support groups that I have led, that there were no clear signs that their former spouse or mate was an abuser while they were just dating. Fortunately, a great deal of research has been done and much information has been gathered and documented that will help us in this area.

I must iterate that we must accept responsibility for the quality of mate we choose to bring into our life and the lives of our family members. This means paying close attention to our mate choice's – facial expressions, jokes, critical remarks, any sarcasm used and so on. We must study the above-stated information about abusers so that we will know how to spot the signals in that person's language, behavior and gestures.

We must learn about our choice's background and study it carefully. Become knowledgeable regarding the kind of home in which he or she was reared. Find out if there was domestic abuse in the home and by whom it was perpetrated. Discover if an abuse mentality runs in that person's family. Observe if our mate choice seems to be harboring any anger or rage for anyone.

Uncover information to determine if our mate choice was a victim of abuse and if so, which therapies have he or she employed to deal with those issues. If there has been no therapy involvement at all, he or she may very well be in denial; we might save ourselves some frustration and disappointment down the road and move on without him or her.

If we choose to continue our involvement, with him or her, we may find out at the worst possible time that, when under pressure or unable to deal with problems in life, he or she resorts to abuse. It may be punching a wall or breaking things but it is just a matter of time before he or she hurts us or our family.

We can be smart; move on and tell everyone we know what we have discovered. We are helping the next intended person who is the target victim in this way. This will only help the apparent abuser to realize that there really is a serious problem.

If our love interest does admit to abusing others (and many will) but he or she will tell us that it was a long time ago or that he or she has been through therapy and anger management, demand to see proof: name of therapists, billing statements, journal notes, dates and locations of treatment and so on.

Ask to visit with the therapist (the patient must be in attendance by law) and ask any questions and seek the advice of the therapist. Never take his or her word for it; this person is an abuser. We must guard our safety and that of our family. Be responsible.

Wisdom from a Professional Dater

I was watching late night cable television several years ago when I noticed a promotion for a sexually oriented program for adults only. It involved an interview with a prostitute. She had no pimp and routinely charged several thousands of dollars per evening to her international clientele of highly influential businessmen. She did very little traveling. Her clients would fly in to see her and they would schedule their appointments with her months in advance.

You can imagine my curiosity so I stayed up to watch this one. Of course, I wanted to see this perfect looking woman whose body obviously emanated sexual energy throughout her entire being. I wanted to observe her non-verbal signals: her looks, smiles, gestures and poses. I wanted to see the woman who the world's most influential men were betraying their mates to support. After waiting for virtually the entire broadcast, her segment finally aired. I was completely stunned by her appearance.

She was an average looking woman in her 40s. She was "pleasingly plump" and appeared to be just over five feet tall. She appeared to be quite intelligent and well educated. She admitted to being a great cook, an imaginative conversationist and a great listener. Obviously, the interviewer was just as perplexed as I was because he kept bringing the subject of sexual prowess to the fore. Each time she answered, she kept her remarks short and frequently changed the subject.

Finally, the interviewer asked, 'What, exactly, do you do with these men?" Her reply surprised me. "About 95 percent of the time we just talk," she confessed. "Talk?" the interviewer exclaimed, "These guys are paying you thousands of dollars for a night and you mostly talk?" Very sheepishly, she said, "That's right."

"Do you have a sliding scale according to how much talk versus sex or something like that?" the interviewer inquired. "No, I charge them what I want and they just pay me," she admitted. The interview continued in this fashion and I remained just as confused as the interviewer. He finally asked a question that made the interview worth waiting for.

"You obviously understand what these men want and you know how to get what you want from them. What is your secret that wives everywhere could use to improve their relationships with their husbands and enjoy the same harmony and mutual respect?" the interviewer asked. She shared quite freely and her answer created a respect in me for her, to this day. This is what she counseled to the women of the world.

She said that women need to understand that the men have the same basic wants of a six-year old child. Now a six year old boy can feed himself, bath himself, dress himself and follow simple directions like to get on the right school bus and know which stop to get off. He likes to go play with his friends; he likes to feel important; he like to feel independent and he knows right from wrong. She said that these men come to her because their wives or mates don't understand this; evidenced by the way they (the men) are treated by them (wives or mates). She continued to explain.

"Men like a good home-cooked meal made with love and I give them that when they arrive. I play their favorite music softly in the background. I make the atmosphere clean and homey; I have their favorite childhood toys, board games or whatever they like in the room." She often leaves them alone while they dine so they can enjoy some unpretentious peace. She is only a room away so, if she is called, she comes.

She allows them to talk about whatever they want; it is usually not about work. They are in control and making big decisions all day; sometimes they just want to talk about simple things from their past. After he finishes his meal, she likes to bath him and continue talking. Afterwards, he may request a massage or he may want to wrestle around and just play. Sometimes they blow bubbles or play with clay and continue to talk. Sometimes there is a brief sexual encounter of one kind or another and sometimes not.

She continued to explain that she always gives them rules to follow like not to eat certain foods that deplete their energy, to be in bed by a certain time each evening, to talk with their family certain times of the week.

If she finds that they disobeyed for any reason, just as she would punish a six year old for disobeying, she punishes them. Once she decides on a proper punishment, she administers it. After she has made her point and she is sure he has learned his lesson, she restores him to his previous position of respect. "See, it's simple," she added.

This woman continued to give example after example that illustrated the finer points of her wisdom. I was offended at first – a six year old? As I pondered her words, I realized that she was right, at least in my case. I made it a point, over the years, to observe both happy and unhappy men with their spouses or mates with her philosophy in mind. Her wisdom has consistently stood the test. Over the years, I have shared this information with several of my female friends who were experiencing conflict in their personal relationships.

Once these women adopted this perspective and applied it to their communication with their mates, the tension in their relationships simply evaporated. In every case, I ended up losing my 'girlfriend' status; I was no longer needed (talk about feeling used and tossed aside).

Rather than go through all of the examples that this lady of the night espoused, I will summarize the highlights of her remarks. I must caution you that she had already established solid relationships with each of these men. I do not know that this information is applicable for use in the courtship phase of a relationship but is quite useful in a committed relationship. Use what you can of it according to your need. With that said, here are the highlights:

- **Food** – There is no surprise here. Men love to eat; especially good food. Use this point to demonstrate love by preparing healthy and filling meals whenever you choose to feed him. Keep the atmosphere friendly and relaxed. I know that many women abhor the idea of domestication these days; so, just have him help you in the kitchen. You may be surprised how eager he is to participate. You may find that he has a talent for food preparation. You would do it for a six year old; do it for the man in your life. We enjoy affection and displays of closeness too.

- **Intimacy** – This area included every aspect of human closeness especially hugs and caresses. How many six year olds don't want a hug or kiss? It seems that they can't get enough. Men are no different.
- **Independence** – Men enjoy being free to come and go as we please. We realize that when we are in a relationship, we have someone else to consider. However, because we enjoy the FEELING of independence, it does not mean that we want to exercise that independence if there is someone in our lives who really values us. Six year olds like to go out and play with their friends if they have been good and finished all their chores. Again, men are no different.
- **Importance** – Men really value feeling important. If your six year old wasn't chosen play in the neighborhood softball game that day, what would you do to lift his spirits? How would you let him know that he is special too, in his own way? You wouldn't tear him down about his fitness level or his athletic limitations. Men want to feel important too. That is a common reason why many men cheat with someone who doesn't appear to measure up to the primary woman in their life. The 'other' woman usually supplies him with that feeling of importance that he does not receive from home.
- **Discipline** – If your six year old child accidentally damages something you told him not to bother, should he be punished? Of course, he should. If defiant behavior is not dealt with in the early stages of life, the incidences of defiance only become more frequent and the offenses become greater. The severity of punishment should fit the crime so that he knows not to repeat it or anything like it. Apply the same thinking to the man in your life. If, for any reason, he makes you feel that you are less than you are, you may have a basis for administering punishment. You must retard and possibly eliminate his tendency to engage in defiant behavior from the first incident.
- **Business** – Men, like children, often exhibit a short attention span. Who usually demands to hold the remote control when the two of you are watching television? Remember those girls in school who had an army of male friends at her beck and call; yet, she rarely dated any of them? This usually confounded all of the other girls. The other girls did not understand that guys like to feel useful (important). The best way to demonstrate to a guy that he his is useful is to ask him to help you do something or do something for you. Keep your man busy but not with mindless tasks just to keep track of him; he will definitely leave you alone for that. Ask him to do 'manly' tasks like lifting, repairing and servicing. What would happen if you left your six year old with nothing to do all

day? Obviously, he would find something to do to amuse himself, possibly something that you might not agree that is in his or your best interest.
- **Play** – Did you know that men love to play? We love to play with you. We enjoy practical jokes, wrestling (this gives us a reason to touch you), racing you (you've seen those beach scenes in the movies), playing tag, throwing balls, playing in the water. Basically, we like doing about anything a six year old would enjoy. Haven't you noticed how well men get along with kids? We enjoy it even more with you so take care of yourself and stay in good shape so that we don't accidentally hurt you. You don't want your man to need to find a new playmate, do you?

Selecting a suitable mate is already a very difficult process for so many reasons. It can mean the difference between a life of prosperous, loving fulfillment and a drama-filled life of misery marked by emergency hospital visits, police reports, court appointments and conferences with social service professionals.

It is all under our control when we choose to accept complete responsibility for our life condition and choices. There is one last area in the mate selection process that I suggest that we examine before we settle on the person who we choose to invest our time with to begin a relationship.

Study Your Intended Mate's Character

Because even the most decent of men have been known to misrepresent themselves, I would like to discuss the concept of good character. Let's say that you found the right match. He is a good and decent man. He is intelligent, responsible, employed and good natured. It appears that all is well; you both move forward in your plans to enter into a relationship together. Eight months, later, you discover that he is still having periodic relations with his "former" girlfriend or that his best buddy, a guy, is also his "forbidden" lover.

Men have been gifted with the talent of carrying on elaborate deceptions for literally years to the dismay of their disappointed mates. I think a discussion of men's character is a proper subject at this point. If you aren't familiar with this subject, it involves a person's ability to make ethical behavior a priority over his or her own ego and selfish needs, especially in a committed relationship. This means that both of you should commit to being honest with and completely supportive of each other regardless of the consequences.

Here is an illustration. If we should be willing to purchase a used 8-passenger boat at the owner's asking price, would we want the selling owner to disclose to us that the boat leaks, slowly, if the additional weight load exceeds 900 lbs; this would impact the number of people and supplies we could load for a trip. Suppose that we made the purchase without this knowledge and we found out this important information while we were several hours into our inaugural journey?

The engine starts sputtering. We go to examine the engine only to learn that it is sputtering because a substantial amount of water has been leaking into our vessel. How would we feel about this? Scammed? Betrayed? If the former owner were in front of us at this moment, what would we say or do to him? The previous owner had a chance to disclose this information to us but he did not. He chose to ignore his opportunity to demonstrate good character by doing the right thing in favor of making a few extra dollars. Let's continue with this a little further.

Let's say that we make the necessary emergency calls to avert a real disaster for us, our family and friends. When we have the money, we get the proper repairs done to our boat. On our way home that day, we happen to see a "For Sale by Owner" sign on a good-looking used car and several people showing interest. We stop to see the vehicle too. To our surprise, it is the same person who sold us the boat we just had repaired. How are we likely to handle this situation?

Whether we choose to forgive and make nice with him or expose him as a scam artist is up to us. What I want each of us to understand is that doing the right thing regarding the boat would only have helped the seller in this follow up scenario.

The seller knew that we would have wanted to negotiate for a lower price if we had known about the leak. The seller would have suffered a minor setback, financially but he would have preserved his reputation for being honest in his dealings. He would not have to worry about any future repercussions from his level of honesty.

It is the same in a relationship. Be certain that you have a realistic understanding of your prospective mate's character. After this much time with him, you should be able to figure this out by the various character indicators. For example: Is he stingy with tips for deserving restaurant servers? Does he harass and belittle fast food employees when he orders? Is he rude and pretentious with hotel employees? Does he tell lies about things that really don't matter just to see if he can get away with it: like his pizza was cold the last time so he wants this one for free or he didn't like the last movie so that he can justify a discount on this movie?

These seem to be rather minor matters, I know. Look at it this way; the employees are paid to do a job. If they do it correctly, why cast dispersions on them? Many people work jobs that are quite thankless in nature. How does what he is doing add to their day or to their desire for appreciation? He could just as easily say, "You guys usually do such a good job, just keep the change!" If he cheats others, he will eventually cheat you. There are about 50 different character qualities. Do your research and get to know as much about your mate choice as you are able.

Unaddressed Trauma Can Damage Our Relationship

It doesn't matter who we are or what our background is, we are going to have many unpleasant surprises in our life. These unpleasant surprises will range from the unexpected loss of loved ones through death to tragic mishaps that will permanently change the course of our life.

Some challenges will be significantly more devastating for some than others. Some will have these mishaps more frequently than others will have. The only consistency is that there will be sufficient heartaches and setbacks for each of us in our lives. (Deborah Tannen, 1990)

When all else is well, never under estimate the impact of a loss or tragedy on our relationship. We may have the best relationship potential with our latest mate selection. We may be entirely confident that we are in the right situation with the right person; we may very well be. Just to be on the safe side, examine the last sixteen months of both of each other's lives for any periods of mental or emotional disruptions that concern a loss (of a job, home, loved one through death, divorce, incarceration or geographic separation) or tragic emotional setback (resulting from a physical illness, accident, attack or natural disaster).

If any such disruptions are in our recent past, we must proceed slowly. The effects of loss or other tragedy aren't always obvious immediately after it has been dealt with. Sometimes the effects on our emotions, attitudes and behavior are delayed for months and sometimes years.

Professional counseling might be needed but at least we should stay open to sharing our feelings about what we have experienced. The panic attacks, depression, periods of indecision and other irregularities may be related to the loss or tragedy that we experienced some time ago. It is not always apparent if we have convinced ourselves that, that particular episode in our life is over. The incident may be over but the effects of it may still be haunting us, in some way.

It is up to us as to how we may choose to proceed. I will not pretend to know what is best for anyone else in their situation; however, in my personal experience, I was eventually forced, on more than one occasion, to face the reality that we cannot turn a blind eye to the effects of these very real issues on our life. It will catch up with us and it can devastate even the most stable of relationships.

I want to share with you, the natural process that human beings go through when dealing with traumatic events. It is a process of grieving; what has been lost as a result of the tragedy. Psychological researchers and other mental health professionals have consistently documented the reality of this process. Not everyone experiences the stages of this process in the same order nor does each person progress through the stages of grieving at the same pace.

Here is what we want to observe in our mate or ourselves:

> **Denial** – In this stage, the person suffering the loss is numbed by shock and disbelief by the news or experience that creates the trauma. This is a natural defense mechanism that is engineered into our being for our protection. We are not always in a position to "fall apart" so to speak. This denial stage typical will last so long as the actual, undeniable proof is

available and presented, that documents the reality of the loss or tragedy. To the person who is most deeply affected by this event, there is no doubt at this point. Usually, this is when we begin to move from this stage to the next.

Anger – At this stage, the person(s) most affected begin to experience deep feelings of anger. The person usually becomes angry because he or she feels abandoned or damaged in one way or another. The anger doesn't appear to have a specific target. In the case of death or disaster, we know in our heart that no one intended for this to happen, yet we are suffering and being inconvenienced, nevertheless. When someone moves to this stage, he or she will remain here until the anger issue is resolved. That will depend upon how each person chooses to deal with the anger. If one does not deal well with anger, one could remain at this stage for years.

Bargaining – Since the most effected person may feel cheated by this event, he or she may take it upon himself or herself to 'fix' this new circumstance by replacing the person or at least the qualities that were lost as a result of this event. This will involve some kind of negotiation with a higher power or finding a person to take the deceased person's place. We usually fail at this phase and move rather quickly to the next phase.

Depression – Once we realize that our life will never be the same again because of this event, we become depressed. At this point, we are truly in mourning. We will grieve as long as we choose to focus on our recent past life. It is only after we make the conscious choice to look positively at the many reasons we have to be thankful, despite this event, that we can consider relinquishing our depression. From this point, we choose to look positively toward building our future and moving on.

Acceptance – When we reach this phase of grieving process, we begin our healing. We finally accept the finality of our circumstance. We are able to talk about it without losing our composure. We are able to share with others the learning and growth that this event has brought to us. We are able to help others who might find themselves at the beginning of such a loss.

Some of these issues will be the result of our own doing resulting from our own negligence and short sidedness. Other issues, we will have no control or power over them; we will simply have to deal with the consequences to the best of our ability. When we can, we will want to blame others. In other cases, there just will not be anyone on whom to place blame.

Whatever the case and result, we will always have a choice in how we choose the move forward with our lives. We can whine, complain and wallow in our own self-pity or we can accept that we have no power to change what has just happened in our life and make plans to move forward. Whatever we decide, it will not be easy and we must understand that we will not be clear in our thinking until we have completed a process of grieving for a period.

The term grieving implies that we have permanently lost something that is essential to our overall well being. This may concern the loss of a loved one through death to a close friend who has moved away. The process is the same regardless of the loss. The depth of the attachment will determine the length of the grieving period. The effect, in each case, will be different for each person.

If we are to deal with someone who is going through the grieving process, it will require an extra special effort on our part. Through each of the grieving phases, we must exercise great patience and understanding as those who go through this process usually do not have a solid command over their emotions because the pain, disappointment and frustration can be so overwhelming. We must be creatively, loving in how we choose to deal with our loved one. Of course, as with any loving endeavor, it will always be worth our efforts, in the end.

I hope that I haven't offended anyone too much in this chapter. I don't pretend to understand the multiplicity of issues that women face in life. I realize that one can only appreciate the world of another by actually living in it for a time. That is not going to happen with me, I enjoy being a man.

I believe that we both (men and women) should raise our standards for how we love and support each other and that begins with each of us taking responsibility for what we create in our relationships. I directed this chapter to women because women ultimately hold the power and influence in virtually every area of dating mate selection and relationship wellness.

Since men historically will do what women permit us to do, women must take the lead in dictating the terms of the mate selection protocol. I have shared with you the most important things you should know in making this leadership a reality. I am risking being shunned by guys everywhere. That means, possibly, no courtside and ringside seats at cherished sporting events, bachelor and Super Bowl parties and being the last chosen at picnic softball games. Please, women of the world; I implore you; do not let my sacrifices be in vain!

Chapter 12

The source of all health, mental, physical and sprititual, is the limitless Life Energy of the Universe, from which all life in Nature springs. Every human being is equipped by Nature with the physical means to contact and use that Life Force.

— *Baron Eugene Fersen*

Use The Power of Your Spiritual Energy

For some of us, the concept of Spiritual matters is synonymous with what we believe within our religion. Believe it or not, one has nothing to do with the other. Spirituality and Religion are completely different subjects. People from different religious backgrounds, cultures and intellects have everything in common spiritually. It is one of many facts of our lives that universally connects and bonds each of us together the way that music, art, sports, beauty, happiness and love does.

We do not have to give up our religious beliefs to embrace a spiritual life. We will be just as welcome at our place of worship as we have always been. We can still participate in all of the ceremonial and social activities that we always have. The only difference is that the quality of life that we enjoy may improve significantly when we focus on our spiritual development.

We will find that we will begin connecting with people who, typically, have been outside of our social purview. We will begin attracting other spiritual people into our life who have a great deal of interesting perspectives to share with us. We will find ourselves enjoying trips and outings that we never considered taking before.

We will engage in thought-provoking discussions that are both stimulating and mind expanding. We will find ourselves losing the desire to engage in self-damaging behaviors like getting high, drunk, gossiping, judging, stealing, illegal activities, violence, criticizing others, blaming others and so on.

Once, we learn to use the power of our spiritual energy, the quality of our existence begins to escalate. It will be the most positive addiction that we can imagine. Even our appearance with change, although we may not see it visually but everyone we encounter will appear to see it.

We will even notice a difference in the way that animals and even insects perceive us. Even if we have not been an animal lover, we will begin to notice a familiar connection with them. Our perception for nature and the stars will experience a heightened sensitivity. We will find our lives positively evolving to a new order with compatible priorities.

Religious Education versus Spiritual Education

Religious education teaches us how to exist within the boundaries of a particular, predetermined belief system; our chosen religion's doctrine will often appear at the beginning of its hymnals or book of sacred writing. It literally dictates what each person believes about important areas in life if each person chooses to be aligned as a member of that institution or order of faith.

Spiritual education teaches us, specifically, about the Eternal Spiritual laws. These Eternal Spiritual laws govern all aspects of life whether or not we choose to believe that they exist. Spiritual education simply teaches what these laws are, how they work and the proper way to use them so that we, each, can achieve the quality of life that we want.

Many of us are taught that our destiny, in life, is predetermined before we are born; that we can do nothing about the eventual quality of our lifestyle, work choices, mate choices and so on. There is no truth in such teaching at all. (Price, Empowerment: You Can Do, Be, And Have All Things!, 1992)

Many of us have heard of "Karma" or the "Law of Attraction." These are two, of many, very powerful spiritual laws (not philosophies or teachings). These laws are quite real and are in full operation in every area of our lives. Through our personal experience, any of us can prove their undeniable impact in our lives.

To deny their existence and power is as foolish as recklessly denying and challenging the physical law of gravity. If we work with gravity, we enhance the quality of our lives tremendously. If we choose to work against gravity, we will quickly meet our death. It is just that simple.

A common question regarding spiritual laws is, "why aren't we taught about these laws in our schools or places of worship?" The answer is quite simple – these laws have been hidden away and shrouded in mystery for millennia by spiritual guardians because they are extremely powerful. (Ambrose, 2007)

We must develop the character and mental appreciation to use them ethically. If we attempt to use them against others, to hurt others, to feed our ego, or to perpetuate any negative agenda (at any level), such a practice will backfire and will quickly plunge our lives into ruins.

The guardians of the knowledge of these spiritual laws have chosen to teach us about moral responsibilities and value judgments with the expectation that respect for these eternal laws would be accomplished through the formulation of memorable expressions and popular sayings that are easy to remember in situations where important decisions or choices have to be made.
Unfortunately, over time, this idea has yielded many flawed expressions that have embodied half truths. As such, they have created more problems than they were intended to solve. For example, "Treat others the way that you would want to be

treated," "A house divided itself cannot stand," and "Charity begins at home" have each stood the test of time. Each has effectively solidified an important moral or value judgment that respects the eternal laws for which each was intended.

The problem is that just as many negative sayings and expression have been coined by influential people who were frustrated, angry, damaged, disillusioned and disappointed in life. Many of these people were only venting but they did so in public forums and their words were adopted and supported by the masses and became entrenched in the international human consciousness. These sayings and expressions do not support any eternal laws and their power has led millions astray. Here some examples of such expressions:

- "History is a set of lies agreed upon." (Napoleon Bonaparte)
- "Democracy is a form of government that substitutes election by the incompetent many for appointment by the corrupt few." (George Bernard Shaw)
- "Love your enemies just in case your friends turn out to be a bunch of bastards." (R. A. Dickson)
- "You can never underestimate the stupidity of the general public." (Scott Adams)
- "A jury consists of twelve persons chosen to decide who has the better lawyer." (Robert Frost)
- "Learning to dislike children at an early age saves a lot of expense and aggravation later in life." (Robert Byrne)
- "Gratitude is merely the secret hope of further favors." (François de la Rochefoucauld)
- "A man with a career can have no time to waste upon his wife and friends; he has to devote it wholly to his enemies." (John Oliver Hobbes)
- "You just can't escape the conclusion that half the people you know are below average." (Scaramouche)
- "Think about how stupid the average person is, then realize that half of us are stupider than that." (George Carlin)

We might find that some of these quotes are both humorous and true, based on our experience. No argument there but none of them do not support any of the Eternal Spiritual laws that govern life. Yet, many of us base our approach and philosophy of life on such popular expressions as these. They are based in negativity and fear. Further, they are not life affirming at any level.

The Law of Attraction states, quite plainly, that we attract to us, what we think about the most (our most passionate beliefs). If we truly believe the worst in people, then, clearly, we will attract only those to us who openly demonstrate those qualities most passionately. To confirm our personal beliefs, whatever they might be, take a look at those people who have found their way into our lives over the last twelve months.

Let's compare what we believe about people, in general, to those people who have recently come into our life. They see what we see whether it is true or not. In fact, we will consistently seek out those who support what we believe so that we can feel validated in our views, whatever they might be.

This is why, within the same neighborhood, we can find those, of us, who are genuinely content with every area of our lives are living in the same vicinity of those, of us, who have an absolutely miserable daily existence. It comes down to how we use the power of our spiritual energy.

As we progress through our discovery about spiritual energy, we find that our experiences, not our study of literature or instruction received, shape our learning. Our experiences from our proactive contact with our spiritual energy will lead us to the undeniable conclusion that our lives are filled with boundless beauty, endless opportunities to enjoy good health, great success, wondrous relationships and perfect love.

Spiritual education teaches us that we are all connected as one. It emphasizes only the highest values, perfection of character, all motivations based in love and total fulfillment of our life experience, now. Religious education teaches us that our lives must be a road of "trials and tribulations" to achieve eventual salvation.

Our Spiritual Energy

In numerous conversations, about spiritual energy, with people, over the years of my life, I have found that, collectively we have many misperceptions about spiritual energy. Some people have told me that we receive it in church. Others were convinced that it was acquired from listening to the sacred music that is played from their place of worship.

Others appear to believe that it must be bestowed upon us from the anointed leaders within our places of worship. Consistently, each person held the common belief that spiritual energy was 'outside' of the human body and had to, somehow, be acquired through some ritual, performance of an act, solicited favor from "God" or an earthly representative of God or a some chance "miracle."

The examination of written records, from numerous ancient civilizations by modern-day archeologists, world historians, linguists and religious scholars have revealed that throughout human history, the most knowledgeable religious and spiritual authorities have held that human energy resides within the human body. (Bruce, 2007)

This has been confirmed through the most recent instruments of modern medical technology. From the Electro Encephalograph (EEG) to Magnetic Resonance Imaging (MRI) medical researchers and scientist have confirmed that, indeed the human body is bursting with its own subtle energy. Although it is conscious energy, it is usually unconsciously directed. (Powell, 2005)

Further, our greatest modern-day researchers have confirmed that it is entirely possible to direct and control this conscious energy within our bodies to change our heart rate, control our blood pressure, change and control our moods, to develop or improve talents and abilities, to control our appetite, to communicate our thoughts to others (even our pets), to become more sensitive emotionally, to improve the effectiveness of our natural senses, to expedite physical healing and much, much more. (Barty, 2008)

At this stage of discovery, I know of no researcher (or research group) who has established a limit for what the conscious energy within the human body can achieve, whether it is consciously directed or undirected. So until proven otherwise, all things are possible with the conscious eternal life energy that resides within us. (Massey, 2009)

This conscious spiritual energy is at work in every area of a healthy human body. It is found to be with us at physical birth and it resides in the sacrum (tailbone) of each person. Our autonomic nervous system directs a minimal amount of this energy to run the biological systems and functions within our bodies so that we develop and grow as our DNA dictates that we should. These would include our nervous system, digestive system, muscular development, cognitive development, adrenal and glandular systems and so on. (Bruce, 2007)

The vast potency, of this conscious energy that resides in our sacrum lies dormant until it is summoned by the brain into action for a specific task. Imagine going through life, battling one dreaded condition after another, when we never had to endure such discomfort. Imagine our body being ache and pain free for the greater part of our aging in later years. (Carolyn Miller, 1995)

Imagine having an alert, aware and energetic mind to be the normal state of our existence. Imagine developing our ability to learn and achieve whatever we wish and then enjoying the rewards without owing anyone else. Imagine directing the conscious energy within to assist us in creating beautiful lasting relationships, of our choosing, for the rest of our lives. Changing the quality of our lives, to what we consider ideal, is completely at our disposal. (Reid, 2007)

Gaining control of this conscious energy within, for those who knew of its existence, has been a goal of human beings for centuries. For example, mind altering drugs have been used to access this conscious energy to a very limited degree. Users, of these stimulants, report having a glimpse of images, music and concepts that changed the direction of their creativity, to such a degree that they were inspired to pioneer their own path of development within their chosen discipline.

Music, art and philosophical histories are replete with people who used mind altering substances to expand their awareness, perceptions and thought development. Unfortunately, this avenue of conscious energy activation often carried with it debilitating side effects.

Fortunately, the last quarter of the 20th century ushered in a safe, consistent and reliable way of accessing this important conscious energy that lies within each of us. It has no negative side affects whatsoever; it is completely safe. It costs no money. Anyone can learn to do it and it can be done at home, at school or work while on a break or in public social situations. Children and elderly people can do it with equal effectiveness and mastery. It improves our overall wellbeing in immeasurable ways that cannot always be expressed in words. This method is meditation.

Access The Power of Your Spiritual Ability

Over the last forty years, I have studied meditation and the techniques for each progressive level. The practice of meditation can be very complex at its most advanced levels. At the most basic level, Sahaja meditation, one merely sits in silence for at least three minutes.

The arms and legs are uncrossed with hands resting on the thighs (palms facing up). With eyes closed, we simply allow ourselves to reach a state of "Thoughtless Awareness." This means that we are fully awake without engaging our brain with any thinking activity at all (although images will come, we simply allow them to pass by us).

This form of meditation, "Sahaja," yields an amazingly peaceful state of being and it allows the dormant conscious energy that resides in our sacrum bone to become active in a way that we have never experienced before. The most immediate effects are a deep reduction of physical, mental and emotional stress. (Powell, 2005)

When we have finished, we will find that our energy level is renewed and we are very alert. We will find it much easier to focus our attention and concentrate. It is even more beneficial to meditate with others who desire these benefits. Once we experience this conscious energy becoming active in our body, it is called a "Realization."

We actually realize that a positive, loving and conscious healing energy is actually inside of us. With this new awareness, we realize that we have a nurturing influence that wants the best for us and wants an even greater role in the care of our body than the basic assignments it receives from the autonomic nervous system. This conscious energy will actually send signals to us when it finds that something is wrong within the various systems and processes of our body.

As we begin to meditate daily, we develop a sensitivity; a vibratory awareness to the movement of this conscious energy. We will sense its rising along our spinal column. As it does so, we will sometimes feel tingling, heat, vibrations, shivers, dull throbbing and so on. This is usually an indicator that something is out of balance in one of the seven most important energy centers it encounters. (Powell, 2005)

Each of these seven important energy centers is concerned with the care of specific areas of our being. When any one of them is out of balance (malfunctioning), this conscious energy will send regular signals indicating that action must be taken to correct the issues in that center. Those energy centers are located in the following areas of our vertebrae: groin, abdomen, solar plexus, heart, throat, forehead (between eyebrows) and at the center of the top of our skull.

The first energy center, located along the tailbone in the groin area, is concerned with our innocence, wisdom and our childlike nature. This energy center malfunctions as we embrace negative traits like gossiping, spreading rumors, greed, arrogance, judgment, sarcasm, wilfull ignorance, blaming behavior, antagonistic and self-damaging behaviors.

The flow of natural energy distribution is, eventually and virtually, shut down until those traits are abandoned. Our reproductive organs are usually adversely affected when we have a malfunction in this first energy center.

The second energy center, located along the lower backbone in the abdomen (around the naval) is concerned with our creativity, artistic abilities and pure knowledge about ourselves. This energy center will malfunction when we neglect our efficient use of time, our physical health, loved ones, relationships, sense of humor, need for learning and creative urges.

We, literally, must re-prioritize our lives accordingly. Neglecting these important areas of anyone's life can cause boundless stresses to our physical health, family life, educational efforts and workplace activities.

The third energy center, located along the backbone at the solar plexus, is concerned with domestic satisfaction, peace and generosity. This energy center malfunctions when we lose respect for the rights and conditions of other people and embrace selfishness, paranoia and competitiveness.

When this center is not functioning properly, we will only be comfortable around others with these same energy issues. Of course, we will find it easy to turn on one another, thus further isolating ourselves from a peaceful and happy coexistence in the world. We must accept that we are ultimately responsible for ourselves and make our decisions accordingly. Our physical energy level suffers when this energy center malfunctions; we will feel lethargic and depressed.

The fourth energy center, located along the backbone at the heart, is concerned with love, security, joy and compassion for others. This energy center malfunctions when we stop giving love to others, when we stop sharing openly, when we stop caring genuinely for others and when we become insincere in our positive dealings.

It is important to have an open heart in order to receive and give love. It is important to have a strong heart to experience true physical vitality. It is important to have a compassionate heart to make sound decisions. It is important to have a loving heart to influence others, positively. We must release every form of non-loving qualities. The health of our physical heart is adversely affected when this energy center is not functioning properly.

The fifth energy center, located along the upper backbone in the throat (thyroid area), is concerned with respectful communication, objectivity, humor and collective relationships. This energy center malfunctions when we choose to take offense regarding matters, of which we are a part, personally when clearly we should not; we refuse to see physical and mental activities as separate.

Feelings of guilt are a common reason for problems in this energy center. For example, our quality of guilt directly affects our level of illness, performance issues and other disorders, This center malfunctions when we refuse to listen or be understanding when someone truly desires to be heard. Its proper functioning is also affected when we purposely limit our communication, when full expression will accomplish our objective, as required.

The sixth energy center, located slightly above the center of our eyebrows, is concerned with perception, insight, vision, forgiveness and memory. This energy center malfunctions when we allow ourselves to focus on anger, revenge and punishment for any wrong that is done to us; when we choose to be unforgiving and critical; when we allow and perpetuate destructive and hurtful thoughts to dominate our thinking.

We must forgive, excuse, pardon or grant amnesty to anyone (including ourselves) with whom we have sharp differences so that we can move forward in our spiritual development. In many cases, we, ourselves, are the accused who must be exonerated. Self-directed anger is a common reason for problems with this energy center. Headaches, tension and stress are common physical manifestations when this energy center is malfunctioning.

The seventh energy center, located in the center of the top of our skull, is concerned with spiritual connection, collective consciousness, expanded awareness, healing, intention and enlightenment. This energy center malfunctions when we limit our perceptions to our five natural senses only (sight, sound, smell, taste and touch).

Other reasons for improper functioning of this energy center are when we refuse to acknowledge our equality with all other people and our connection to all living organisms; when we deny the presence of divinity, from which all life and creation originates (Light and Love), within us; when we choose to delegate responsibility for our lives to others and when we willingly relinquish our power to exercise our free will.

As this conscious energy within us rises to this final energy center before it exits the body, it will teach us about who we are and where our place in life is to be. Our life purpose is revealed to us along with how, in specific ways, we are to fulfill it. This information will clarify with each successful meditation.

Each of the energy centers affects the physical organs within its vicinity. For example, if the energy flow of the second energy center, located in the abdomen, is malfunctioning, it will also affect the proper functioning of the digestive system too. If the energy center, located in the heart area is malfunctioning, it often times affects the physical operation of the heart organ as well.

Making a conscious decision to release negative qualities, thoughts and behaviors so that the affected energy center will begin functioning properly, will often begin to restore the physical health of the affected organs, systems and processes in the body as well.

The diagram below depicts the subtle conscious energy system that is inside each of us. The dormant conscious energy, that is with us from birth, housed in the sacrum (tailbone), is represented as a spherical, coiled energy inside an inverted triangle.

Each of the body's energy centers, located along the spinal column, is numbered as explained above. Notice that the hands (fingers, palm and thumb) are numbered according to the corresponding energy center to which each is connected. Finally, the broad quality that each energy center concerns is labeled accordingly.

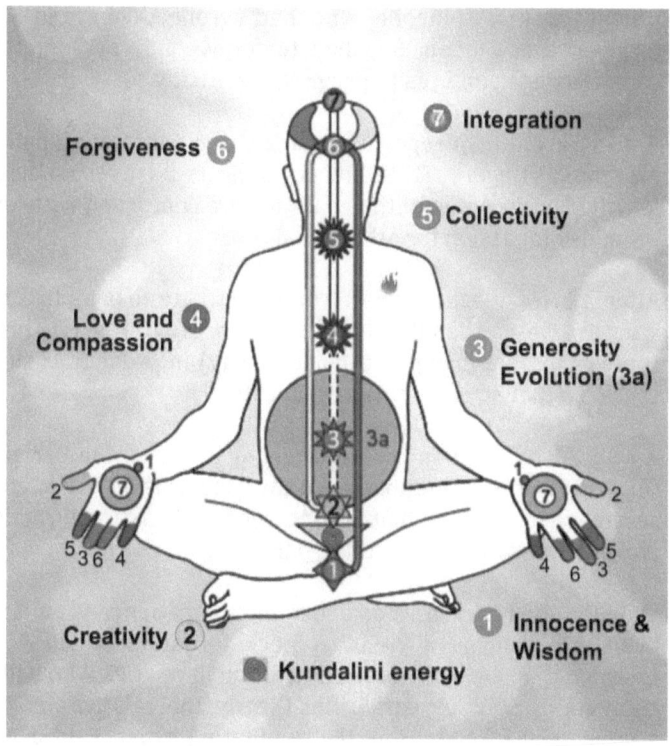

Conscious Energy System

Earlier, in this chapter, it was stated that this dormant, conscious energy would give us signals indicating when it found that an energy center was out of balance. These signals would be in the form of tingling, heat, vibrations, shivers, dull throbbing and more. These signals usually register along the spinal column as the conscious energy travels up from the sacrum (represented by the inverted triangle) during meditation in the region of the energy centers.

More often than not, the meditating person will feel the signal sensations at the energy centers themselves, in the hands or in the feet. Each signal has a specific significance and should be addressed, sincerely, before the next meditation session. Each meditation session will sharpen our "vibratory awareness." (Powell, 2005)

Here are some examples from first-time meditation participants, each of whom reported having a very positive experience, who were under my supervision:

- A 32 year old woman reported feeling an alternate dull throbbing in the temple area of her head. This is located in the area of the sixth energy center which concerns perception, insight, vision and memory.

  After a few brief questions, she admitted that she had been holding a grudge against someone who had wronged her and she had not forgiven that person. She had to forgive this person, sincerely and completely, to continue to progress spiritually.

- A 45 year old man reported feeling sharp penetrating pains in both of his "pinky" fingers. These fingers indicate a correspondence with the fourth energy center, at the heart and are concerned with love, security, joy and compassion for others.

  After a brief questioning, he confided to me that he had been lusting after a close friend's fiancée. He had to release his obsession (preferably in a loving and positive way) in order to clear this energy center so that he could progress spiritually.

- A 63 year old woman reported feeling a sickness in her abdomen and tingling in her left thumb toward the base. This indicated an issue in the second energy center that is concerned with creativity, artistic abilities and pure knowledge about her, personally.

  She identified herself as an artist, by occupation, and said that she had been experiencing a creative block for quite a while. She further revealed that she had been caring for an ill relative who had treated her badly for most of her earlier life. Clearly, this relative was experiencing a great deal of guilt. She, the meditating artist, held a great deal of resentment for this person. She vented about her discomfort with this situation to anyone who might listen.

It was important that she see the truth of this 'damaged' person so that she could release her resentment and forgive him or her. She might have, perhaps, used the emotional turmoil that they both were experiencing as inspiration in her creative artwork.

- A 25 year old man reported a stinging sensation on the heel of both of his hands and thumbs. This indicates that there is an issue with the first energy center that is concerned with innocence, wisdom and childlike nature and in the second energy center that is concerned with creativity, artistic abilities and pure knowledge about us, personally.

This man was obese and he revealed, to me, that he had been having digestive issues for quite some time. After learning about the concerns of the first energy center, he confessed that he was a manager of a fast-food establishment and did not like many of his employees.

He further admitted that he unfairly abused certain employees by manipulating their work schedules, position assignments and performance evaluations. He also suffered from insomnia. He further confessed that he had neglected everything that he felt was important to him for the sake of keeping his establishment operating properly. Through our conversation, he revealed to himself, what he had to do to correct the disorders in his life.

That is the beauty of spiritual living. Once we understand how our actions, behaviors, attitudes, emotions, thinking and decisions affect us, per the Eternal Laws of life, we can correct the difficulties in our lives, ourselves. There is no need for pressure from law enforcement, courts or any outside organizations.

Unfortunately, I have no follow up information on any of these individuals as we (the meditation group with whom I work) often provide meditation opportunities at public events and we do not often see some of these people again. This point is to get them started by teaching each person about the conscious energy within and allowing each person to decide how to use it for his or her own life enhancement. We also expect each of those people to teach someone else, too.

We, all, have a powerful conscious spiritual energy inside of us. We were born with it. Jesus, the master of love and virtue, reportedly told his followers that "the kingdom of God was within." This is part of the spiritual wisdom that was guarded for several centuries. Those guardians were convinced that the masses of people would abuse such power if they knew about it. So, it remained hidden.

There are no negative side effects to this form of meditation. If we express a desire that is not life-affirming, the conscious life energy within us simply does not respond. This conscious energy is only programmed by the Divine to do positive, loving work inside and through of us; not to do damage to itself or our body.

It only responds to positive, productive and loving desires for personal improvement. So we can use it to create the state of health that we want; the relationships for which we long, to attract the quality of people and opportunities that we desire and so on. It is OUR personal power to use. It keeps our secrets, works quietly, it knows no limits, works while we are asleep and never fails to deliver the results we desire (although its timing is still a mystery to me).

Discovering Our Dharma

"My what?" was my response when I first learned of the concept of "Dharma." Dharma is a term from the eastern religions that simply translates to mean: Do Your Part as Expected. Wherever you find yourself in life at this point, do everything that you are supposed to do in light of the positions in life that you occupy.

Simply put, if we are a student in junior high school, we are responsible for diligently learning and mastering our course work while being courteous and respectful to our classmates, teachers and school employees. If we also happen to be a pet owner, we are also responsible for taking the best care of our pet (or pets) for which we have accepted responsibility.

As a member of our household, we are also responsible for making contributions to the daily operation and maintenance of our home. This means doing our fair assignment of chores, keeping our room clean, greeting guests, taking and passing along phone messages appropriately and so on.

If we are also a sibling, we must be a caring, considerate brother or sister in all the ways that such a role implies. (If you are a parent reading this aloud to our children, we may want to stop now.)

Every parent wants children who do what is expected of them. Parenting would go a great deal smoother if that were the case. So how many of us parents would relax and take it easy if our children did everything expected of them? Is it possible that many parents would take advantage of this situation by increasing the burdens on their children while enjoying a more leisurely existence themselves?

If we would be one of those parents, we would only be damaging ourselves. Not only would we be demonstrating the highest level of parental irresponsibility but we would damage our credibility with our family, friends and community. Dharma is only operationally sound when ALL concerned embrace it completely.

That means that as a parent, our responsibility supersedes just feeding our children to feeding them the healthiest foods that are available for them. Further, it is our responsibility to make the meals appetizing as well. It also means not just asking our children about how they are doing school but getting involved in their educational experience in every way that we can make a contribution.

Imagine that everyone actually did his or her part in every facet of their world to the maximum extent of his or her ability. Conceivably, we each would be so engaged with working together, at every level that every area of society would turn into a place of joy and comfort.

Envision how each of us, embracing our Dharma, would play out in personal relationships, family relationships, casual friendships, workplace relationships, places of worship, social gatherings, school environments and so on. With everyone, sincerely, doing his or her part, there would be no reason for gossip, bickering, jealousy, anger, sarcasm, judgment or personal attacks of any kind.

It is easy to think that everyone will not do this. Everyone doesn't have to do it. Only those, of us, who are reading this book, need to be concerned. If those, who are now familiar with this concept of finding their Dharma, would practice this sincerely and then encourage those closest to them to do the same, consider how much stress and tension would be released from our mind, body and emotions.

Think about how smoothly our household would run. Think about how much better and more productive our workplace would become. How would applying this concept of finding our Dharma impact student success? The greatest reward in all of this is that we and our ilk would become a shining example to others who are stumbling through life because they are not familiar with this concept.

So how does finding our Dharma apply to our life? Let's start with the condition of our life now. Take note as to which areas could be better. Next, state exactly why those areas aren't what they should be. Finally, be clear about how thoroughly we have embraced doing our part, in every area of responsibility that we have chosen to undertake, at this point in our life. Once we have finished our personal examination of our life, we have laid the foundation for finding our Dharma.

Let's take a look at our chosen line of work at this point. It is important that we live up to the spirit of the stated mission of our position. If our job is to serve the public, can we honestly say that we do the best every day, for everyone, that we are responsible for serving? Is our attitude one of full service and respect? If so, then we have found our Dharma in this area of our life.

If we have not, then it is just as important that we figure out why. If we are not fulfilled by our current work, what is (or are) the reason(s)? Each reason must be addressed and dealt with as sincerely as possible. No one else can do this but us for ourselves. If we aren't happy with our line of work, it is important that we make preparations to transition into a line of work that is more in line with our passions.

Always Seek Wisdom Our Creator

Chapter 13

Don't ask yourself what the world needs; ask yourself what makes you come alive. And then go and do that. Because what the world needs is people who have come alive.

- Harold Whitman

Our Sense of Entitlement

Many of us have become discouraged from wanting to improve our position in life because we have lost, forgotten or never learned a responsible sense of entitlement. This concerns our ability to perceive ourselves as being deserving of a higher quality of life, greater respect, substantially higher income and so on.

We all deserve access to any good thing that we want in life. We are entitled to explore whatever we choose in life as long as we do so positively, productively and without infringing upon anyone else's rights, privileges and freedom.

Children have a strong sense of entitlement. This is a natural sense that we all have from infancy. Unless, we are taught differently, we will never hesitate to demand what we want and need to enjoy our lives to the fullest extent of our capacity. A child's sense of entitlement is, at first, based upon learned dependence from his or her parents. They expect their parents to supply all of their most important needs.

Children learn and develop abilities to become increasingly independent as they grow and mature. Their sense of entitlement usually does not diminish. For example, once a child learns where and how to retrieve cookies from the cookie jar, that child will exercise his or her independence often. That child, armed with the proper knowledge and experience, will feel a sense of entitlement to enjoy these snacks as often as he or she pleases, unless the parent intervenes.

As parents, whether we are consciously aware, we teach our children to manage their sense of entitlement. We do this in many ways. We do so in the form of limiting their behavior, encouraging assertive behavior, allowing aggressive behavior, permitting passive behavior, brokering their requests or by ignoring their requests altogether. The mental and emotional health of the child and eventual life success in adulthood will be determined, to the greatest extent, by how thoroughly and carefully we teach them a healthy sense of entitlement.

- A) **Limiting** – Those of us who are parents, who teach our children a limiting sense of entitlement, do so by teaching them a "poverty" mentality. (Eker, 2005) Often, we do this unwittingly. This happens in families where we have limited financial and material resources.

When our child expresses a specific desire that would cause a financial or logistical burden on the family, we will often retort with such discouraging statements as, "We don't have the money!"; "We just can't afford for you to be able to do that;" "We just don't live that way!"; "You don't come from one of those families;" or we might just say, "No!" These teachings have no positive benefit to the children now or when they mature to adulthood.

When we handle our children's' demands this way, in effect, we condemn them to a life of lack, limitation and poverty. They may secure a great education and solid employment with an excellent career path in a thriving industry, unfortunately, because of their "poverty mentality," they will tend to squander their earnings and mismanage their material resources to support their belief that their just is not enough for them to have what they want.

An easy example of this mentality can be found by observing young adults who are sports or entertainment celebrities who were from families who taught this mentality to them. Despite the millions of dollars they earn, they never seem to have enough.

The money is spent recklessly and foolishly on expensive luxury items that they were never taught to appreciate. Once, they have no other material items to acquire, they turn to outlandish recreational activities. This often results with episodes with excessive illegal drug involvement, gambling or one or more versions of racketeering.

Once their careers have ended, usually within a matter of months, these celebrities very often find themselves in an impoverished condition that is often worse than they experienced in their youth. The resulting fines and fees, to settle their legal entanglements, are often sufficient to deplete what remains of their savings, after their celebrity status has diminished. The "poverty mentality" will surely endure.

B) **Assertiv**e – Wise parents encourage their children to make their needs known. The children benefit from knowing that they have been heard. The children also expect a response from their parents as to their ruling regarding their requests. It is important that parents realize the opportunity to solidify their children's' sense of entitlement using this style of teaching.

As parents, we may have limited resources, financially, influentially and materially. This should not be seen as a barrier to teaching children a positive sense of entitlement. We can teach our children that, yes they can have what they have asked for if they are willing to earn, work or sacrifice for it.

If it is at all possible for parents to secure what their children are requesting, this will buy them some time so that they might begin saving the money or gathering any other resources to eventually fulfill the request(s). As parents, we could tie the conditions for acquiring the requested item(s) or privilege to such variables as grade performance, household chores completed in a timely fashion, community volunteer work, behavior in church or school or some other area of need.

This way, our children are never refused a request for something in which they feel they are entitled. They will determine the value of what they have requested by balancing it against the price of the acquisition, which is determined by the conditions set by the parents.

Of course, as parents we should always be prepared to "deliver the goods," so to speak, as our children will, sometimes, surprise us by measuring up to and sometimes exceeding the challenges that, we parents, propose. Realistically, what parent is going to complain about that kind of demonstrated growth and maturity in their children?

C) **Aggressive** – With this approach, children are encouraged to let everyone, extended family, family friends, school associates, community members, workplace associations, church members and so on, know their requests. These are requests that we, as parents, know the children deserve but we cannot bear the burden alone.

These are generally once-in-a-lifetime opportunity requests like an international student exchange study request, senior trip abroad, scientific study opportunity, and extended volunteer opportunity out of state or other opportunity on this level.

This is the kind of request where it really will take a community effort to bring it to fruition. This is where it is beneficial that the youth has chosen to accept full responsibility for the condition of his or her life at an early age (see Chapter 5). This means that the youth is willing, at all phases of the project, to demonstrated leadership, good character, discipline, persistence, a solid work ethic and superior social skills.

As parents, we must be willing to work tirelessly to do our part and to be superior representatives for our children, especially in this matter. Whenever we allow ourselves to be a part of the aggressive style of entitlement teaching, we must accept that it as a teaching opportunity for, literally, everyone who is involved and at every level.

This will involve fundraising through staged events, donations collection, and special sales and so on. As parents, we should keep a journal of the project, as a whole, noting the important successes and shortfalls and the lessons we learn, as someone we know may benefit from our experience soon after. The neighborly thing to do is to make ourselves available as volunteer consultants for the next child, in the community, who choose to accept such a challenge.

D) **Passive** – This is a style of teaching about entitlement that will solidify a child's sense of entitlement but in an extremely unhealthy way. When children are allowed to have whatever they request, it will appear to outsiders that the child is being 'spoiled.'

This may actually be the case as the child may not fully be committed to most of the requests but, as parents, we are inclined to comply with the request for such reasons as 1) we don't want to upset our child. 2) We want our child to like us or love us more. 3) We have the extra money or resources at this time. 4) Our beautiful child is so sweet and lovable.

This style of teaching entitlement is flawed because it does not require any effort, commitment or sacrifice from the child him or herself. They do not learn to earn, work or sacrifice for what they want. As parents, we might rationalize that we can live with that. However, when the child reaches adulthood, he or she might be devoid of the skills necessary to acquire adult level resources, independently.

That, now adult, may have to resort to marrying someone for financial reasons, instead of for love and companionship. He or she may have to resort to less honorable and perhaps controversial means to secure the quality of life that he or she has always enjoyed. Parents never want to witness their child failing in adult life this way.

This could lead to a life of criminal or illegal activities that would bring disgrace to the family. As parents, we should think through our decisions to give our children everything they want for such reasons as, "I want him to have more that I did," or "I don't want her to have to work as hard as I did" (see Chapter 7).

E) **Brokering** – As parents, many of us feel that we have no choice but to provide for our children at a 'reduced' level of quality. This is known as "brokering." It has its benefits and its disadvantages. This is most effective when children are age seven or less. Its value as a teaching option, to instill a healthy sense of entitlement, tends to diminish in its effectiveness over the next 11 years of youth.

The benefits of brokering are these: 1) we save money, consistently. 2) Our children get a reasonable measure of what they requested. 3) We maintain peace and harmony in the home for all concerned. 4) We have the secrecy to pull off grand deceptions and manipulations. These advantages are only viable in relation to the level of the requesting person's innocence and gullibility – seven year olds and younger.

The disadvantages of brokering are these: 1) our time of use is limited. 2) We breed mistrust in older family members, especially our spouse. 3) We develop a relationship with our children based on dishonesty. 4) Pertaining to toys and other material possessions, we risk being found out, as a liar and a cheat, at some point during our child's advanced years.

Here are some examples of instilling a sense of entitlement by using brokering as the teaching method. We can all relate to how television advertisements exaggerate the attractiveness of products that are marketed to children. Children learn to ask for those products by name. We can generally satisfy a child's wishes through replacement.

For example, a child may request a specific multi-colored cereal that is also made in generic form. A family that wishes to save money may by one box of that cereal and replenish it with the generic product periodically.

Children would not recognize the difference as long as they recognize that it comes from the container with which they are familiar. The evidence of deception is consumed and will not be available for scrutiny, later in life by that, now deceived, child.

This method will work for toys that are not classics and which may not appreciate in value. As our child edges closer to age seven, he or she will develop reliable reading and product recognition skills. He or she will become a moderately discriminating consumer.

We are still able to negotiate with them but they will never be satisfied with us because, we all want what we want, not what someone else wants us to have. In adulthood, our children may be particularly prone to manipulation by more skilled personalities like those people who work in sales, customer service, and collections and so on.

F) **Ignoring** – We disregard our childrens' requests, for what they tell us they want, by cutting them off with a stifling and final, "No." We are actually teaching them that their wants and needs are not important; that their fate is in our hands only, not their own.

This position gives a child a very unsettling feeling of powerlessness. We are teaching them that their lives are predestined, regardless of what they do or want. We are pushing them into a mentality of dependence and away from eventual independence and self reliance.

It is important that we think back to when we were children, ourselves. We may have forgotten how damaging the word 'No' was to us at that stage of our lives.

It is as word that told us that we did not matter; it was a very minimizing word. The word 'no' can damage a child's self esteem. If the word 'no' is not used for the purpose of protecting us or correcting bad behavior, it is a very disempowering word.

Ignoring or suppressing a child's request to be heard, regarding what he or she wants and needs is most damaging in teaching him or her about the concept of entitlement. This practice can erase any child's sense of entitlement for many years to come. This child is likely to develop a passive, approval seeking mentality; a child who has virtually no sense of entitlement for even the most basic necessities in life.

As parents, when we aren't focused on teaching our children to manage their sense of entitlement, we tend to appear, to others, to be buying our children's' love and affections by attempting to supply our child's needs when, clearly the child can supply his or her own needs at some levels. As parents, by our inability to say "no," teach our child to abuse his or her sense of entitlement.

There are situations where the exact opposite happens. As the child develops and becomes increasingly independent, we parents refuse, more often, to meet our child's needs. When the child really is unable to fill an important need and the parents do not have the resources to be of assistance, we simply discourage the child from expressing such a need to us.

As this happens more often, the child loses a sense of entitlement for the better things in his or her life. They become all too familiar with their parents excuses. By the time they reach adulthood, we find that some of them have a very strong sense of entitlement and some of us do not.

Of those people who have a strong sense of entitlement and have been taught to manage it, they are likely to enjoy a fulfilling and productive existence because they have been taught to earn and seize the opportunities that are afforded them.

Of those people who have a strong sense of entitlement but who have not been taught to manage it, they are likely to become the insensitive bosses, family leaches, criminals and abusive bullies in life. In short, they will use whomever they can to get whatever they want at someone else's expense, if they do not possess the skills, abilities and resources themselves, to acquire what they want on their own.

For many of us, who are reading this section, this is the first we have heard about our sense of entitlement. This kind of conversation may have never have taken place in our home where we grew up. When this is the case, we must decide where we are in the development of our own sense of entitlement. If we do not feel as strongly about the importance of this area of our lives, we should. It is as important as understanding our self worth, self esteem and our self image.

Those who have a strong sense of entitlement will fall into one of two categories: 1) Those people who have been taught to manage their sense of entitlement positively; and 2) Those people who have no understanding of how to manage their sense of entitlement. People who fall into this second category are those who have a stifled sense of entitlement.

Those, of us who have a stifled sense of entitlement can be divided into two groups: 1) Those who have become the discouraged procrastinators and under achievers in life; and 2) Those who give up on their life goals before they begin; these are the habitual quitters and whiners with whom we are familiar.

Those, of us, who have a stifled sense of entitlement and who become underachievers, or the habitual quitters and whiners, are likely to pass these perceptions and attitudes onto our children Regardless of where we find ourselves, it never hurts to examine our present circumstances as it pertains to our sense of entitlement.

Ideally, we will want a solid, positive sense of entitlement and we will want to strengthen our ability to manage this strong sense of entitlement. More important, we will want to teach our children a responsible sense of entitlement. That begins with teaching them that they are responsible for the condition of their lives and the consequences of their decisions and actions as early in life as is practical.

We, sometimes, believe that the world's 'non-natural' resources are somehow limited. They are not. No matter what we are told by people who are trying to sell us something or profit in some way from our fears and insecurities, we must understand that opportunities, and resources to enjoy them, are limitless.

That is like someone attempting to have us seriously believe that we will deplete the earth of its grains of sand. There are deserts and oceans full of it; opportunities and resources are just as plentiful. It is true that we may not see it that way right now but we must consider changing our perspective about this for just a few moments.

Now that we have opened our thoughts to the possibility that there could be limitless opportunities and resources, please get a paper and pen. Now, let's pick five of our favorite movies. I want us to watch them and as we normally would; I want us to note all of the modern day inventions and technology that weren't available when that movie was made.

Some people, from those days, understood that there was much to be created to improve our quality of life. Oh sure, there is always some of us who are into futuristic movies; that is fine. Note all of the technology and inventions in the movie that do not actually exist today – these are just a few of those limitless opportunities that exist right now.

Keep that pad and pen handy; we're not finished with this yet. I want us to think of things, about which, we routinely complain. What do we find annoying, inconvenient or poorly serviced in this world? What do we find that other people we know are constantly complaining about?

Now suppose that we could get all of these people to stop complaining so much and work on finding solutions that would satisfy each of these situations. Imagine how energized our days would become. There would be nights when we would not be able to sleep because we would begin to obsess on these solutions.

Sure, we would get all excited but we would not have the money to do anything about it. Well, believe it or not, not every solution requires a large sum of money to make it work. We have all observed poor children at play. Observe any of our toddlers at play, virtually anywhere. They are amazingly creative in making up games and finding ways to amuse themselves with whatever resources they find. They, definitely, aren't thinking about money while they are playing.

I know that we are adults and we are thinking about money. So let's go look in our kitchen. Look at some of the gadgetry that we use all the time. Someone invented them. We could have actually made some of these in our spare time. Look at some of the school and office supplies that we and our children use. If we work on cars, or other motorized vehicles, look at some of the latest tool inventions that we use.

Some of them aren't more than a few years old. Notice the cleaning and sanitizing solutions for our hands and tools. We can just look around our home and see what we have been purchasing in the last few years. Someone invented, financed and marketed all of these because they recognized the opportunity. They only moved forward from the idea stage after reassessing their own sense of entitlement.

Keep it simple. I know that many of us, who are prone to road rage, have already jumped to the idea of putting the retractable bazooka, which vaporizes the car in front of us, in the hood of our car, for when we are behind those terribly cautious drivers, when we are running late for work. The rest of us are thinking about hypnotizing devices to get our mates to do what we want and stay out of our hair while we are watching television or talking on the phone.

We are entitled to whatever we want, as long as we are willing to work for it and don't do so at the expense of others. If we are willing to make a contribution to the world community so that someone else's life can be better, we will be rewarded for it.

A responsible sense of entitlement is good for everyone, including us. We can think it through and decide how we are going to begin accepting full responsibility for the condition of our life in light of our new perspective regarding a healthy sense of entitlement. Next, make it happen.

Once we choose to accept full responsibility for our life condition and choose to take control of the direction of our life, we will begin to examine what needs to be changed in our life. Our sense of entitlement must be one of those areas. When we have solidified our responsible sense of entitlement, we will begin to see the many opportunities to be seized in our lives. Many of us will discover that we can turn our greatest challenges into profitable opportunities. Here are three examples from what I have observed in my personal life:

> **Hambry** was a coworker and friend who was absolutely the kindest person who anyone could ever know. He was obese, under confident and he was, admittedly, unfulfilled with the condition of his life. He blamed a great deal of his unhappiness on his self image and self esteem. He decided, one day, that he deserved to be happy and that he was going to stop doing things that were adding to his unhappiness and only do things that were going to support his overall happiness. He felt entitled.
>
> He decided to be more social, eat healthier food, drink more water, exercise and only see the best in himself and in other people. His change of mentality affected everyone in his life and we each responded in kind.
>
> He did reduce his body weight considerably through diet, exercise and drinking a lot of spring water. His marital relationship improved dramatically from what I observed. He stopped complaining about what he earned and decided to engage in developing one of his many passions: Smoked Barbeque.
>
> He invited several of us over for a barbecue at his home one weekend. We had a great time. Everyone loved his cooking, especially his barbecue sauce, meat preparation and grilling techniques. He received such positive feedback that he actually decided to go into business. Inside of one year, he and his sauce were a familiar entrance-way fixture at local grocery stores throughout the city.
>
> **Jeanine** was a sanitation worker who felt under paid and underappreciated. Her communication was extremely negative and critical. While her team was cleaning up a banquet facility late one evening, she came across a folder carelessly discarded from one the event managers. She placed it aside to be returned to the proper manager after she completed her work duties.
>
> As she unlocked the office door of the event manager to place the folder on the desk, her curiosity got the best of her. She peered inside to see what it contained. She found mostly billing and contract information. Carefully, she studied the itemized pricing of the event.
>
> She could not believe what decorations, equipment and food cost for these special events. She thought she could do a better job with many of the decorations as she replaced the folder and locked the office door.

She was more filled with negativity than ever, as she waited for her bus home. The bus driver for that evening turned out to be an old friend from her high school. They caught up with each other from the many years apart. When Jeanine reached her stop, she was in a much better mood and had forgotten about the earlier incident.

The driver stopped her before she exited the bus to give her some information and make a request that changed her life. The bus driver admitted to Jeanine that she was engaged to be married and asked Jeanine if she would make the center pieces for the reception. At that moment, it all flashed back to her.

In high school, Jeanine was highly regarded for her arts and crafts mastery. She had built a reputation for being a supremely gifted event decorator. She hadn't even thought about it for several years. She agreed to meet with her friend to discuss it.

As Jeanine entered her home, she could hardly contain her excitement to return to her former status of a decorating authority. Ideas raced through her head about additional decorating amenities that might be included. Maybe she would volunteer to head up the entire reception event. This kind of encouragement and appreciation was long overdue; it was just what she needed. She prepared for bed thinking about center piece ideas.

Around 3 am, Jeanine woke up. Apparently, she dreamed about reclaiming her sense of entitlement in a most responsible way. She arrived at work about 30 minutes early the next day. Instead of going to the employee break room to clock in, she went to the administrative offices to meet with the events manager.

When she did report to work, 45 minutes late, she had a smile on her face and a transformed personality. She was genuinely positive, engaging and humorous as she announced that she was going into business as an Event Decorations supplier. She did just that with a fair amount of success.

Paul treated animals with more respect than he did people. He hated his retail job. He was about as impersonal as a salesperson could be and still keep his job. He recited specials and discounted items and the like, in a monotone voice.

He rarely looked at his customers as he counted their change back to them, as he thanked them and wished them a good day. His transformation came when was walking home and noticed a puppy tearing at a carefully tended flower bed of an elderly neighbor.

He retrieved the puppy and returned it to the owner. When he returned to the elderly neighbor's home to explain what happened, no one answered the door. He looked through a window to see if he could see any movement. He did. He saw the foot of someone in a doorway struggling. He had the presence of mind to go home and call 911 to report an emergency.

When he returned, he found that a back door was unlocked. So he went in and found that his neighbor was unable to get up. He waited for the emergency medical personnel to arrive, all the while assuring his neighbor that everything would be all right.

The emergency medical workers were so impressed with Paul's handling of this situation, that they invited him to explore joining them as an employee. The idea was completely new to him. He had never thought of himself in such a heroic role. He never felt entitled to consider it before.

After several months of classes and training certifications, he resigned his retail job and became an emergency medical technician (EMT). It was much more rewarding personally and financially. He enjoyed giving presentations about various areas of person safety at schools, recreation centers, community centers and places of worship for different organizations.

Paul's entitlement issues concerned his work. He did not see that he had anything meaningful to offer to anyone so he stayed in a job where he just "went through the motions." He revisited his sense of entitlement and found that he was entitled to something better. He proves it daily to the delight of many grateful emergency patients.

There is something better waiting for us, who aren't fulfilled in life. Maybe it is a forgotten talent, as in Jeanine's case, or a skill that we kept hidden as in the case of Hambry. Maybe some of us are like Paul in that we just haven't considered the many options available to us in this day and age.

When we consider and assess our sense of entitlement in terms of being responsible, we are well on our way to finding our special place. We will fit perfectly. It will be the most natural thing for us to do. It is time for all of us to enjoy a responsible sense of entitlement, if we have not already.

Chapter 14

"We are born free. Every self-damaging habit and vice that we have now, we learned from people who chose dysfunctional alternatives to their own difficulties in life"

The Power of Our Natural Freedom

"Freedom isn't free" became a popular catch phrase in the early 21st century as a means of justifying military activity for one nation against other nations. So far as the physical freedom, of any nation of people is concerned, this is a wholly true statement.

For as long as there are people, of corrupt or questionable character with any political, economic, financial or social influence, anywhere in the world, physical freedom will never be free for anyone, including those of corrupt character who wield such power.

There are areas of freedom that we all possess that are completely free and when collectively used, in consensus, are ultimately more powerful than the collection of all corrupt leaders and their respective areas of influence, combined.

Time and again, throughout human history, the one influence that has continually corrected injustices through legislative changes toppled the most powerful leaders and the strongest empires have been that of 'public opinion.' Popular public opinion in societies, around the world, has placed common people to positions of greatness and removed the most stubborn of hated leaders from power.

Public opinion is like a great tidal wave. Whether it is flowing in a favorable or unfavorable direction, it is extremely difficult to neutralize. Advertisers, politicians, business people, entertainers, artists and celebrities, of all descriptions, eventually come to revere the power of public opinion.

The most powerful fuel that powers public opinion comes in the form of ideas (and concepts, thoughts, mindsets, intentions, views, perspectives and so on). Every leader absolutely abhors any ideas that are contrary to the one that is most beneficial to him or her personally, to be introduced to those under his or her control. This is true of every level of leadership in government, politics, business, religion and social organization.

The wisest leaders will appear to be open to new ideas but the introduction of those ideas will result in one of two fates: 1) Leaders do permit the introduced changes within their organizations when they, themselves, are the greatest beneficiaries of those ideas or 2) Those ideas will eventually be rationalized, by the supporting leadership group, to be unfit for all concerned, often with no further discussion permitted. An example of this is illustrated in organizations that take on multi-level marketing (MLM) projects as "fundraisers" for their organizations that may also fund programs that help the poor. So, if the leadership does not personally benefit, the end consumers suffer.

These ideas, that fuel public opinion, come from us, people from all backgrounds and walks of life. These ideas are born of our conscience, experience, educational research, imagination, wisdom and observation. Sometimes these ideas are purely selfless in intention and sometimes, they are not.

They are usually consistent with the character and ethics of the one who bears the idea. The intentions, of such ideas, often lose their purity as those with less honorable agendas become involved.

In cases where the author, of the idea, is a person of questionable character and reputation, there may very well be hidden agendas. When this is the case, the selling of the idea, to the masses, is usually shrouded in complexity, mystery and ambiguity.

Bitter infighting often will result; something that rarely happens with ideas that have a purely selfless motivation. Simple and selfless ideas are the easiest to adopt and implement. They tend to benefit everyone involved equally; no one person or organization has a particular advantage over another as a result.

Always Side With Responsible Public Opinion

Once the masses of people, in any population, become knowledgeable, desirous and focused in any direction, the tide of public opinion will shift. The more it is opposed, the stronger it will become. Through realization, enlightenment, education and understanding, the masses will demand higher standards in leadership output in every area of society. The leadership of the enthusiastic masses of people will continue to pressure for change until that desire is fulfilled.

For example, in commerce, we desire a greater selection of products and services in quality and availability; in education we desire more learning options, more efficient implementation and improved quality of teaching personnel; in government we desire stricter accountability, equal treatment for all, consistent application of the law and stable results from our leadership, as it pertains to the ideas introduced.

The tools that the masses of people will use to signify their expectations, respectively, are their combined financial spending power, level of personal involvement and solicited support, their public outpouring of vocalized demonstrations and political vote casting. Then, the often overlooked, artistic community representatives, of the mass thinking, will usually frame and focus the popular thought, of the day, in the form of songs, art, poetry, novels, theatrical productions, movies, documentaries, museum exhibits and so on.

I spent most of my childhood in a small village in Ohio. Each year, a small traveling circus would come to town. They would setup for about a week at our local community park. I was always fascinated with the elephants and being an animal loving enthusiast, I was fascinated with the way they were handled. I noticed that adult elephants were always anchored with a long rope, around their necks, tied to a small, six to eight-inch stake pounded into the ground. These large creatures would never stray from their assign areas.

Conversely, I noticed that the calf (baby) elephants were always anchored with a rope of similar length around their necks but tied to a large tree or telephone pole. They constantly struggled to get away. When I approached a handler about this, he asked me if I had ever heard that elephants 'never forget?' I told him that I did but I thought it meant that they always remembered how much they loved peanuts or salt (I wasn't a very bright child).

The handler explained to me that they never forget their futile struggles for freedom as calves. So when they are anchored to a small stake in the ground as adults, they don't bother to pull away because of the lesson of struggle they learned in their youth. I thought to myself, people are that way too.

So many of the adults that I knew on my paper route seemed to be stuck, in their thinking, to so much of what they experienced in their youth. In many ways, they appeared to have trouble moving fully into adulthood. They would talk about their lessons learned in their youth and apply that thinking into adult life.

For example, because they did not do well in a junior high school math class, they labeled themselves as 'bad in math' without ever revisiting the effort to master it later in life, when their brain had matured. I never understood that but I am sure that we are all guilty of that to some extent.

When we feel powerless, personally and collectively as a society, we begin to consider unhealthy ways of escaping what we perceive as an inevitably unfulfilling existence. We first, justify smoking as a way of reducing stress. Then we accept progressively larger doses of alcohol during non-working hours to unwind and position ourselves for proper social interaction.

When those feelings of powerlessness permeate our friendships, we turn to gossip, sarcasm and judgmental behaviors. When our love life is affected, we (guys) turn to various forms of pornography (videos, magazines, strip clubs, private clubs and so on.) In extreme cases, we consider hardcore street drugs or suicide.

All of the above-mentioned behaviors are extremely self damaging to our physical, emotional and mental health. Imagine that on one of our worst days, our car broke down and we had to walk home. While walking home, we notice a brown paper bag that appears to have been thrown sloppily into the brush on the side of the road. We check it out and find that it is stuffed with hundreds of thousands of unmarked bills of money.

For most of us, we would experience a sweeping change of attitude regarding our outlook for our lives. I don't see most of us inviting our friends to our home to get "falling-down drunk or high" with this bag of money in our midst. Consider, at this moment, the rush of energy we are feeling by just thinking about this possibility.

Simply the mention of better times ahead has changed our attitude about how we would handle our lives with just an infusion of a large quantity of cash. With this renewed perspective, it is important that we remember that the vast majority of issues, in our personal lives, center around our quality of life, personal comfort, appropriate companionship, a healthy self image and good health. We can do something about each of these right now.

We can free ourselves of the common disappointments that we experience everyday at home, in our workplaces, in our schools, in our places of worship and in our social establishments. We simply make a commitment to accept full responsibility for exercising the power of our natural freedom. Our power for freedom and positive change, in every area of our collective existence, lies within each of us.

Let's consider some common areas of discomfort in life and your freedom to improve upon them.

1) **Workplace** – A high pressure, tension-filled workplace breeds negativity, terrible attitudes and poor health among the employees. Employees tend to treat each other as badly as the employer's lower management is treating them collectively.

   There were many jobs that I have worked where I could count on one hand the number of coworkers that I found that I actually liked. One day, about twenty years ago, it occurred to me that I could be one more person, at my job, who I actually liked. I made it a rule to be kind to myself and, as often as I thought about it, extend such kindnesses to my coworkers. It worked!

   Eventually, the mentality of my workplace changed, in every way, for the better. It has worked everywhere I have tried it since. I am now used to working in positive, harmonious work environments where people work together and treat one another with respect.

   It begins with us as individuals making the change in ourselves. We have the natural freedom to do this. The few people that we like at our job have already made this decision. We can join them by making the decision to treat one another with the highest respect, compassion and importance.

   Without changing the quantity and quality of our work output, we can make every effort to be polite, courteous and considerate to as many people as we encounter in our work area. We can find ways to be helpful to the next person by positioning the work we pass on in the most convenient way to him or her.

Share the load with another coworker whenever you find yourself idle. You stay busy while helping a coworker through a busy period. We have the freedom to do this. It costs us nothing and we gain so much.

2) **Home** – A household were responsibilities are unequally divided can be a difficult place to enjoy. It simply does not matter who brings home the most money or the difficulty of each person's job, it is nice to get help with clearing and washing the dishes. If we are behind on the laundry, we always feel better when our mate or other family members, selflessly, pitch in to help.

No one wants to live in a home where the closet doors are off the tracks or hinges. No one desires to live in an environment that is ragged and poorly maintained. So organize, clean up, repair, landscape or whatever needs to be done so that we all can feel good about where we live. We can create countless projects to encourage togetherness, sharing and opportunities of "catch-up" conversation. We have such freedom at our disposal.

Children never understand that we are too tired to play with them, when we get home from work, so we might as well indulge them. The escape from reality that children can provide is always better than getting high or drunk. They stimulate our creative thinking abilities, encourage healthy exercise and will cause us to end up looking so silly, that our neighbors will have funny stories to tell about us for years to come.

When we get our second wind, we find ways to dazzle them even further. Remember, these are the people who will, one day, make a decision to take us in or drop-kick us into a nursing home! They will have such freedom at their disposal.

3) **Friendships** – We all want good, reliable friends who are loyal and ethical. Psychological research consistently reveals that most of us can only identify just a few people in our lives, of all of those we know, who truly fit this description.

We have the freedom to change this in our lives. It begins with each of us. As we are taught in sacred writings, if we want good friends, we must first be a good friend. If we want more good friends, we must be a good friend to more people.

Whatever qualities we desire in our circle of friends, we must cultivate those qualities in ourselves as friends. We must beware to think these qualities through as we may demand qualities that we may not honor when the positions, within a situation, are reversed.

For example, decide if we really want to be told, by our close friend, that our 'amazing' love interest is really interested in our close friend and not us. If we demand that level of honesty in our friendships, we must also be clear that there will be no repercussions for such revelations for anyone concerned.

The tone and quality of our friendships are entirely within our control. We have the freedom to extend our friendships to whomever we desire and the number of potential friendships that we choose to maintain is completely ours to decide.

If we are at a point in our lives that we are losing most of our friends through death, we must realize that we have the ability to create new friendships with younger people who may very well benefit from our years of experience and wisdom. Making new friends keeps us young and vibrant in every way.

4) **Mates** – Affairs of the heart can be complicated. Once we attract the loving relationship, with a companion who fits our desired criteria, we must decide on exactly how we will preserve and protect the relationship with that person. We must also establish the value of the relationship to us and set the limits of what we are willing to endure to hold on to that relationship.

Mutually, we have the freedom to establish rules on how to handle conflict, shared time, personal alone time within and outside of the residence, personal activities and shared activities and so forth. We can also decide on many other issues such as family planning, couples friendships, extended family involvement, dealing with undesirable family members, recreation, diet and health and so on.

How our personal love relationships develop and thrive is our decision, individually and as a couple. We do not have to tolerate lying, cheating, childish behavior and abuse under the guise of being in love. We have the freedom to demand, prepare for and expect the best for ourselves.

Once we realize that our mate choice is not so committed or fulfilled by the relationship that we might value highly, we have the freedom to downgrade or end the relationship accordingly. We have the freedom to make ourselves available for a more perfect relationship with a more suitable mate choice. We have the freedom to look forward in our lives without questioning if we should look back.

5) **Education** – We never have to be satisfied with our current level of knowledge and experience in life. We have the freedom to investigate, explore and add to our personal body of knowledge everyday of our lives.

We have the freedom to acquire new skills, develop new talents and cultivate latent abilities for which we seem to have a knack.

We have the freedom to learn from virtually everyone we encounter. We simply must maintain an awareness of the lesson(s) that person brings with him or her. Those lessons may not be taught directly by that person. The lesson may be something that we must observe in that person's ability to adapt, create or survive.

We have the freedom to open ourselves to learning from our past mistakes as well as our current experiences. Many of us find ourselves, repeatedly in the same situations over and over again. The names and places may change but the situations are the same. This is our fate when we choose not to learn from our experiences.

For example, we find ourselves in the same kinds of financial difficulties time and again; or, we find that our love relationships seem to turnout the same way, over and over. There are lessons that we have failed to notice and learn, in the past. We have the freedom to review these situations for our own educational enrichment.

6) **Mental** – One of the greatest freedoms that we neglect is our freedom to think for ourselves. We tend to believe, almost entirely, anything we learn from talk radio and television, television news programming, television commercials, movies and the like without any serious questioning at all.

The greatest gift we have, second to life itself, is the ability to use our mental faculty. With our mental faculty, we are able to use our imagination to create, fascinate and entertain ourselves endlessly. We can use our mental abilities to study, rationalize, discriminate, reason and research.

These abilities alone hold endless possibilities on what we can accomplish individually and collectively. So many of us seem to be relegated to allowing ourselves to be entertained by video games, repetitious puzzles and preprogrammed media sources instead of engaging in productive thinking activities.

Our thinking activities are what allow us to find solutions to issues that prevent us from reaching a better quality of life. When we engage our mental faculties, we create great stories, songs, poetry, art, crafts, inventions (from which we can profit quite richly) and much more.

There is literally no limit to what we are able to accomplish when we choose to think proactively every day. There are infinite ideas to be conceived. Most of these ideas can have a life altering effect on our situations. We will never experience them if we do not include free thinking as a daily activity. (Cooper, 1999) This can be accomplished in groups too. Anyone can start a thinking club.

7) **Emotional** – We have the freedom to choose our emotions. Dr. Candace Pert, Ph.D., has engaged in research that conclusively proved that our emotions are chemically based within our body. This simply means that chemical imbalances can drastically affect our emotions.

Anyone who has observed the dramatic mood swings of teenagers can readily see evidence of this. As they progress through puberty, they are dealing with wildly fluctuating hormone and adrenaline levels. Their moods can change from serious to playful and from panic to completely relaxed within the span of an hour.

This research is helpful to adults in understanding the popular expression that, 'happiness is a choice.' Of the many emotions that we can exhibit, we find that we can choose to be miserable and our body will serve up the chemical mixture to sustain that emotion.

We can choose to be optimistic and our body will respond with a chemical cocktail accordingly. Now think about all of the time we have spent engaged in negative thinking. Because energy follows thought, our body created chemical combinations to support where we were putting our thought energy. Optimistic people are emotionally infectious.

We tend to want them around when we are troubled because of their sunny disposition and optimistic outlook. These people are doing what we all can do. We can exercise our freedom to be happy, optimistic, and creative or whatever we would like for ourself and our body will produce the chemical combinations to sustain those emotions.

The consciousness of the world community would be positively transformed, if everyone were to participate, routinely, in generating only positive emotions while abandoning all fearful and negative emotions. By the way, fear and negativity do nothing to benefit our health and wellbeing at any level. Fear and negatively are completely destructive emotions when we choose to harbor them for more than a few moments at a time.

8) **Spiritual** – We have the freedom to exercise our spiritual nature any time we choose. This does not mean that we have to turn away from our family's religious faith and traditions. It does mean that we should take full advantage of the opportunities to learn about the divine powers that were infused within us from the time of our conception.

We are endowed by the Divine Source, of all life, with the power to connect, our entire being, to Eternal Life energy for the purpose of healing, creative mastery, high-level learning, intense loving, enhancing our natural beauty, correcting unhealthy habits, connecting with animals, plants, insects and all of nature.

We have a divine right to choose the life that we desire and to make positive and meaningful contributions to humanity while we are here, in this life, on Earth. Through our spiritual nature, all things are possible, all of the time. We simply need to spend the time to learn how to make the best use of our spiritual nature per the Eternal laws that govern its operation.

We position ourselves to connect with Divine energies through basic meditation techniques that progress from relaxation, to silence, to thoughtless awareness and finally to Divine connection. When we connect to the Divine Source, we receive a regular "tune-up" for our entire being that balances, heals and energizes us to operate at peak efficiency.

9) **Health** – Our total health and fitness is another area where we consistently neglect to exercise our freedom. We have the freedom to take care of our body, emotions, mentality and spiritual nature. We have the freedom to create unrestricted superior healthfulness. We have the freedom to choose healthy foods, lifestyles, exercises, recreation, social activities and friends.

We have the freedom to create safe environments for ourselves and our loved ones. We have the freedom to create comfortable environments within our homes and communities. We have the freedom to protect our earth home from destructive forces and influences that will eventually compromise the quality of our health.

10) **Self Expression** – We all have the freedom of personal, self expression to some extent. For example, we can dress ourselves, style our hair and adorn our bodies in ways that express our individuality. We should do this for a variety of reasons. Our freedom of expression begins and ends with us, however.

When our self expression is intentionally offensive and antagonizing to others, we are abusing our freedom of expression. Most of us have been to outdoor, family events where someone chooses to wear a t-shirt or jewelry that displays a humorous adult-themed or X-rated message. We often chuckle to ourselves, quietly until the child in our company says to us, 'I don't get it' while pointing to the source of the message.

When we are attending a concert, where only adults will be in attendance, we can be a bit more risqué with our choices in self expression. As people who have chosen to accept full responsibility for our lives, we have the responsibility of enhancing the quality of life around us. Exhibiting good character is a priority for us now. This includes making responsible contributions to the development of those around us, including children.

11) Society – We have the freedom to be an asset within our local society. This does not mean that we should not live as we desire. It does mean that we do not have to be "useless consumers." For example, if we are going to panhandle, we must be willing to honor our donors with an uplifting song, prayer or, at least, genuine good wishes.

Most of us understand that economic fluctuations eventually affect everyone. Some of us subsist closer to the bottom of the economic strata than others. Sometimes, we must ask for support from others to continue to live. We never have to lose our self respect to do so. That is entirely our choice.

Those people, in every society, who will help us to maintain our dignity and self respect, far outnumber those who have no concern about us at all. So we can look for opportunities and take advantage of opportunities to demonstrate our value in many important ways.

The first and easiest way is through genuine acts of kindness. We can become an angel for someone who is burdened with substandard health. We can do things like inform a bus driver that someone who cannot run is trying to board the bus but will require an extra minute to finish the journey. While that person is making his or her way to the bus, we can engage the driver in light, stimulating conversation just to pass the moments.

When we notice visitors in our city, who appear to be lost, we can offer directions or to physically lead them to their destination, if they are walking. In this way, we make ourselves ambassadors for our city or town. Our, previously, lost visitors will have positive comments to share with future visitors to our locality. With one act of kindness, we enrich the public image of the place where we live.

When we are proactive in our thinking, we can find a multiplicity of ways to help others. This will ultimately help us, as many experienced visitors often show their gratitude for our kindness in the form of a cash tip, although, the money should not be our motivation for helping others in need.

We can offer recommendations to those who are looking for a place to dine or seeking local entertainment for their families. We can lead lost visitors, who do not speak our language well, to local police for special assistance.

We can also actively engage ourselves as a volunteer in places that serve the poor and undervalued people in our society. If we are also partaking in the benefits of such organizations, we can also donate some of our time as a way of showing our personal appreciation for the assistance that the organization provides to us.

If we are receiving any kind of state or federal assistance for such circumstances as disability, unemployment, incompetence or anything else, we can still volunteer at our local schools as a tutor, teacher assistant, recess monitor, community representative or mentor. Schools always need extra help. If we do not have a documented history of being a threat to minors, this is a wonderful way to exercise our freedom to be an asset to our local society.

This is just a small list of the natural freedoms that we can exercise that will make important differences in the quality of our lives and in the lives of those with whom we are closest. When we exercise these freedoms, we open ourselves to a great deal of personal fulfillment. We definitely enrich the quality of our community.

It is normal and natural for each of us to show, give and love freely. We were that way as toddlers. As we learned about the world, we were eager to share what we learned with anyone we encountered. We loved pointing out the new, the different, the amazing and the shocking things that attracted our attention.

We loved to give and share. In addition to showing what we discovered to those in our world. We enjoyed sharing our most precious toys and other possessions. When we were around a fussy and crying infant, we would rush to bring the baby our favorite toy, blanket or stuffed animal that always made us feel better. We would even do this with our older siblings and parents.

At our most innocent stage, we are always open to giving a loving hug to someone who wasn't feeling at their best. We would give pats on the back, reassurances that everything would be 'all right,' and hugs as we decided that it might help. Being a showing, giving and loving person is our natural state of being. This is the truth of who we are inside right now.

These qualities, that are associated with our natural state of being, are susceptible to suppression as we have non-supportive experiences in our growth. We may be introduced to other ways of dealing with misfortunes that befall us in life, by our family, friends, teachers and other community members. We might have been taught that "we play through the pain" or that, "tears are a sign of weakness." We must forgive those who force these transgressions upon us.

We can never go wrong when we decide to be true to ourselves; that is to do what we feel is right for us. We are happy and fulfilled people when we are this way. Even those who are tempted to bully or make fun of us are only paying attention to us because they want to learn from us. They want, desperately, to be free, to be true to themselves, too.

Chapter 15

"The Devil Made Me Do It!"
— Clerow "Flip" Wilson, Jr

The Satan Experiment

I was not reared in a church. My mother was forced, as a child, to endure the dogma and ceremonial rigors of an extremely charismatic religious organization. Church was an all-day event on Sunday. She was forced to learn and play the piano so that she could entertain church members who might visit the family's home throughout the week. Her religious issues notwithstanding, she enjoyed an otherwise typical childhood for a family of her background. She enjoyed the love of her family, friends at school. She did chores in the home and engaged community activities.

I was the first born and my parents made a decision that good character, a solid education, a strong work ethic and broad life exposures would be the cornerstones of my rearing. I was not a very bright child so the area of education was a struggle for me for most of my pre-adult years.

As individuals, we tend to acquire our learning primarily through visual, auditory or kinesthetic (physical touch and handling) sensations. To compensate for my lack of intelligence, I, naturally, developed a multi-sensory (a blend of all three styles) learning style. Regardless of the subject matter, I had to see it, hear it and touch it, to learn it properly.

In the area of religion, neither of my parents were convinced that, what was being preached from the pulpit of the church, was entirely accurate, based on their brief exposure to adult life. For example, I discovered long ago, that few teenagers believe that 'honesty is always the best policy.' If they actually practiced that, the majority of them would be grounded most of the time.

Class grade point averages would drop significantly. Parents would never be surprised by calls from authorities to pick up their child from the school, police stations, clinics and hospitals. Parents would be able to predict, quite accurately, their child's life-altering setbacks resulting from self-damaging activities. My parents were no different in their thinking.

Because my parents weren't sure which direction they should pursue, regarding my religious education, they decided to allow me to make up my mind when I was mature enough to express such an opinion and they would comply. They kept their word and their support.

They really did not want me to experience the frustration and mistrust about religion, in general, that each of them had experienced. They trusted that wherever,

I ultimately chose to place my faith and spiritual energy, it would be in a positive and productive way, if they provided the correct moral foundation.

My religious journey started when I got my driver's license as a teenager. There was a rumor circulating that if guys went to church, we could find girls! So, I went to my [paternal] grandmother's church and sure enough, there were girls there. They were gorgeous and they were my age – Hallelujah!

I joined and had a great time making friends, enjoying new experiences and learning about God, Satan, Heaven, Hell, Good, Evil, Love and Hate. I was given a 'Holy Bible' and I was instructed, frequently, by the church leadership to "read my Bible." I did just that. I actually read each page, from cover to cover. I wasn't a very bright teenager, either.

In reading my bible, I was happy to learn that it was the home of so many of the clichés and wise sayings that I had always heard while growing up. I was happy to learn the origin of the world and life as we were experiencing it. I was thrilled that I could actually find and read the "Ten Commandments" first hand.

I was impressed with learning about all of the obscure figures and their contributions to the world of religious understanding. I marveled at the stories of Moses, Joshua, Daniel, Nebuchadnezzar, and Isaiah, Kings David and Solomon, Jesus and his disciples and so on. It was my belief, for a while, that every answer that anyone could ever need, could be found in the Holy Bible.

I read my Bible again a year later to solidify my understanding of the scriptures. Since, I was already familiar with the material, I expected my reading to be a pleasurable review. It was not. I missed a great deal during my first reading. I noted many curiosities and inconsistencies that I simply did not understand. I could not find the answers that I sought by cross referencing the pages either.

For example, I did not understand why our prayers had to end with the word or name, "Amen." I found no clear reason for it anywhere. Also, I did not understand why God was so vengeful, angry, vindictive and insecure in the Old Testament yet to so kind, loving and forgiving in the New Testament.

There was no mention of animal or human sacrifice whatsoever in the New Testament, yet in the Old Testament God was constantly demanding that we sacrifice an animal, food or a child. Yet, it was clearly stated in the scriptures, "I am the Lord your God, I change not." Malachi 3:6 (Holy Bible: King James Version, 1979)

I stated earlier that I was not a very bright child or teenager. As it turned out, I haven't been a particularly bright adult either. Like everyone else, I have made mistakes, had misunderstandings and taken several wrong turns in life. Though, my intentions have usually been honorable, I still found myself, consistently, in situations, predicaments and drama that I would not wish on anyone, for any reason.

At some points in my life, I honestly believed that there were forces working against me that I could not overcome. Because of the nature of some of the circumstances, I was convinced that no physical person had the influence to create the silly and stupid scenarios in which I found myself. No one else could possibly benefit from my going through such madness. I opened myself to the possibility that Satan, the infamous, fabled devil in the Holy Bible, was wreaking havoc in my life.

My Search for Religious and Spiritual Truth

I investigated these phenomena in my life for many years. I studied with every Christian denomination that I could find. I studied with the Seventh Day Adventists, who added to my knowledge regarding the importance of diet to our health and educational excellence. I studied with the Jehovah's Witnesses, who turned out to be some very nice people, who taught me a respect for life, creation and the Earth that I found tremendously enlightening.

I studied, "The Urantia Book" and learned about the angelic and celestial hierarchy and how they are charged with serving all living creatures, including mankind, spiritually. I studied ancient and eastern sacred writings like the Kybalion, Kabbalah, The Bhagavad-Gita, The Science of Mind, The Metu Neter, and The Egyptian Book of the Dead: The Coming by Day and By Night.

I was still not satisfied with the sketchy information that I was uncovering regarding Satan, Hell, Evil and Hate so I decided to go directly to the source, despite warnings from religious leaders that I would be adversely affected by such peering. In my childhood, I was extremely trusting and quite gullible. I fell for tricks, rumors and stories that the other children told me. After so much of that treatment, I became the kind of person who investigated everything anyone told me before I formed an opinion.

I grew up as a fan of the movie, "The Wizard of Oz." I loved that the frightful Wizard was eventually exposed as a fraud. That is the mentality that drove my search to understand the above-mentioned concepts. My life was constantly in turmoil so I had no fear of things ever getting any worse and they never did.

I studied books on Witchcraft and Witches and learned that they prefer the terms Wicca and Wiccans, respectively. I found that they practice "White Magic" and "Black Magic." I learned that White Magic was spell casting using the various Earth energies to help others, whether that person was aware or not. Black Magic was the ole, "Let's turn Bob into a dung beetle because he broke my heart" kind of spell casting, using the same Earth energies. That is why the Wiccans need hair, clothing and animal tissue samples. Each of those contain energy unique to the person in question.

I studied esoteric psychic sciences to gain a formal understanding of such subjects as astral projection, mental telepathy, extra-sensory perception (ESP), divination, zodiac, runes, numerology, the tarot, quantum travel, and so on. All of these subjects were extremely interesting, fascinating and sometimes very complex.

All were important and valuable in the context of their intended, respective purposes. I still did not have the definitive answers that I originally sought. I decided to go back to where I started in light of what I had discovered to see if I could connect any of the information. To my surprise, I did.

My father had to work a great deal while my brother and I were still children. On nights when he could not be home, we were on our mother's bed watching television until we were sent to our own beds. My mother was fond of the "Billy Graham" Crusades. We watched them often.

One evening, Graham answered a question rather brilliantly, I thought. He said that he was asked "What is Hell?" by someone who did not want to hear about scenarios involving afterlife images of torture chambers supervised by Satan, the devil. This is the answer that I heard and remembered: He said, 'Hell is complete and total separation from anything to do with God and His love.'

If a relationship with God is complete joy, harmony and fulfillment in every area of our lives, then, it stands to reason that total separation, from God, would bring the opposite quality of life. That made sense to me. It also made sense to me that if we were not aligned with the laws that govern all of life – God's laws, we would experience the effect of someone or an unseen force working against us; like swimming upstream against the current of a downward-flowing river.

I was told by many religious leaders with whom I have talked that God is indefinable in human terms and that the only way we could truly learn about God is not through the scriptures but through 'personal' experience. This also made sense to me. Metaphysical experiences are usually subjectively described. Even when two people encounter the same kind of experience, like near death or out-of-body, their accounts are never identical.

It occurred to me that, the only way, any of us, can say that we know one another, or anyone else, is through personal experience. Surely, this had to be the case with Satan, the devil. Every account that I ever heard about was an individualized account. In the autumn of 2006, I decided to devise an experiment that would deliver an answer to me, conclusively.

I have never been in a hurry to make friends with, or get involved with, anyone who was intent on doing any harm to me. This applies especially if it concerns someone who is more powerful and influential than I thought myself to be. If there is a devil named Satan, I definitely do not want to get to know him and have him cause further damage and confusion in my life.

Since my life was perpetually chaotic, confusing and unpredictable. I decided to create an experiment that would alleviate that. That way, I could note when satanic influences appeared in my life. Further, I would also note the form and manifestation of these activities. I also wanted my experiment to run for an extended, defined period that I could compare to previous periods, in my life, to compare differences.

My Search For Satan: The Experiment

Here is my experiment. I decided to arrange and order my life so conservatively that I would remove myself from any chance of brushes with danger, drama or conflict. I was careful about where I went (and what time), with whom I kept company (and for how long), activities in which I chose to engage and so on. It should have been a really boring year for me but it was not.

I set certain guidelines that I was sure would insure that I had as bland an existence as possible, for that year. I was ready to perceive the satanic influences immediately whenever they surfaced. Here are my guidelines that I decided to follow regarding my experiment:

1) It should last for a period of one year (365 days)
2) I would not make any decisions based on fear of an outcome
3) I decided to accept responsibility for every decision I made, right or wrong
4) I would not be neither afraid nor intimidated by neither people nor circumstances or feel compelled to make any decisions that are not in my best interest.
5) I would follow some basic Eternal laws that I uncovered in my "search for spiritual truth:"
   A) **The Law of Attraction** – We attract to us and become what we think about the most.
   B) **The Law of Cause and Effect** – When we change the cause we change the effect.
   C) **The Law of Harmony** – Go with the flow whether we understand why or not.
   D) **The Law of Karma** – Give good, receive good. Give bad, receive bad.
   E) **The Law of Wisdom** – Pay attention and make informed decisions based on what we learn.
   F) **The Law of Love** – Our motivations for everything we do should be based from love. (Holliwell, 2005)
6) I would not change what I truly wanted on any day just to avoid a satanic encounter
7) I would not change my priorities in my life
8) I would disregard all thoughts of Satan, Hell, Evil and Hate in every form where I had control
9) I would be ready to take notes regarding any satanic intervention by keeping a pen and notepad handy at all times.

My experiment started in the fall of the year. Many good things happened. Many unpleasant things happened. I made new friends and I lost some friends to misunderstandings and death. I discovered new communities of people who were spiritually curious like I was and I found some communities that were not a good fit for me.

Some people were very kind to me and some people were very mean to me. I gained some weight and I lost some weight. I felt a little under the weather during the change of seasons and I felt great the rest of the time. At the store, I overpaid for some items and I found really low prices sometimes on things that I wanted. I learned many new things and I forgot many things. I was lonely and unfulfilled sometimes and at other times I was content. Sometimes my life was quiet; other times, it was filled with drama, conflict, misunderstandings and mistakes (lots of them).

In evaluating my issues, I decided to focus my attention on the very unpleasant and troublesome situations that I encountered each week. I wanted to see if I could identify evidence of satanic intervention, conclusively, in my life. I took special note of personal conflicts at work and in my social life.

I also watched, very closely, those situations, where I found myself in a position of disadvantage with others. Finally, I wanted to see how many situations that I found myself at the center of, that had nothing to do with my efforts.

My life that year had exactly the same pattern as it did in previous years. It was filled with chaos, misunderstandings, mistakes and wrong turns. As I analyzed each situation, I decided to be as honest as I could about my role in bringing any of the situations about that I did not like. After all, I had been living like this for several years.

Continuously, I seemed to get the opposite of everything that I wanted. It was extremely frustrating to me. For years, I was not and had not been making any progress, material or otherwise, in my life. I was simply logging negative experiences. None of them were adding any value to my life, in any way that I could identify or measure.

To my surprise, as I examined each situation, I found that I did, in fact, play a significant role in every situation, pleasant and unpleasant where I found myself. I could not believe how many times when I intervened in someone else's life in an attempt to rescue them from a challenging situation.

At other times, my communication was an issue. I either said something or implied something about myself or about my ability to influence a certain favorable outcome for them. I didn't really understand why I would do that when my life was such a mess.

Last, when I did not say or do anything to influence the development of a negative situation, I realized that my attitude, mentality and emotions were often negatively focused for vengeance, provocation and intimidation. For example, my employer leadership became corrupt, incompetent and devoid of integrity. The would routinely bark to the employees, "If you don't like how things are run here, go find a job somewhere else." Instead of rising above the workplace dysfunction, by choosing to be responsible for my own life, I chose to compete for superior influence within the workplace.

So far, there was no sign of Satan; just me being obnoxious and divisive. It was at that point that I realized that I was not practicing good character as I was reared to do, honoring the eternal laws that I committed to follow nor minding my own business, as I should. After some serious self examination, I was forced to release myself of responsibility for the synergistic operation of my workplace to those who were employed to manage it.

I began to consider that, perhaps, I was my own worst enemy; that maybe I should look within myself before I pass blame for my life situations off onto someone who I really cannot prove is interfering with my life. I decided to correct my random and convenient deviations from practicing good character. I made a more rigid effort to honor the eternal laws that I promised myself that I would follow.

In addition, I decided to mind my own business. No matter, what I witnessed from anyone, I decided not to get involved unless I was specifically asked to do so. If I did choose to get involved, after being asked, I imposed rigid conditions and boundaries that guaranteed that I would not be overly involved or taxed by the situation.

For example, no matter what issue someone would bring to my attention concerning their situation, my first question was always, "Well, what are you going to do about it?" Their answer would communicate to me the seriousness with which they took the matter. Whatever level I was petitioned to be involved came with conditions that had to be met before I committed my time, energy or resources.

After I made these adjustments in my own life, something did happen that I did not expect. The drama, conflicts, misunderstandings, mistakes and stupidity all vanished. There has been no repeat of any of these negative situations. My stress level dropped dramatically.

I found that the quality of my relationships with everyone became enriched. I found that my finances were more easily managed. New opportunities to learn and grow seemed to appear out of nowhere. My social life improved significantly. In short, every area of my life seemed to improve. It was as though I had "fallen in love" except this was not a temporary phenomena, it became my normal life.

Though my life had improved to a level where I was deeply satisfied, there was still the question of Satan's intervention into my life. In light of my discoveries about my behavior, communication, attitude and decision making, I could not prove that there was or had ever been any satanic intervention into my life.

Every issue, that I could identify, even in my childhood, I could trace to an action, decision or behavior that I had chosen or was taught to choose. We can only respond to any situation based on the information that we have at the time. Sometimes, that information is flawed or incomplete. It is our responsibility to find the truth, wherever it is.

After more years of study, I found the following: a) According to John Randolph Price of The Quartus Foundation, the word "Hell" was never a part of the original Holy Bible scriptures. Further, when it was added, it never referred to a place of eternal damnation. (Price, The SuperBeings, 1981) b) There are only two primary emotions that influence the mental states that guide our motivations, behaviors, decision making and actions – Love and Fear.

Love guides our positive and productive progress in life. Fear is the basis for the negative, destructive, selfish, judgmental, blaming, drama-filled lives that many of us live each day. (Henry Grayson, 2003) c) Energy follows our thoughts. If we are taught to fear something or someone, our concentrated energy gives it life and power. (Hay, You Can Heal Your Life, 1989)

Consider how a child, who is taught that there is a "Boogie Man" who will terrorize him or her for misbehaving, will give life and power to this imaginative character. Without ever seeing a picture of him, a child will expend tremendous energy thinking about him, to the extent that the Boogie Man will eventually have life and a great deal of baseless power and influence over the child.

He will live under the bed, in a closet or outside of the window and only at night. The child will live in constant fear of this creation because the parents choose to delegate their responsibility for teaching their child, through loving means, correct and acceptable behavior. Adults exhibit the same mentality when it comes to such colossal creations as Santa Claus, the Tooth Fairy and the Easter Bunny.

There is nothing wrong with enhancing a child's world with fantasy but most adults refuse to teach their young children, upon introduction of these cultural creations, that none of these persons actually exist. Lies are seeds of separation planted in the fertile soil of a child's mind. Those lies have an interesting way of growing through the perceptions of our offspring as they progress through their youth and throughout their adulthood.

Notice the level of separation that teens exhibit when, only a few years earlier, they had to find out from their friends in elementary school, that there is no Santa Claus, Easter Bunny and Tooth Fairy. They were not able to depend on their parents to tell them the truth. Is there any wonder that they trust their friends more than their parents, as teens?

Parents who continue to widen this divide through misinformation and manipulation of their children's mate choices, sexual aspirations, career choices, social choices often find ever-growing, extended periods of separation with their offspring well into adulthood. This separation will manifest itself in extended absences, minimal communication, apathy in family matters, guarded interaction with grandchildren and delegation of obligations regarding life-altering, family decisions.

Regardless of the satanic intervention in our lives, it is still our responsibility to hold ourselves to the absolute highest standards of good character and respect for the laws of life, at every level of existence. As people, there are a great number of things that we can accomplish when we work in concert with one another and respect one another. This becomes considerably easier to do when we choose to accept responsibility for every area of our lives and follow all of the laws that are intended for our overall wellbeing, from family laws to Eternal laws. (Cottrell, 1979)

My Satan Experiment results brought my attention to one other experience that we commonly share; that of "Evil." In movies, music, novels, operas and theater, we collectively enjoy the thrill of experiencing evil through the story's characters. We love the influence of evil in comedies, horror, mysteries and dramatic storylines. In the arena of entertainment, evil is a staple of human culture.

The issues develop when those, of us, who decide to forgo our responsible development and maturity as adults, choose to romance and glamorize the qualities of evil in real life. This is a problem because we do not truly understand evil at its core.

Evil is destruction. It is complete annihilation at every level where it is found. From what is stated in the Holy Bible, Satan is synonymous with evil. If that is so, then evil will destroy everything around it, including Satan. Once it has destroyed everything that can be destroyed, by its very definition, it must turn on itself.

Should this happen, there would eventually be no evil, according to Eternal Law, because of its very nature to separate from life as we understand it. If the entertainment industry were to internalize this understanding, we would have a lot of extremely short books and movie productions.

In the end, through my personal experience, I was never able to neither confirm nor deny the existence of Satan. Through an epiphany, I was able to confirm that I could never deny my ability to get in my own way when I set out to reach any goal that I set. From the day of this epiphany, I decided that I need to keep an eye on the person between my ears, who drives the vessel that I inhabit.

I recommend to anyone, reading this work, to try the Satan Experiment. Do it as an individual or as a group for a project in school, place of worship or as part of an experiment of your choosing. Because of it, I have a profound respect for the words that appear at the entrance of so many ancient mystery schools in history – "Know Thy Self."

In conclusion, we each must keep in mind that all responsibility, for our lives, ultimately resides with us, regardless if we choose to accept it. When someone approaches us for recruitment into organizations that support or encourage us to do physical, emotional, mental, social, moral, economic or public damage or harm to innocent people in support of a political, religious or business agenda, it is our responsibility to be true to ourselves.

If being true to ourselves compels us to support such organizations, then it is our responsibility to weigh the consequences of our personal support and involvement. We must be completely accountable for our part of the damage and dysfunction that we have created for others and ourselves. We must be willing to face the public scrutiny, legal consequences and damage done to our personal image and reputation as well as that of our family.

We always have the choice to do what is right, honorable and uplifting for all people concerned. When we choose to ignore the positive and productive choice, we are opening ourselves up to scandal, public ridicule and permanent disgrace. We are also, unfairly, condemning our loved ones to a legacy of suspicion, judgment and prejudice.

When we allow others to convince us that it is right to harm others, in any way, for Divine, religious or business reasons, it is our responsibility to face the truth: If God truly wills anything to be, anywhere in the universe, God never requires munitions and people bent on hate to do destructive acts on any Divine creation.

Every culture on Earth has established, for centuries that God is all powerful, infinitely loving and ever extending Itself through creation. In short, base on Its own Laws, God can do no harm to Its own creation. By extension, any harm or damage that any of us do to anyone, at anytime and for any reason does not serve a Godly purpose.

Accepting responsibility for our lives means that we cannot use excuses that we were tricked, conned or manipulated into doing bad things. We know right from wrong. When we do not, it is our responsibility to spend the required time researching and investigating those unknown or uncertain matters in our lives until we have the information that we need to answer any questions that we have about those concerns.

We are accountable in every way for our lives. We are accountable for everything we do when we choose to get 'high' or drunk. We are accountable for everything that happens to us when we willfully deprive ourselves of proper rest, nutritious food and adequate exercise. We are accountable for what happens to us for not gaining proper knowledge for our everyday living and caring for loved ones.

We are accountable and responsible for verifying any information that we receive regarding foods, medications, household cleaning products and environmental toxins that might be a threat to our health and that of our children. We are accountable and responsible to investigate, thoroughly, any invitations we receive to be a part of business schemes, civic organizations, political or religious organizations that make demands upon us that we know, in our hearts, are wrong and discriminatory against other people, regardless of who they might be.

For example, when someone uses 'allegiance to God' to justify killing, murder or bringing harm against anyone, in any way, they are not being truthful with us and it is our responsibility to expose anyone with this intent, publicly. It is just as absurd to recruit people to make the sun shine or to cause the wind to blow. Whenever God requires the fulfillment of any purpose, it will be done independent of human participation. Should anyone attempt to convince us otherwise, rest assured that it is not really about God at all.

The ways to honor God, if anyone so desires, is to share, genuinely and freely, love, information, happiness and truth that permits each person to have complete independence in fulfilling his or her own destiny in life. In service, we can help those who demonstrate that they are helping themselves and be compassionate and generous to those who are in need of comfort and assistance.

In this way, we do not violate anyone's freedom or privileges, in life. We are still good neighbors and citizens of the community who are blameless when others make choices that create serious issues in their own lives. Further, we are true to ourselves and we are living positive and productive lives for which we accept full responsibility.

Citations

Aitken, S. (2007, December 06). Is the Standard American Diet (SAD) Bad for Your Health? *Natural News.com* , p. 1.
Albrecht, M. C. (1982). *Reincarnation: A Christian Critique of a New Age Doctrine.* Downers Grove: InterVarsity Press.
Ambrose, K. (2007). *9 Life Altering Lessons: Secrets of the Mystery Schools Unveiled.* Foresthill: Reality Press.
Amy Jamieson-Petonic, M. R. (1995). *Avoiding Dehydration, Proper Hydration.* Cleveland: The Cleveland Clinic Foundation.
Anderson, G. (1995). *The 22 {Non-Negotiable} Laws of Wellness: Feel, Think, and Live Better Than You Ever Thought Possible.* New York: Harper Collins Publishing.
Anderson, M. (2008). *Healing Cancer: From Inside Out.* RaveDiet.com.
Andrews, T. (1993). *The Healer's Manual.* St. Paul: Llewellyn Publications.
Ann-Williams-Heller. (1990). *Kabbalah: Your Path To Inner Freedom.* Wheaton: Quest Books.
Armstrong, T. (1993). *7 Kinds of Smart: Identifying and Developing Your Many Intelligences.* New York: Penguin Books.
Associated Press (Washington). (1974). *Energy Crisis: Is It Real or Not?* Madison: Wisconsin State Journal.
Ausubel, K. (Director). (1987). *Hoxsey: How Healing Becomes A Crime (DVD Documentary about a Successful Cancer Cure)* [Motion Picture].
Barbara De Angelis, P. (1999). *Passion.* New York: Dell.
Barbara De Angelis, P. (1991). *Secrets About Men Every Woman Should Know.* New York: Dell.
Barbara De Angelis, P. (2001). *What Women Want Men To Know.* New York: Hyperion.
Barty, B. (Director). (2008). *Spirit Space (DVD) Documentary: A Journey Into Your Consciousness* [Motion Picture].
Berg, Y. (2001). *The Power of Kabbalah.* San Diego: Jodere Group, Inc.
Berry, D. L. (1997). *Internal Cleansing.* Roseville: Prima Publishing.
Bradley, M. (1978). *The Iceman Inheritance: Prehistoric Sources of Western Man's Racism, Sexism and Aggression.* New York: Kayode Publications LTD.
Bristol, C. M. (1948). *The Magic of Believing.* New York: Pocket Books.
Brown, W. S. (1985). *13 Fatal Errors Managers Make And How To Avoid Them.* Old Tappan: Fleming H. Revell/Berkley.
Bruce, R. (2007). *Energy Work: The Secret of Healing and Spiritual Development.* Charlottesville: Hampton Roads Publishing, Inc.
Cameron, I. A. (Director). (2010). *Leap! (DVD) Theoretical Interviews: Let Your Adventure Begin* [Motion Picture].
Candace B. Pert, P. (1997). *Molecules Of Emotion: The Science Behind Mind-Body Medicine .* New York: Simon & Schuster, Inc.
Carmen Herra, P. (2009). *The Eleven Eternal Principles: Accessing the Divine Within.* New York: Crossing Press.

Carolyn Miller, P. (1995). *Creating Miracles: Understanding the Experience of Divine Intervention*. Tiburon: H.J. Kramer, Inc.
Christie-Murray, D. (1981). *Reincarnation: Ancient Beliefs and Modern Evidence*. Bridport: Prism Press.
Christy, M. M. (1994). *Your Own Perfect Medicine: The Incredible Proven Natural Miracle Cure That Medical Science Has Neve Revealed!* Mesa: Wishland Publishing.
Cicero, C. C. (2004). *The Essential Golden Dawn: An Introduction to High Magic*. St. Paul: Llewellyn Publications.
Clason, G. S. (1926). *The Richest Man In Babylon*. New York: New American Library.
Clow, B. H. (2004). *Alchemy of Nine Dimensions: Decoding the Vertical Axis, Crop Circles and the Mayan Calendar*. Charlottesville: Hampton Roads Publishing Company.
Conze, E. (1951). *Buddhism: its essence and development*. Oxford: Bruno Cassirer Limited.
Cooper, P. (1999). *Secrets of Creative Visualization*. Boston: Red Wheel/Weiser,LLC.
Cottrell, J. (1979). *His Way*. Cincinnati: Standard Publishing Company.
Cunningham, S. (1985). *Cunningham's Encyclopedia of Magical Herbs*. St. Paul: Llewellyn Publications.
Cunningham, S. (1997). *Wicca: A Guide For The Solitary Practitioner*. St. Paul: Llewellyn Publications.
Dale, C. (2009). *The Subtle Body: An Encyclopedia of Your Energetic Anatomy*. Boulder: Sounds True.
David J. Schwartz, P. (1959). *The Magic of Thinking Big*. New York: Fireside/Simon & Schuster.
Deanna M. Minich, P. C. (2009). *Chakra Foods for Optimum Health*. San Francisco: Conari Press.
Deborah Tannen, P. (1990). *You Just Don't Understand: Women and Men in Conversation*. New York: Ballatine Books.
Desai, M. (2004). *Miracles of Urine Therapy: A Practical Guide To Auto-Urine Therapy For Every Man, Woman and Child*. New Delhi: Pankaj Publications.
Doreen Virtue, P. (2000). *Divine Prescriptions: Using Your Sixth Sense - Spiritual Solutions for You and Your Loved Ones*. New York: St. Martin's Press.
Dr. Earnest Holmes, P. (1938). *The Science of Mind*. New York: R.M. Mc Bride and Company.
Dr. Joel Fuhrman, M. (2008). *Eat for Health*. New York: St. Martin's Press.
Dyer, D. W. (2009). *Excuses Begone!:How to Change Lifelong, Self-Defeating Thinking Habits*. Carlsbad: Hay House, Inc.
Eker, T. H. (2005). *Secrets of the Millionaire Mind: Mastering the Inner Game of Wealth*. New York: Harper Collins Publishing.
Elaine Weiss, E. (2000). *Surviving Domestic Violence: Voices of Women Who Broke Free*. Salt Lake City: Agreka Books.
Esser, P. D. (1990). *Chi Gong: The Ancient Chinese Way To Health*. New York: Marlowe & Company.
Extreme Nutrition Ltd. (2009). *Understanding the Importance of Hydration*. Wooton Bassett: Extreme Nutrition.

Fersen, B. E. (1923). *The Science of Being.* New York: J. F. Tapley Company.
Fox, L. (Director). (2009). *The Story of Stuff* [Motion Picture].
Fromm, E. (1956). *The Art of Loving.* New York: Harper Collins Publishers, Inc.
Gawain, S. (1978). *Creative Visualization: Use the power of your imagination to create what you want in your life.* San Rafael: New World Library.
Gimbel, T. (1994). *Healing With Color and Light: Improve Your Mental, Physical and Spiritual Health.* New York: Simon & Schuster.
Gina Kemp, M. L. (2011). *The Smart and Safe Use of Vitamins and Supplements.* Santa Monica: Help Guide.org.
Giuliani, R. W. (2002). *Leadership.* New York: Miramax Books.
González-Wippler, M. (2004). *Keys To The Kingdom: Jesus & The Mystic Kabbalah.* St. Paul: Llewellyn Publications.
Griscom, C. (1991). *Feminine Fusion: The Power To Transform Strength With Sensitivity, Logic With Intuition, and Sexuality With Sprituality.* New York: Simon & Schuster.
Halevi, Z. B. (1976). *The Way of Kabbalah.* York Beach: Samuel Weiser, Inc.
Halsey, R. (Director). (1990). *Joe Versus The Volcano* [Motion Picture].
Hart, D. L. (1987). *The Winning Family: Increasing Self-Esteem In Your Children and Yourself.* Oakland: LifeSkills Press.
Hay, L. L. (1991). *The Power is Within You.* Carlsbad: Hay House, Inc.
Hay, L. L. (1989). *You Can Heal Your Life.* Carlsbad: Hay House, Inc.
Henry Grayson, P. (2003). *Mindful Loving: 10 Practices for Creating Deeper Connections.* New York: Gothem Books.
Hicks, E. a. (2006). *The Law of Attraction: The Basics of the Teachings of Abraham.* Carlsbad: Hay House, Inc.
Holliwell, R. (2005). *Working With The Law.* Camarillo: DeVorss & Company.
Holmes, E. (1948). *This Thing Called You.* New York: Jeremy P. Tarcher/ Penguin Books.
Holy Bible: King James Version. (1979). *Holy Bible.* Nashville: Thomas Nelson Publishers.
Hunt, V. V. (1989). *Infinite Mind: The Science of the Human Vibrations of Consciousness.* Malibu: Malibu Publishing Company.
James F. Balch, M. a. (1990). *Perscription for Nutritional Healing.* Garden City Park: Avery Publishing Group, Inc.
Joseph Murphy, D. P. (1972). *Miracle Power for Infinite Riches.* Paramus: Prentice-Hall.
Jude C. Williams, M. (1994). *Jude's Herbal Home Remedies.* St. Paul: Llewellyn Publishing.
Kaku, M. (1994). *Hyperspace: A Scientific Odyssey Through Parallel Universes, Time Warps and The 10th Dimension.* New York: Oxford University Press.
Kelly, E. (1997). *Spiritual Journey: How To Get Through The Day.* Yellow Springs: Cimarron Books.
Kelly, M. (2005). *The Seven Levels of Intimacy.* New York: Beacon Publishing.
Keltner, D. (2010). *Hands on Research: The Science of Touch.* Philadelphia: The Psychology of Wellbeing.
Kloss, J. (1972). *Back to Eden.* Twin Lakes: Lotus Press.
Korda, M. (1975). *Power: How To Get It, How To Use It.* New York: Ballantine Books.

Kremer, G. R. (1991). *George Washington Carver: In His Own Words*. Columbia: University of Missouri Press.
Leek, S. (1973). *Sybil Leek's Book of Herbs*. New York: Cornerstone Library.
Marciniak, B. (1992). *Bringers of the Dawn: Teachings from the Pleiadians*. Rochester: Bear & Company.
Marciniak, B. (1995). *Earth: Pleadian Keys to the Living Library*. Santa Fe: Bear & Company.
Marciniak, B. (2004). *Path of Empowerment: Pleiadian Wisdom For A World In Chaos*. Novato: New World Library.
Marilyn Mc Dirmit, D. (1990). *Reincarnation: A Biblical Doctrine: ...whose time has come for the Evangelical Church*. Maggie Valley: Eagle Publication Company.
Martin, R. (1995). *The Coming of Tan*. New Hope: Historicity Productions.
Massey, G. B. (Director). (2009). *The Living Matrix (DVD) Documentary: New Insights Into Our Bodies, Minds and Health* [Motion Picture].
McWhorter, J. H. (2000). *Losing The Race*. New York: The Free Press.
Merton, T. (2000). *Essential Writings*. Maryknoll: Orbis Books.
Michael Newton, P. (2004). *Journey of Souls: Case Studies of Between Lives*. St. Paul: Llewellyn Publications.
Murphy, J. (1965). *The Amazing Laws of Cosmic Mind Power*. West Nyack: Parker Publishing Company, Inc.
Murphy, J. (1963). *The Power of Your Subconscious Mind*. New York: Prentice Hall.
Newell, A. W. (2010, April 30). The Hazzards of Microwave Cooking. *Health-Science.com*, p. 1.
Packer, S. R. (1988). *Creating Money: Attracting Abundance*. Novato: H.J. Kramer Inc./ New World Library.
Paulson, G. L. (1991). *Kundalini and the Chakras: A Practical Manual*. St Paul: Llewellyn Publications.
Peirce, P. (2009). *Frequency: The Power of Personal Vibration*. New York: Atria Books.
Perkul, A. P. (Director). (2008). *Water (DVD) Documentary: The Great Mystery* [Motion Picture].
Pierce, T. H. (2009). *Outsmart Your Cancer: Alternative Non-Toxic Treatments That Work (Second Edition)With CD* . Stateline: Thoughtworks Publishing.
Powell, N. (2005). *Sahaja Yoga Meditation*. London: Corvalis Publishing.
Praagh, J. V. (1997). *Talking to Heaven: A Mediums Message of Life After Death*. New York: Dutton.
Prabhupāda, A. B. (1968). *The BHAGAVAD-GĪTĀ AS IT IS*. Los Angeles: The International Society for Krishna Consciousness.
Price, J. R. (1992). *Empowerment: You Can Do, Be, And Have All Things!* Carlsbad: Hay House, Inc.
Price, J. R. (2003). *Nothing Is Too Good To Be True*. Carlsbad: Hay House, Inc.
Price, J. R. (2000). *The Jesus Code*. Carlsbad: Hay House, Inc.
Price, J. R. (1981). *The SuperBeings*. New York: Ballantine Books.
Production, Z. Z. (Director). (2007). *The Rise and Fall of a Scientific Genius: The Forgotten Story of Royal Raymond Rife* [Motion Picture].

Reid, N. (2007). *5 Steps To A Quantum Life: How to Use the Astounding Secrets of Quantum Physics to Create the Life Your Want*. San Fransico: Winged Horse Publishing.
Robbins, T. (1986). *Unlimited Power*. New York: Ballantine Books.
Rusha, L. D. (2010). *The Secrets of Knowing: The Science of Intuition*. Boulder: JDP Corporation.
Scott, S. K. (2006). *The Richest Man Who Ever Lived: King Solomon's Secrets to Success, Wealth and Happiness*. New York: Doubleday.
Sereda, D. (Director). (2009). *Quantum Communication (DVD): Documentary* [Motion Picture].
Sherwood, K. (1988). *Chakra Therapy: For Personal Growth & Healing*. St. Paul: Llewellyn Publications.
Siegel-Maier, K. (2009). *Coming Clean - The Hidden Dangers in Common Soap*. El Segundo: Better Nutrition Magazine.
Smallstorm, S. (Director). (2007). *9/11 Mysteries Part 1: Demolitions (DVD Documentary of Facts Purposely Surpressed)* [Motion Picture].
Stone, R. B. (1976). *The Power of Miracle Metaphysics*. West Nyack: Parker Publishing Company, Inc.
The Urantia Foundation. (1955). *The Unrantia Book*. Chicago: Urantia Foundation.
Three Initiates. (1912). *The Kybalion: Hermetic Philosophy*. Chicago: The Yogi Publication Society.
Toy, A. D. (2009). *We Are Not Alone: A Complete Guide to Interdimensional Cooperation*. San Francisco: Red Wheel/Weiser Books.
Trudeau, K. (2004). *Natural Cures: "They" Don't Want You To Know About*. Elk Grove Village: Alliance Publishing Group.
Uth, R. (Director). (2007). *Tesla* [Motion Picture].
Waite, A. E. (1972). *The Book of Black Magic*. Boston: Red Wheel/Weiser, LLC.
Waitley, D. D. (1984). *The Psychology of Winning: Ten Qualities of a Total Winner*. New York: Berkley Publishing Group.
Wallce Sampson, M. a. (2000). *Science Meets Alternative Medicine: What the Evidence Says About Unconventional Treatments* . Amherst: Prometheus Books.
Ward, P. V. (2003). *Gods, Genes and Consciousness*. Charlottesville: Hampton Roads Publishing Company, Inc.
Wattles, W. D. (1976). *The Science of Getting Rich: Attracting Financial Success through Creative Thought*. Rochester: Destiny Books.
Weed, J. L. (1968). *Wisdom of the Mystic Masters*. New York: Reward Books.
Williams, J. R. (1988). *You Can't Afford The Luxury Of A Negative Thought: A Book for People with Any Life-Threatening Illness*. Los Angeles: Prelude Press.

Index

A

Abusers 150, 151
accept full responsibility 8
advertisers 9
after-school fights 60
Annie Leonard 125
annoying aches 64
Autointoxication 70

B

be my parents 58
Billy Graham 200

C

Caring 44
character . 1, 6, 8, 12, 27, 28, 30, 41, 42, 43, 45, 46, 47, 49, 51, 52, 54, 57, 58, 59, 61, 67, 94, 99, 100, 102, 115, 118, 120, 125, 127, 128, 138, 139, 143, 145, 147, 156, 157, 162, 164, 177, 186, 187, 194, 197, 203, 205
cheap-shot artists 56
children 8, 10, 16, 32, 35, 36, 37, 40, 44, 51, 52, 54, 58, 67, 68, 74, 80, 84, 85, 94, 95, 112, 113, 118, 119, 120, 122, 124, 128, 129, 130, 135, 143, 144, 145, 146, 147, 148, 151, 155, 163, 172, 175, 176, 177, 178, 179, 180, 181, 182, 190, 194, 204
Choices
  Negative .. 5, 6, 36, 38, 42, 43, 53, 54, 55, 59, 62, 96, 105, 111, 113, 114, 117, 120, 122, 127, 145, 156, 162, 194
Christina 3
Citizenship 44
cleaning lady 11
Coaching 31
Commitment 17
Counseling 31

D

Dharma 172, 173
Discipline
  Development . 17, 23, 43, 61, 67, 79, 87, 112, 114, 115, 138, 139, 140, 165, 177
Distractions 18
do not date 60
don't be discouraged 37

E

education 20, 23, 27, 29, 30, 31, 32, 34, 35, 37, 38, 40, 42, 43, 44, 50, 85, 96, 111, 112, 118, 130, 133, 138, 140, 144, 145, 146, 162, 164, 176, 187, 197
emotional attunement 78
Emotionally 67
Enablers 25
energy center .. 167, 168, 169, 170, 171
entitlement 16, 175, 176, 177, 178, 179, 180, 181, 182, 184, 185
Eternal consciousness 79
Eternal Intelligence 79, 82
Ethics 43
Examine the messages 46
experiment 32, 89, 200, 201, 205
Expert 47
expositions 25, 37

F

failure 148
Fairness 44
fear 27, 48, 52, 75, 78, 81, 121, 147, 148, 150, 151, 163, 193, 201, 204
Financial
  Emergency . 7, 14, 17, 30, 32, 33, 34, 48, 49, 50, 95, 96, 104, 108, 122, 123, 125, 134, 135, 138, 148, 175, 176, 178, 186, 187, 192
financial literacy 33
Foods

Processed 10, 20, 42, 48, 54, 67, 70, 71, 72, 87, 154, 172, 194
Formal Education 30
Functional Education 32

G

gamblers... 78
George Washington Carver.............. 80
Geronimo 94

H

Hambry 183
Health issues 54
Health Resource Bank...................... 89
High Nutrient Dense Diet................. 71
Holy Bible............... 198, 199, 204, 205

I

Impatience 16
influential people 42
Informal Education 30
Integrity 44
Internal Body Cleansing................... 70

J

Jeff Barrie 125
Jehovah's Witnesses 199

K

King Solomon.................................... 38

L

Lack of Discipline 17
Lack of exposure............................... 20
Life Experience 31
Lifestyle options 54
Lou Holtz... 114

M

mate......7, 17, 26, 30, 35, 50, 54, 55, 62, 68, 84, 95, 113, 118, 122, 128, 146, 147, 150, 151, 152, 156, 157, 158, 160, 162, 190, 191, 204

meditation .92, 166, 168, 170, 171, 194
Mentally.. 67
Mind is aware.................................... 79
Modern Toxins 70

N

Negative growth................................ 56
negative stress 87
new parents....................................... 57
News
  Sources........ 9, 10, 14, 18, 42, 50, 78, 113, 158, 192
nobody's-going-to-change-me 62
no-excuses... 12
Notice the timing 46

O

Ohio University 3
oil industry 45
our life..... 10, 11, 16, 17, 18, 19, 21, 22, 23, 24, 25, 27, 29, 30, 32, 34, 35, 36, 37, 38, 39, 40, 41, 42, 49, 54, 55, 57, 59, 60, 61, 62, 63, 66, 81, 83, 86, 89, 90, 95, 98, 99, 107, 110, 112, 124, 127, 128, 129, 130, 131, 132, 133, 134, 136, 137, 139, 140, 141, 151, 152, 156, 157, 158, 159, 161, 164, 173, 182
Our mentality 20
Our world 127
out-of-school conduct...................... 61

P

patriotism... 18
periodic contact with others 68
Poor Social Skills 21
Positive growth................................. 56
Positive stress 87
profane language 54
public image 61
public school teachers 23

Q

Quality of Execution........................ 18

Quality of Knowledge 17

R

Ralph Nader 45, 49
relationship 7, 17, 23, 30, 35, 36, 52, 54, 58, 74, 81, 109, 120, 124, 129, 138, 142, 143, 144, 146, 148, 149, 154, 155, 156, 157, 158, 160, 179, 183, 191, 200
religion 81, 161, 162, 186, 197
Reputation
 Good..7, 8, 12, 21, 22, 27, 44, 46, 47, 57, 61, 62, 100, 103, 108, 113, 120, 124, 129, 132, 138, 157, 184, 187
respect...6, 8, 24, 26, 27, 28, 29, 30, 31, 32, 37, 38, 40, 42, 51, 56, 57, 59, 60, 66, 68, 94, 95, 98, 108, 112, 113, 115, 118, 119, 120, 121, 122, 138, 142, 143, 144, 146, 148, 153, 154, 162, 167, 173, 175, 184, 189, 195, 199
Respectfulness 43
Responsibility 43
responsible behavior 54

S

Sahaja 166
Santa Claus 130, 204
Self-damaging
 Behavior .6, 7, 8, 35, 41, 85, 86, 105, 113, 161, 167, 197
self-damaging behavior 85
self-damaging choices 35
Self-education 32
Seventh Day Adventists 199
Sex Issues 54
solutions..10, 11, 14, 15, 18, 24, 25, 29, 32, 45, 82, 88, 89, 91, 92, 93, 98, 109, 125, 182, 192

sorry parents 56
spiritual .. 23, 64, 67, 81, 83, 86, 88, 89, 92, 124, 149, 161, 162, 164, 165, 168, 171, 193, 194, 198, 201
Spiritually 68
Spokesperson 46
Standard American Diet 71
Steve 117
Stress 86
supplements 47, 48, 73, 74
surrogate parents 59

T

The 'Good Enough' mentality 16
The Akashic Record 80
The Urantia Book 199
Time Constraints 19
Training 31, 102
Trustworthiness 43

V

vibrant health 65
Violence 54

W

we exist on many levels 67
weak people 57
Weight-loss
 Issues 11
what is right for us 24
willful ignorance 18
wisdom . 4, 7, 21, 27, 30, 33, 37, 38, 39, 40, 44, 57, 58, 60, 61, 62, 82, 85, 109, 114, 122, 127, 130, 132, 134, 136, 154, 167, 171, 187, 191
Witchcraft 199
Work 94

www.ingramcontent.com/pod-product-compliance
Lightning Source LLC
Chambersburg PA
CBHW032023230426
43671CB00005B/185